MAKING MANAGERIAL PLANNING MORE EFFECTIVE

MAKING MANAGERIAL PLANNING MORE EFFECTIVE

LOUIS A. ALLEN
Chairman, Louis A. Allen Associates, Inc.

McGRAW-HILL BOOK COMPANY

*New York   St. Louis   San Francisco   Auckland
Bogotá   Singapore   Johannesburg   London
Madrid   Mexico   Montreal   New Delhi   Panama
São Paulo   Hamburg   Sydney   Tokyo   Paris
Toronto*

Library of Congress Cataloging in Publication Data

Allen, Louis A.

　Making managerial planning more effective.

　Bibliography: p.
　Includes index.
　1. Corporate planning.　　I. Title.
HD30.28.A38　　　658.4′012　　　81-13669
ISBN 0-07-001078-1　　　　　　　AACR2

1 2 3 4 5 6 7 8 9 0　DODO　8 9 8 7 6 5 4 3 2 1

ISBN 0-07-001078-1

The editors for this book were William Newton and Carolyn Nagy,
the designer was Elliot Epstein, and the production supervisor
was Sally Fliess. It was set in Melior by J. M. Post Graphics.

Printed and bound by R. R. Donnelley & Sons Company.

for Ruth

CONTENTS

PREFACE

This book has a long history. After some 25 years of research and consultation with companies in many parts of the world, I recently undertook a survey of planning in 27 companies to identify current needs and new developments.

After interviewing managers at all levels, I arrived at two basic conclusions. First, planning technology is changing rapidly, but it is changing haphazardly and in all directions at once. There is little or no agreement on a logic or system or even a vocabulary of planning to define and guide that technology. Second, most planning effort is devoted to planning for the enterprise as a whole. A great need exists for managerial plans that will provide direction for individual managers planning for their own positions, in their own areas of responsibility.

This book aims to help fill that gap. The objective is to distill from current thought and practice a clear statement of concepts, principles, and techniques and a vocabulary of planning so that you can develop your own position plan and use it to improve performance in your area of management accountability. The focus will be on helping you develop a managerial plan for your own position, not for the enterprise as a whole, with the proviso that if you are the chief executive officer, your position plan will be the basis for the enterprise plan.

CAN PLANNING BE SCIENTIFIC?

Planning at present is far from being a science; if we wish to improve it with greatest certainty and economy of effort, we can well follow the same steps that have led to the gradual unfolding and eventual formalization of the sciences we know. The two key words are "logic" and "order," and one inevitably leads to the other. We need much more of both, and we begin with the most basic element, the language we use in planning.

When conducting interviews in different companies, I found that planning terminology was so varied and contradictory that it was often impossible to understand what my informants tried to tell me until I physically examined the processes and documents they described.

Planning systems in current use have evolved largely from the budgeting process. Rarely have they been constructed on the basis of a clear and understandable logic. Most often the inevitable carry-over of accounting conventions is still the molding influence in the development of planning systems.

To confound the situation further, the planning done in many enterprises has been divided into little fiefdoms. I found strategic planners, management by objectives (MBO) experts, controllers, zero-based budgeting specialists, members of financial staffs, and environmental analysts advocating special approaches and developing their own plans, often without coordinating their efforts.

POSITION PLANS AND ENTERPRISE PLANS

I found that many of the larger, more mature companies carry on two kinds of planning simultaneously. First, there is the overall set of strategic, operational, and financial plans that guide the enterprise as a whole. But these are broad, comprehensive, and long-range. Second, there are the plans managers develop to cover their own areas of accountability. These may be called MBO Plans, Work Plans, or other names. Even if they exist at all, these plans usually are maintained apart from the business planning system and they may have little consistency as to contents or use. They mark a gap between the strategic plan for the enterprise as a whole and the planning of the individual managers who must carry out the strategy.

It is clear that one of the greatest needs among practicing managers is for more sharply focused plans which will state the results that must be accomplished, the work that must be done, the costs of that work, and a means of evaluating how well the plans are accomplished. I have identified these as "Position Plans," plans that define the accountabilities of each position, as contrasted to "Enterprise or Corporate Plans," which pertain to the organization as a whole.

As I have worked with position plans, I have found that they have many uses which at first I did not foresee. They serve as the building blocks for the enterprise or corporate plan. Since organizations are a means for implementing plans, the structure of the position plan also serves as the structure for the organization. Position plans provide a framework for delegation of responsibility and become the basis for criterion-referenced controls.

We expect to appraise people in terms of the results and work for which we hold them accountable; therefore, the position plan, which defines this accountability, also becomes the best basis for performance appraisal.

There are areas of ordered and logical progress in current planning. Many companies have assessed their needs, have captured the best of what is available in theory and practice, and are using rational and effective planning approaches. Bits of this have leaked into general circulation. However, most successful practitioners guard their planning expertise as carefully as they guard their proprietary technical and marketing information.

I have attempted to winnow the mass of data available, to reinforce this with firsthand knowledge of current practices, and to derive fundamentals for practicing managers. You will find that I have placed great emphasis on the logic of planning. It is satisfying to discover that there is a clear, orderly rationale underlying the process which ties all of its parts together. I have gone to some lengths to state universals, to define terms, to describe methods, and to rationalize and clarify a vocabulary so that we all can speak meaningfully to one another about planning.

I hope this will provide a general framework within which you can unify and focus the planning methods you use already. It will give you a means of arranging your planning work into logical categories and a structure within which all parts of planning can fit logically. The framework will provide techniques you can put to work at once in your own position to help you improve your planning.

Planning currently is in a most interesting and significant developmental phase. With the knowledge that is available for sharing, we can develop more useful planning approaches for our own positions and for our organizations. Since plans are the best means we have of mastering the future, instead of being mastered by it, the effort to become more proficient in planning is worth all the time and effort we can devote to it. I hope this book will help.

Louis A. Allen

ACKNOWLEDGMENTS

I would like to thank the following corporations for providing and confirming the information cited in the text:

Alcan Aluminum Corporation, The American Management Association, The American Red Cross, Ameron Inc., Anchor Hocking Corporation, Arcata Corporation, Armco Inc., Atlantic Richfield Company, Avco Corporation, Avery International Corporation, Avon Products, Inc., Bank of America, Bowery Savings Bank, Bristol Myers Co., Inc., The Carborundum Company, Celanese Corporation, Chase Manhattan Corporation, The Cleveland Electric Illuminating Company, The Conference Board, Digital Equipment Corporation, Eaton Corporation, Emerson Electric Co., FMC Corporation, Ferro Corporation, General Electric Company, General Mills, Inc., General Motors Corporation, W.R. Grace & Co., H.J. Heinz Co., Hewlett-Packard Company, Intel Corporation, Kennecott Copper Corporation, Lear Siegler, Inc., Magic Chef, Inc., A.C. Nielsen Company, The Northwestern Mutual Life Insurance Company, Ohio Bell Telephone Company, Oil Development Company of Texas, Pacific Gas and Electric Company, Palm Beach Incorporated, J.C. Penney Company, Inc., Pfizer Inc., Raytheon Company, RCA Corporation, Rockwell International, Rohm & Haas Company, Sea-Land Industries, Inc., Sears, Roebuck and Co., Singer Company, SmithKline Corporation, Swift & Company, United Airlines, U.S. Industries, Inc., Western Electric Company, Inc., White Motor Corporation, Wm. Wrigley Jr. Company.

I wish to express my gratitude to the members of Louis A. Allen Associates, Inc. for their valuable contributions, both in concept and application, based on their consulting and educational assignments in many parts of the world. I am most appreciative of the contributions of John A. Murden, Henry W. Seeley, Gerard J. Carney, Howard H. Cook, Francis G. Edwards, John A. Foley, Beverly T. Galloway, Lewis McClellan, Larry Munson, William Nelson, Clive Pack, Anacleto Del Rosario, Van'Ro Van den Berg, Ron White, and Terryl C. Wilson.

Finally, I wish to thank Janet Helson for her dedication and excellent help in preparing the final manuscript.

Louis A. Allen

ABOUT THE AUTHOR

LOUIS A. ALLEN, who heads the international consulting firm of Louis A. Allen Associates, Inc., is well known for his contributions to the professional practice of management. Mr. Allen has had wide experience as a business executive, consultant, and management educator. His management experience includes twelve years with the U.S. Air Force, Aluminum Company of America, and Koppers Co., Inc. His three-year study of management in 150 companies for the Conference Board is considered to be the most comprehensive of its kind. He has served as consultant to the staff of Booz, Allen and Hamilton.

Mr Allen has advised many companies and lectured extensively all over the world. Based on this broad experience, he has been a leader in rationalizing and defining the concepts, principles, and techniques of management. His writings, which have been translated into nine languages, include books such as *Management and Organization*, *The Management Profession*, and *Professional Management: New Concepts and Proven Practices*. He has received the Academy of Management-McKinsey Award and is a Certified Management Consultant and a Fellow of the Academy of Management.

MAKING MANAGERIAL PLANNING MORE EFFECTIVE

1

PROBLEMS IN PLANNING

Far from feeling glad when I see some time-honored fallacy exploded, I think of the new one that will come to take its place, and ask myself the anxious question: Will it not perhaps be more inconvenient and dangerous than the other?
ANATOLE FRANCE

THE CHAPTER IN BRIEF Planning has great potential to facilitate progress, improve productivity, and increase human satisfaction. While we have made significant advances in the technology of planning, we have become so immersed in the mechanics that we have not been able to take advantage of its real capacity. Both behavioral and organizational problems beset managers who wish to plan effectively.

Problem areas that need attention are semantics, the artificial gap between planners and doers, and confusion about staff and line roles. The tyranny of the budget and confusion in control are central issues. Difficulties also arise because planners proliferate paper and tend to forget that people make plans, not the reverse. And, too often, managers fail because they don't know how to plan systematically and effectively.

Planning is the single most important, and most misunderstood, factor in the *continued* success of any enterprise. If the past has any validity in predicting the future, we know that over half of all companies we consider successful today can expect to be acquired, merged, or in a state of decline within 10 years. The significant difference between the losers and gainers uncontestably will be their sustained ability to *plan* their success.

THE SCOPE OF THE PROBLEM

The mandate to plan is understood well enough by virtually every manager. But the willingness that is everywhere evident is handicapped by plans that too often have become paper exercises developed by planners and sanctified by top executives. And they have little relationship to the daily work that determines failure or success.

For example, the president of one $800 million enterprise showed me his planning documents. First was a large, leather-covered, spiral-bound book which contained the 10-year strategic plan. It was accompanied by a three-ring binder with a comprehensive 1-year budget.

1

Questioning indicated that the strategic plan was updated yearly and was used primarily to justify major capital commitments. The budget was policed rigorously on the basis of a monthly reporting system.

The only means the president had of evaluating the work of the five product divisions reporting to him was in terms of their ability to meet the profit targets and the budgets that were given to them at an annual planning meeting in December. Within the past year the company had acquired one new enterprise and divested itself of two. None of the three was logically related to its primary business.

In another large company, an MBO system had been vigorously maintained for 5 years by the organization development staff. But it applied only to managers up to grade level C, a middle-management level. The planning-staff department had nothing to do with it. It was used to appraise performance but was not made part of operational plans and had no bearing on the budget or on incentive compensation.

The facts seem to demonstrate that while the time and money poured into planning are multiplying rapidly, commensurate results are not being realized. The problems that have arisen are complex, but their solution is well within our grasp. A primary cause of these problems is that planning has grown spontaneously. In the process, it has acquired a varied and often contradictory terminology, a patchwork of theory, and a miscellany of techniques. Planning, the discipline of logic and order, cries for logic and order.

In my research and work with companies, I have found that practicing managers are often baffled by the disorder they find in planning. This seems to be especially true of those accustomed to the precision and discipline of the technical professions and the sciences. Probably the most frustrating, because it is the most unnecessary, of these problems is that of language.

THE SEMANTIC JUNGLE

The Bible relates that the children of Noah attempted to build a tower that would enable them to climb into heaven. God prevented this impropriety by confounding their language so they could not understand one another.

Planning seems to have created its own Babel. Misunderstanding begins with the very fundamentals. To begin with, we have not yet even agreed what planning is. Some equate it with the whole of management. After all, we plan organization, we plan controls, we plan our leadership; in fact, we must plan all phases of the management functions.

Some say that planning is part of decision making. Others conclude that it is integral to control, and still others that control is an extension of planning.

Company practice helps little. While interviewing managers, I found that from one enterprise to another the same words often are used to identify different planning actions. A very large and successful company calls its profit plan a "rolling forecast." Another, equally large and successful, refers to its annual budget as its "profit plan." In some organizations, budgets always contain objectives; in others, objectives are developed without regard to budgets. I found that some companies establish budgets, then develop programs to achieve them, while others first prepare programs and then develop budgets to determine whether they will have the resources to undertake them.

"Strategy" is a semantic chameleon. It can mean such things as the purpose of an enterprise, the means the enterprise will use to achieve that purpose, the basic objectives of an organization, the process of making long-range decisions, and the approach to be followed in carrying out a plan. It is also commonly used as a synonym for "method," "approach," or "plan."

Many managers speak of determining strategies, then developing plans to carry them out. We are thus led to believe a strategy is something other than a plan. On the other hand, planners and top executives are prone to make strategy the capstone of the planning process, and nowadays there are few corporate plans that do not derive from long-range strategies.

The Jungle Closes In

Semantic uncertainty affects the ability of managers to discuss planning meaningfully; it blocks improvement because managers are not always sure what they're trying to improve. As a result, planning loses its integrity; it fails to achieve unity and coordination because the basic ideas on which a planning structure must be built are tenuous and changeable. This "semantic jungle," as Harold Koontz characterizes it, is as great a problem for professors of management as it is for practitioners. As Dr. Koontz points out, "One of the greatest obstacles in the development of a more unified and useful theory and service of management has been the problem of semantics. Those writing and lecturing on management and related fields have tended to use common terms in different ways." However, he refers to attempts at standardization and concludes that "while this semantics swamp still exists, and we are a long way from general acceptance of meanings of key terms and concepts, there are some hopeful signs on the horizon."*

Can We Have a Common Vocabulary of Planning?

We need a common vocabulary of planning, in which planning terms are directly related to the work that is done and are defined in clear, simple language. Since great variations in terminology now exist, it will be necessary to adopt some criteria for selection and, at some point, to make rather arbitrary choice of the terms to be used.

Most people who are concerned with planning have already suffered the penalties of confused communication. For managers who must base their actions on a precise understanding of their planning responsibilities, the semantic clutter they encounter may prejudice vital decisions. A common vocabulary will enable us to delineate what actually happens when we plan so that managers everywhere can benefit from our common experience, learn from our mistakes, and innovate with confidence.

Ameron, Inc., provides a case in point. After some 8 years of formalized planning, Ameron found that vocabulary was a continuing problem because different people understood different things by such common terms as "forecasting," "objective," and "budgeting." The difficulty was compounded when new functions were organized and outside companies were acquired. Ameron's solution was simple and direct: it developed a glossary of terms, defined a standard terminology, and educated managers to use it.

Experience indicates that an important precaution to take in standardizing planning terminology is to avoid "jargon," that is, special terms that have no clear meaning or that are coined in order to make it appear that what is described is new or different. However, new ideas sometimes require new terminology, and when this is in order, we will want the new words to fit within the same logic we have already adopted for our common vocabulary.

WHAT ROLE FOR STAFF?

In many organizations, plans are developed by one set of people and carried out by another. This gives rise to serious problems, because too

*Harold Koontz, "Toward a Useful Operational Theory of Management," in Melvin Zimet and Ronald G. Greenwood (eds.), *The Evolving Science of Management*, AMACOM, New York, 1979, pp. 327–347.

often there is little meaningful communication between the two. As a result, we find top executives developing ambitious plans that are neither understood nor followed by the operating people who are expected to carry them out, while staff groups labor over careful scenarios that never find their audience.

Where Scientific Management Went Wrong

The artificial separation of planners and doers is one of the undesirable legacies of the movement that revolutionized our ideas about management—mostly for the good—between 1910 and 1930. This was scientific management. A key idea of scientific management that continues to prompt the way we organize our planning efforts is the assumption that greater productivity results if planning is separated from performance.

The Staff Crutch

A consequence of this assumption is the persistent tendency to turn planning over to staff specialists. Managers and operators accountable for results are expected to follow the staff plans, and their performance and rewards are determined largely by how well they accomplish the intent of planning staffs. Managers often lean upon staff planners because the work of planning can be time-consuming and difficult. An easy solution is to have skilled specialists take it over. As planning needs have expanded, planning activities have been parceled out to different staff groups within the organization. It usually requires little time and only small opportunity for each group to stake out its own planning territory. This turf must then be defended, and potential or actual interlopers fended off. Organizational walls are thrown up, and planning becomes a house divided against itself.

As the proprietors protect their planning fiefdoms, the separation of staff from line becomes institutionalized. This further encourages specialized vocabularies. The separate plans take on a life of their own and never fulfill their synergistic potential for guiding and directing the enterprise and all of its parts in one unified course of action. The immediate results are that different plans are developed that have little organic relationship to one another and that Marketing Plans, Operations Plans, Research Plans, and Developmental Plans go marching off to the beat of their own drummers.

Who Owns the Strategic Plan?

In most enterprises, the Strategic Plan is "owned" by the corporate-planning department, which also has possession of such companion activities as the Diversification and Divestment Plans. This ownership has its disadvantages. The strategic plan deals with the long-range future, which appears hazy and uncertain to executives accustomed to dealing with tangible, here-and-now problems. Planning specialists seek to probe this murky future with a bagful of new tools: prognostics, computer modeling, normative forecasts, relevance trees, and portfolio theory. These new methodologies are complex and difficult; chief executive officers are prone to delegate them, along with the strategic plan, to the planning staff and to limit their own personal responsibility to strategy discussions with the board and key officers.

One consequence is that the germinal decisions which eventually shape the strategic plan are made by staff experts who are profoundly knowledgeable in their technologies but who lack the breadth of knowledge and the necessary objectivity and insight to influence the future of the enterprise for success. Because this work is done *for* them, the chief executive and line officers fail to define, weigh, and assess their true options so far as future avenues of growth and profitability are concerned. Strategy becomes a theoretical exercise that changes periodically, rather than a commitment of resources to maintain a consistent position in a changing future.

The MBO Experience

Management by objectives often illustrates the staff-line dichotomy. Introduced to implement the idea that managers should manage in terms of the results they want to achieve, not the day-to-day work they happen to do, MBO programs have often become the special province of the organization development, personnel, or human resources staff groups. I found that in many cases the MBO program requires managers to develop objectives as a separate exercise. These objectives are processed by the designated personnel department without reference to the strategic plan, operating plans, or budgets; in fact, the objectives cited in each will have no relationship to one another.

Minimizing Planning by Staff

Are there ways to bridge the gap between planners and the managers who must carry out the plans? A number of approaches have been successful. All concentrate on lodging planning where it properly belongs—with the manager accountable for results.

The most direct solution is to cut back on staff planners so that accountable managers are forced to do their own planning. This approach is exemplified by Intel Corporation, leader in microprocessors. Intel does not maintain a conventional staff-planning function; rather, planning has been made a primary responsibility of every manager. When help is needed in developing plans, committees or project teams are organized to provide the advice and service that would otherwise be forthcoming from a staff-planning group.

Balancing Staff and Line Planning

More commonly, enterprises attempt to allocate clearly defined planning roles to line and staff groups so that each carries out the part of the total planning task it is best equipped to perform.

General Mills, Inc., for example, walked both sides of the fence before it found the proper balance. Typical of many companies in its first approach to formalized planning, General Mills built a corporate group of over 50 planners, who were berthed in the controller's department. Planning was an extension of the budgeting process, and much of the planning was derived from accounting quantitative data. In effect, the planning process was a response to two questions: "How are we doing now?" and "What does it look like for the balance of the year?"

Those plans were worked out in detail and presented for approval to management. Unfortunately, even after they were approved, the plans prompted no dynamic action. In fact, they were largely ignored. Investigation revealed the reasons. There was no participation and little or no understanding and acceptance on the part of the managers who were expected to carry out the plans. On top of this, strategic planning was so dominated by the immediate requirements and pressures of budgeting that most planning extended no more than 1 year ahead.

General Mills decided that, to be effective, planning would have to be done by the decision makers and not by the planners. In line with this thinking, the company revamped its planning approach. The staff-planning department set up a planning system that holds managers accountable for planning as well as for carrying out the plans. Their performance is measured both in terms of planning competence and operating results, and incentives are awarded based on accomplishment.

Western Electric Co. Inc. also learned to take advantage of the relative strengths of staff and line in planning. Western Electric discovered that when line managers do their own planning, they tend to become immersed in current needs and problems. This leads them to extrapolate from the immediate past and to adopt a short-range, narrow viewpoint which can lead to trouble. As Western Electric concluded, a carefully balanced approach in which line and staff play to their strengths gives the best results.

THE TYRANNY OF THE BUDGET

Planning is often confused with budgeting. I found that a great many managers, when they speak of "planning," are really talking about their annual budget. One reason is that in most companies budgeting came first and what is called planning was derived from the budgeting process.

We might expect this, for the idea of budgeting goes back to France of the Middle Ages. In those days business people kept their money in a *bougette*, or small leather bag. Budgeting then consisted of counting the money in the bag to see if there was enough to pay expenses. As business grew to include many people, somebody had to keep track of the money, so there arose the *contrerolleur*, the one who kept a record of the *bougettes* in order to control receipts and expenditures. So began the "controller" and "comptroller" as we know them today.

In today's usage, the budget is a listing, by categories, of expected receipts and proposed expenditures for a specified period, usually 1 year. Estimates of what is to be received and what is to be spent are prepared on the basis of what happened in the past, adjusted to fit anticipated changes.

The budget may have a forecast and a set of objectives tacked on, but the commitment of money to be received and spent is the governing section. In an attempt to strengthen the inherent weaknesses of this approach, some companies use responsibility budgeting and zero-based budgeting to help them determine the specific uses to which the largest share of available funds should be committed. The majority, however, still extrapolate past expenditures into the future, index them to the expected level of sales revenue, and rigorously control expenditures to fit this procrustean bed.

What is the upshot? Suppose, as is true for almost all managers, you are required to prepare a 1-year budget which will determine how much money you can spend and against which your performance will be judged. At the same time, you are asked to develop a long-term plan in which you set forth what you *might* be able to accomplish 3 to 5 years in the future. There is no question that you and your team will spend most of your time working up the budget. If some activities you consider important have been lopped off in the past because of budget restrictions, you will pour your creative efforts into stratagems that will give you a safe cushion. Just as Gresham found that bad money drives out the good, you have probably discovered already that short-term, quantified planning drives out the long-term, strategic, and more uncertain planning.

This tyranny of the budget appears whenever long-term or strategic planning and the annual budgeting process are placed in close association. As a consequence, too often the budget is the operative plan. As a result, planning becomes past-oriented, short-term, overly quantified, and stereotyped.

One consequence is that the budget is most sharply demarcated and often lives its own life with little reference to other parts of the planning process. Usually it is the exclusive province of the controller, budget director, or financial manager, who uses a separate staff to develop it on a timing and cycle different from those followed by strategic planning, forecasting, MBO, and other planning activities. The outcome is that the budget is developed first and other plans flow from it. Although the incongruity has received little attention, in effect we first allocate to standard categories the money we expect to have available, then we determine what results we want to accomplish and how we will achieve them.

What happens, of course, is that we continue to allocate resources to these standard categories year after year, often assigning the money in proportion to the amount of revenue we anticipate. This encourages the perpetuation of existing projects and operations, with little provision for questioning their value or contribution to objectives.

Is Zero-Based Budgeting an Answer?

Different types of budgets have been developed in an attempt to reorient budgeting so that these problems can be avoided. Thus we have the program-planning system of budgeting, responsibility budgeting, accountability budgeting, zero-based budgeting, bracket budgeting, PERT (Program Evaluation Review Technique)/cost, and others.

Zero-based budgeting has been successful in a number of organizations; in others it has failed. Zero-based budgeting reverses the commonly accepted sequence of the budgeting process by first identifying each activity that is to be performed. The values and costs of the work are determined, and an evaluation is made of the benefits of performance. Only then are priorities established and resources allocated. In short, zero-based budgeting is a method of linking resources directly to results.

Drawbacks in Zero-Based Budgeting

The chief faults of zero-based budgeting are that it may create floods of paper and may demand inordinate amounts of management time for review of the thousands of decision packages it generates. However, the basic logic underlying zero-based budgeting is much sounder than that on which conventional budgeting is based, and its disadvantages can be minimized.

FMC Corporation, an early and successful user, finds that zero-based budgeting subjects each activity to the rigorous criterion: "Is it worth what we pay for it?" By setting priorities for each significant expenditure, the company can concentrate funding on the most important ones and eliminate or reduce those that contribute least.

A California utility company also has had good experience with zero-based budgeting. For many years the company operated successfully with conventional budgeting. Then it found itself caught in the problems created by fast-growing demand, escalating costs, and consumer resistance to rate increases. Looking for ways to make every dollar work harder, the company recognized that its chief tool for cost control—the budget—was commonly regarded as a numbers ritual that was performed yearly by staff people. While expenditures were controlled, there was no way to determine the relative value of individual activities. People were hired because they were "in the budget"; maintenance expenses were justified because this was the way maintenance had always been done. Zero-based budgeting was found to be a means of responding more quickly and effectively to fast-changing conditions. If it is shortened and simplified, there can be little question that zero-based budgeting will help to strengthen planning. By forcing us to think through the specific activities for which funds will be used, to place a value on the activities, and to weigh opinions, zero-based budgeting brings a new and creative aspect to the vital task of resource allocation.

QUANDARIES IN CONTROL

Closely related to the budgeting problem is that of control. That there should be confusion between planning and control is remarkable in itself. After all, there seems to be a distinct difference between deciding in advance the course of action you and others will follow, which is "planning," and checking up to make sure of what was actually done, which is "control."

Common usage does not always bear this out, however. In some companies, the production control department performs virtually the same work as is done by the production planning department in other companies. The control department, where it exists, is usually also responsible for planning. Company planning systems often make provision for reporting against the plans and for taking action to correct deviations from plans, both of which would seem to be control, not planning, activities.

The confusion between plans and controls is commonplace. Because statements of standards often accompany objectives, the standards, as well as the objectives, are counted as part of the plan. Budgets are usually considered a control device, and the budget most often appears as the central factor in control systems. Furthermore, companies that have controllers usually make them accountable for budgeting, although budgets are widely accepted as parts of the planning process.

The chief difficulty in this confusion is that managers who assume that plans are also controls often find they are trying to navigate their craft with a compass but without a rudder. In addition to determining where we want to go, how best to get there, how soon, and how much it will cost (which is the work of planning), we also need to know whether we've finally arrived where we should. The latter is the work of control. Clearly the rudder is as indispensable as the compass and a chart.

THE GAP BETWEEN TOP AND BOTTOM

There can be no question that good planning must begin and end at the top. Recognizing this, many companies have invested heavily in the staff and techniques for developing excellent strategic plans. However, it is equally true that no plan is any better than our ability to carry it out. The work of implementing plans is performed at the line of operations, which is five, six, or more levels down from where the planning work commonly is performed.

This artificial separation of performers from their plans stems from the belief that people at lower levels do not have the objectivity or knowledge to determine their own plans or to make meaningful contributions to product and market decisions. However, this overlooks the fact that the people who make and sell the product have firsthand knowledge of product characteristics and of customer needs and often can provide unique insights that lead to pragmatic solutions. Even when strategic plans are comprehensive and of high quality, if the connection between top and bottom is not made, the painfully wrought corporate plan becomes a paper exercise. Knowledgeable executives recognize the danger of this planning gap and take steps to close it.

As Edward Carlson described it when explaining how he turned United Airlines around from losses of $46 million to continuing profitability and success, "Sometimes they're right and sometimes they're wrong but, by and large, people in various other jobs have a better idea of what's good for the company than someone sitting at corporate headquarters."

The net result of the gap in planning between top and bottom levels is that most first-level supervisors don't have plans—they follow instructions. And not often can those who do plan see a connection between their own plans and those of the managers at top levels who are guiding the enterprise.

In a large midwestern bottling company, for example, the president and his management committee decided that the company would change to computer-controlled filling lines in each of its 12 bottling plants. The costs of the changeover were incorporated in the budget. Six months later, when the quarterly budget reports were reviewed, the controller reported that none of the funds budgeted for the changeover had been spent, so presumably the work had not been started. Investigation showed that the bottling plant managers knew the change was to take place, but since they had not been asked to develop plans for accomplishing the work in their own plants, nothing further had been done.

Planning by Consensus

Japanese companies typically avoid the planning gap by securing a high degree of involvement and agreement from top to bottom. This involves the discussion and analysis of every plan at all levels of the company to which it applies.

In Japan, as in the United States, the introduction of a new product or service has implications for every department of the enterprise. In the United States, these strategic decisions are made at higher levels, with little reference to those who will be dealing directly with customers or actually producing the product or service. The Japanese approach is to discuss the matter both in groups and individually. This brings out a variety of ideas and problems from the different viewpoints represented. These are reconciled before the work proceeds. Securing consensus takes time and slows decision making, but it increases the probability that the decision will be understood and successfully implemented.

Training Managers to Plan

The planning gap between top and bottom may exist because managers do not have the necessary planning skills. It is also true that in many cases accountable managers at lower levels do not plan because they do not know how to.

The fact is that while managers at all levels will accept planning as a primary responsibility, surprisingly few clearly understand what planning they should be doing and how to perform the work required. The upshot is that while planning may appear first in their position descriptions, it consists mostly of reviewing plans developed by others and either concurring or disagreeing with their judgments. As we would expect, when true at the top, this is also the case at lower levels. I have been surprised at how few presidents and vice presidents are able to develop clear, meaningful objectives or a sharply defined, measurable set of performance standards to accompany them. Few can think through and write, or dictate, a terse, meaningful action plan that will elicit confident action from their subordinates. It is also true that a large percentage of those reporting to top executives, as well as managers, section chiefs, and first-line supervisors, are planning illiterates. Surprisingly, this often applies to newly minted MBAs, who have a surfeit of knowledge about the strategic planning done at top levels but do not know how to plan for their own positions.

If managers do not know how to plan for their areas of accountability, they will not. It seems obvious that an accountant who does not understand and cannot do accounting work cannot be a good or even an acceptable accountant. So, also, managers who cannot do the planning work that only they can perform effectively cannot be good managers.

THE PROBLEM OF THE PAPER MILL

We often seem to value a plan in terms of the pounds of paper required to state it. This comes from confusing planning procedures with planning performance. The most important part of a plan is carrying it out;

we need only as much written detail as is necessary to accomplish that purpose. But the conventions of planning too often prevail, and we gloss over content in our concentration on filling out forms.

Planning procedures are necessary if we want to achieve the standardization required to integrate different plans into a unified whole. But we are prone to confuse the medium with the message. Too often I've seen managers labor for days to compile the information required by the company's detailed planning forms and, when they have finished, say with relief, "Now we can go back to work."

Recently I was talking to a top official in a key government agency. "We've finished our 5-year plan," he said. "It will be duly reviewed by the executive council. Three or four questions will be asked. Then we'll file it until we do the same thing next year."

The Form Is Not the Plan

Emphasis upon completing forms and compiling numbers conceals the true purpose of planning work: to encourage people to use their creative abilities in creating mental pictures of what they want to happen—then getting enough of that down on paper to convince and guide those who will *make* it happen. As one manager said to me, "The most stimulating parts of my job are to think about all the things we *could* do in the future and to narrow those down to the *one* we're most capable of accomplishing. Then comes the really difficult part of the job, which for me is to get both my people and my boss to understand and support what we all need to do and, finally, to work like blazes to make it all happen."

There is no question that planning of any kind generates a certain amount of paper. After all, good planning requires procedures so it will proceed in an orderly and uniform manner. However, because procedures prescribe *how* planning is to be done, often we assume that good procedures guarantee good plans. The reverse too often is true: overreliance on procedures tends to make planning perfunctory and stereotyped. People fill in the forms, meet the deadlines, and then "go back to work."

Highly motivated people will do better planning with imperfect methods than poorly motivated people will with technically impeccable forms and procedures. The heart of planning is the thinking that goes into it and the action that results, not the written substance that is recorded and filed. In fact, the written record is useful only to the extent it evokes accurately the sound thinking that has taken place.

PLANNING LACKS SYSTEM

"System" can be a buzz word. It is applied to everything from auto washing to the arrangement of interstellar space. But its meaning has significance for all managers who plan. A system is an integrated whole, made up of diverse but interdependent parts that work together in unison under the influence of an overall logic. Unfortunately, as we have seen, this is the antithesis of too much of current planning, which is often poorly defined, contradictory, overlapping, and incomplete. The parts of planning often are held separate by their "owners" rather than integrated into a cohesive whole.

We see the systems approach in other disciplines. The systems approach enabled NASA to put a man on the moon. Computers must be logical, or they are inoperable; therefore, they must be used in a systems format.

A planning system is unique because its purpose is to enable people to predetermine courses of action, usually to be carried out by other people. In this respect it differs from a computer or mechanical configuration and from engineering and mathematical systems.

A planning system is not optional; it is necessary, because progress by hunch and intuition is halting and uncertain. Without conscious and orderly thought about the best courses of action to be followed in the future, we inevitably repeat the mistakes of the past, fail to benefit from the experience of others, and lack opportunity to involve in our decisions the ideas of those who will carry them out. A logical, orderly system enables us to distill from our knowledge and experience the concepts, principles, and techniques which, if followed, will enhance our probabilities of success rather than prejudice them.

PLANS IGNORE PEOPLE

This brings us to the final problem: plans may be technically sound but fail to recognize the needs of the people who will carry them out.

The technology used to help operate our planning system has been expanded and improved with such rapidity that much of it is startlingly different from what it was only 10 years ago. However, the humans who use this technology have changed very little in their essential characteristics for 10,000 years or more. In the final analysis, it will not be the new-style tools that make the planning decisions. This will still be the task of old-style humans.

Plans work only as well as people want them to. While standardization is necessary, flexibility is equally important. Procedures that encourage participation and generate creative inputs help people to develop an emotional ownership in both the plan and its outcome. Since, by its nature, managerial planning is designed to guide the actions of other people, it can be useful only if it satisfies two requirements. First, it must convince people it will help them perform better; and second, when they do perform, the process must provide recognition and reward. Successful planning is as much motivating people to perform as it is developing the written outlines that guide their actions.

Today the expectations and needs of people are changing, and this is an important factor to build into our planning process. Only a few years ago we thought that we could best satisfy the people of our organizations by helping them to actualize themselves. But we are slowly recognizing a central truth: People must help their organizations become what they are capable of becoming before they, individually, can secure the tangible support and emotional sustenance they need to actualize themselves.

In my many trips to Japan and my work with Japanese companies, I have become familiar with a significant difference in orientation on the part of both managers and employees. The business enterprise in Japan is expected to be paternalistic: a concerned, kindly, and provident parent. Japanese managers strive for consensus, for understanding and agreement on important decisions before they are made. Employees look to their companies to provide social and emotional as well as economic security. The Japanese attitude is: "I will put my company's interests first because I know my company is concerned and will place high priority on my interests."

As Kyonosuke Ibe, chairman of Sumitomo Bank, explains it, the worker gives loyalty to the company, and in return, the corporation gives the worker the assurance of lifetime employment.* This attitude undoubtedly underlies the strong feeling of teamwork that pervades Japanese industry.

In other countries, including the United States, we see the idea of reciprocation also, but now, instead of "What can I do for the company so it will be able to give me security and support," the question seems to be "What can my company do for me?" This is the concept of "entitlement," the expectation of certain benefits as a matter of right.

The General Electric Company states it succinctly. "Few work for the sake of working, or just for the salary." General Electric recognizes

---

*"It Took the Japanese to Build Japan," *Business Week*, October 6, 1980, p. 17.

that "Jobs must be challenging and rewarding, and leave plenty of time for mental and physical refreshment."

And what is the reciprocal entitlement? As General Electric puts it: "We expect the best efforts of people who are dedicated, conscientious, who have a professional commitment to productive output and a spirit of cooperative effort in our mutual enterprise."

Satisfying the "entitlements" of both managers and the people they manage will be more difficult than we thought. A number of companies, including General Motors, Procter & Gamble, and General Foods, for a decade or more have tried to find ways in which unionized workers can become directly involved in the decision-making process. Work teams have been the primary vehicle. Job enrichment and job rotation have been instituted. Delegation of responsibility and authority have been increased within clear limits. There is significant evidence of increased employee satisfaction and morale and of improved productivity in many of these cases. Importantly also, quality circle teams have made valuable contributions to plans for improving production facilities, reorganizing clerical and administrative operations, developing and expanding product lines, and identifying and exploiting new areas of customer demand.

Problems can be challenging as well as frustrating. The difficulties we encounter in clarifying and improving our planning approaches yield to knowledgeable and consistent action. The effort is well worth it, because good plans are multifaceted tools that can provide benefits far beyond those we ordinarily envisage. We will discuss these benefits—and some uses of planning you may not be familiar with—in the next chapter.

KEY POINTS

1. *Planning Has Untapped Potential.* Planning is vitally important to every practicing manager, but its potential has not been realized. The reasons are evident in almost every enterprise and deserve careful study.
2. *The Problem of Semantics.* Differences in the meaning of the most common terms prevent us from understanding what others do and how we can improve our own planning. They impede communication within enterprises and among different organizations.
3. *Strategy or Objectives?* Confusion in the ideas and terminology that apply to "strategy" and "objectives" are cases in point, because both are vital to planning success, but neither can be effective unless made part of a functioning whole.
4. *The Inadequacies of Budgeting.* Budgeting is the forerunner of much of today's planning, but the tight structure, precise detail, and unchanging

consistency vital to budgeting are inappropriate to the kind of creative, flexible planning we need today. New approaches such as zero-based budgeting are helpful, but do not solve the basic problem.

5. *Planning Is Not Control.* Planning often is confused with control. When this happens, planning is hamstrung, for the purpose of control is to assess and regulate both work and results, while that of planning is to guide and facilitate them.

6. *Who Is Accountable?* Often there is no clear accountability for planning. Different parts of what should be an integrated process become the property of groups with different viewpoints and objectives. This often results in a gap between the people who develop plans and those who carry them out.

7. *Both Top-Down and Bottom-Up.* Planning, especially strategic and long-range planning, should be both a top-down and bottom-up process. However, often it takes place only at the top, beginning and ending there. Part of the reason is that top managers do not believe that lower-level people can contribute effectively to top-level plans. This is a mistake, for eventually every plan must be carried out at the lowest operating level.

8. *Staff Can Only Help.* Planning fails when it is not taken as a primary responsibility by top executives but is relegated to planning staff. It fails if it does not follow an orderly, consistent, and logical process and if it does not provide for the needs of the people who must make the plans work.

9. *Planning Needs to Be Creative.* Planning often becomes fixed and arbitrary because it depends too largely on the filling out of forms and too little on creative thinking, the weighing of options, and the formulation of conclusions that have a workable consensus.

10. *Plans Are for People.* We tend to forget that plans work only as well as people want them to. Nowadays, people have different expectations about their work. They expect as a right that their jobs will be mentally and physically, as well as monetarily, rewarding. Our plans cannot succeed unless they provide for these human needs.

QUOTES FROM CHAPTER 1

Significant quotations from this chapter that you will want to consider and discuss in greater detail:

- Planning is the single most important, and most misunderstood, factor in the *continued* success of any enterprise.

- For managers who must base their actions on a precise understanding of their planning responsibilities, the semantic clutter they encounter may prejudice vital decisions.

- Managers often lean upon staff planners because the work of planning can be time-consuming and difficult. An easy solution is to have skilled specialists take it over.

- Intel Corporation does not maintain a conventional staff-planning function; rather, planning has been made a primary responsibility of every manager.

- General Mills decided that, to be effective, planning would have to be done by the decision makers and not by the planners.

- Zero-based budgeting is a method of linking resources directly to results.

- Japanese companies typically avoid the planning gap by securing a high degree of involvement and agreement from top to bottom.

- Newly minted MBAs, who have a surfeit of knowledge about the strategic planning done at top levels . . . do not know how to plan for their own positions.

- Plans may be technically sound but fail to recognize the needs of the people who will carry them out.

2
WHY PLAN?

We cannot cast out pain from the world, but needless suffering we can. Any calamity visited upon man could have been avoided or at least mitigated by a measure of thought. Whatever failure I have known, whatever errors I have committed, whatever follies I have witnessed in private and public life have been the consequence of action without thought.
BERNARD BARUCH

THE CHAPTER IN BRIEF   As we have seen, planning at its present stage is confronted by many problems. However, the benefits planning offers are both immediate and pervasive—so much so that our attempts to make it more logical, orderly, and useful promise rich rewards. In this chapter we will discuss the advantages planning offers in facilitating successful growth and in motivating the people who instrument that growth. We will begin to see the precision with which plans can set the specifications for organization structure and how they facilitate delegation. We will find that sound plans become our most effective communication channels. And, to tie the whole thing together, we will find that, in serving as the basis for controls, plans become the best agents of their own success.

PLANNING IS PREREQUISITE TO SUCCESSFUL GROWTH

Planning is one of the key skills for any manager who wishes to grow in capability and stature. Although today I would estimate that no more than 15 to 20% of managers do a good job of planning, at least 98% know they should. The reason is that almost every alert manager today knows from observation, if not personal experience, that plans both engineer and catalyze success. There is plenty of evidence.

Managers rarely fall short of their real potential for lack of technical competence. Of all the managerial failures I have seen, there most often appears one real cause: a failure to plan logically and consistently so that the limited resources that are available are directed to the opportunities that really matter.

Must Entrepreneurs Plan?

The paradox is that entrepreneurs can be extremely successful with little or no formal planning. Entrepreneurs who begin enterprises carry in their heads a picture of what the enterprise is to become. They know what they want and how to accomplish it. So long as the entrepreneurial genius can handle the really difficult problems and make the important decisions, all the planning necessary can be done in that one brain. But inevitably even the most capable natural leaders find their personal capabilities outgrown. The more diversified and dispersed the enterprise becomes, and the more complex its technology, the sooner this occurs. Because entrepreneurs have always done it on their own and spontaneously, these leaders find it very difficult to pass on to others what they so clearly see in their own minds. But unless they do, the bright picture will fade and success with it.

Typical is an electronics company in the so-called Silicon Valley, south of San Francisco. It was still small enough to be dominated completely by its very able but dictatorial president, who did everything himself and boasted of it. The company was slowly strangulating under this authoritarian leadership. Signs of oncoming crisis were clearly evident, but the president refused to recognize them. A precipitate drop in profits resulted in his equally rapid dismissal from the top post. The first move of his replacement was to institute a formalized planning process.

Most companies that grow have proved for themselves that sound planning is a necessary prerequisite. Sound and flexible plans are the best safeguard against the vagaries of the future. As a case in point, North American Aviation had 90,000 employees and orders for 8000 aircraft when World War II ended. Within 3 months the firm had to cut back to 5000 employees and its orders had shrunk to 24 planes. The company went from having healthy profits to barely breaking even. Expert in technical planning, the company used the same skills to plan its future. Instead of succumbing to early pressure and using its considerable assets to diversify into unknown fields, North American first took the time to develop a long-range plan. Then it capitalized on its strengths by diversifying into new scientific and technical fields basic to national defense. Now part of Rockwell International, the company is a leader in its field.

The Impact of Competition

During the next decade we shall see even greater broadening of the aggressive competition now evident in almost all markets and products. Where once the United States was the great spawner of multinational corporations, today Japan, West Germany, Holland, Belgium, England, and other countries maintain autonomous operating and marketing enterprises in the United States. These multinational corporations can exist only if they plan their far-flung operations to take advantage of the potential synergy of size.

Planning skill is important for both large and small enterprises. Complex technologies, once available only to the heavily capitalized giants, are being simplified and improved with great speed. With careful planning, they can be exploited successfully by small entrepreneurs. Marketing planning has improved greatly, so small companies that know how to plan can identify market segments in which they can exert as much muscle as the big corporations and can successfully chip away at specialized markets.

PLANS ESTABLISH THE ORGANIZATIONAL FRAMEWORK

We generally think of organization in terms of organization charts and job responsibilities. But these are largely a record of the organization we happen to have evolved, and they are built around the conditions and personalities of the past. They are usually outdated almost as soon as they are completed. An organization chart does not help us to determine whether people are doing the right work and too much or too little of it. Moreover, it does not tell us how we should be changing the organization to meet the needs of the future, which we know will be different and probably even more demanding and complex than those of the present.

Sound organizations are derived from sound plans. When we organize, we are determining what work should be done to accomplish our plans, who should do it, and how people can work together most effectively.

A sound organization must directly relate the work to be done to the goals to be achieved. Furthermore, if we establish a logical hierarchy of the plans we have, this also becomes the basis for the organizational hierarchy: the structures of plans logically should become the structure for organization.

PLANS GUIDE DELEGATION

Your success as a manager lies in your ability to get other people to do work and make decisions you would otherwise do and make yourself. Two things intervene in getting other people to do things for us. First, we prefer to do things ourselves, rather than to have them done by others. Second, our subordinates usually learn to delegate upward more quickly than we learn to delegate downward.

There are good enough reasons. All of us who have tried to delegate downward know the impatience and frustration that come from watching somebody else do a job slowly and clumsily when we could do it to perfection in a fraction of the time. And when people make it clear they admire our expertise, it takes inhuman resolution not to assume personally the really difficult chores that others gingerly circle.

Planning can help. The key to effective delegation is to know, firmly and unequivocally, what you must do yourself and what you can best assign to others. A good plan is a mechanism for thinking through with your team the results to be accomplished, the work to be done, the time limits, and the money required. With this information in hand, you can determine who should take each part of the total task. You can also reach agreement on when and by whom work and results should be checked. Given this, you can delegate without abdicating and retain the necessary control.

PLANS HELP MOTIVATE PEOPLE

Behavioral science reveals a number of interesting aspects about human behavior. First, we are all largely dedicated to satisfying our own needs. We work hardest when we are striving to accomplish something that will bring us reward or recognition. Research shows that people will get better results if they have a clear picture of demanding and challenging goals than if they just try to do their best. The greater our feeling of ownership in the results we are trying to achieve, the harder we'll work to succeed.

One fast-food chain I studied, for example, had been losing out to a competitor. The store managers were urged by headquarters staff to work harder, to cut costs, to get more paying customers into the stores. Nothing much happened. Finally a store managers' meeting was held at which plans were developed by the store managers to help them improve their situation. The significant part of it was that on review these plans echoed almost exactly the actions that headquarters staff had been urging. However, these had now become the managers' own plans. With little additional help, they turned the situation around within 6 months.

Having an objective in itself helps improve performance. But the outcome is even more favorable when your own manager discusses your progress and results with you and when you have an opportunity to find out how he or she thinks you're doing and to reconcile any differences of opinion.

The final boost to motivation occurs when, in addition to feedback, you get generous recognition for the contribution you've made. The more tangible the reward and the more clearly you understand what you must do to earn it, the harder you'll work.

A good plan can be a powerful motivator if properly used. It contains objectives that you've agreed are important and you'll work to achieve. It is supported by performance standards that provide the best basis for differentiating between good and poor work and that encourage prompt and generous rewards for accomplishment.

PLANS SERVE AS COMMUNICATION CHANNELS

People have an interest in a great many things; however, the information they need most is that which helps them anticipate and solve problems directly related to the work they are doing. Most communication systems fail to provide this because they do not tap directly into individual responsibilities.

Good plans provide the framework for giving people the information they want. Bank of America, for example, has found that its planning process causes people at all levels to think about the future in a disciplined manner and to commit this thinking to writing. These plans are distributed to managers and help to improve overall communication at the various management levels. Because it is directed at the critical few things that make for success, discussion of plans by those directly concerned ensures not only that they will think systematically about the future but also that they will get at the center of potential problems instead of nibbling at the fringes.

Ameron, Inc., a leader in engineered products, is another company that makes conscious use of its logical and well-defined planning system as a communications device. By requiring managers to prepare a plan and by using staff as expert advisers, Ameron secures a direct interchange of ideas and intentions and reconciles different points of view among key decision makers. This facilitates understanding and coordination. It also reveals a great deal about a manager's interests, capabilities, and management acumen.

The need to maintain communication tells us something about the characteristics of good plans. They must encompass managers' full areas of accountability: all of those things which they must cause to happen and for which they will be called to account if they fail. Plans often fail to communicate because they relate to groups of people and not to individuals. The strategic plan, marketing plan, or operations plan are most significant when they relate to specific individuals who are held accountable both for the plan and for its results.

To communicate, a plan must do more than be read; it must *create* understanding. The active principle needed is injected by providing for regular review and discussion both of the plans themselves and the problems that attend their implementation.

As a case in point, Roy A. Gentles, president of Alcan Aluminum Corporation, regularly reviews performance against plans with the division presidents and corporate-staff heads who report directly to him. "It is a time-consuming responsibility," he says, "but since each performance discussion triggers a series of similar sessions all the way down the line, it is one of the best communication channels we have."

Another company I studied requires that each manager must hold a monthly meeting with all the people who report to him or her. In that meeting two things are done. First, each person reports to the group on progress and problems in carrying out plans for the past month and for the month to come. Second, that individual answers any questions people wish to ask.

As one manager told me, "It is amazing how misunderstandings are clarified in those meetings before they become operating problems. The time I spend in those planning sessions is one of my best investments."

PLANS ARE THE BASIS FOR CONTROL

An important aspect of getting things done is to be able to monitor work without interfering with it and to anticipate problems before they become crises. Controls often fail because we try to control work after it has been completed. That's much like trying to save money after it has been spent. The best we can do in controlling after the fact is to identify mistakes that have already been made and to prevent them from recurring.

To be effective, control involves assessing and regulating both work in progress and work completed. The real need is how to check on work while it is still being done. One answer is to develop programs and schedules to accompany objectives. This makes it possible to use the plan in a dual role: to determine what to do and also to check up to make sure it is being done properly.

We generally recognize that setting standards is the first step in control. A standard is a criterion that will enable us to differentiate between good and poor work and results. Although we often set standards arbitrarily, experience shows that they are most logical and useful when they can be related directly to the work and results to which they refer. This means that standards should be derived directly from the objectives they are expected to measure.

A New York sales manager, for example, set a standard of $200,000 per month sales revenue for each district sales supervisor. This met with universal resistance. "It's unreasonable because we've never done $200,000 in this district before," as one supervisor put it.

The sales manager studied the problem carefully, and then asked the supervisors to determine how much incentive and commission they and their crews wanted to earn, what sales they would have to generate following the commission formula, and what specific steps they would follow to create that volume of sales. The plans that were submitted recognized that several attractive new products presented new sales opportunities and that a revised advertising and promotion program would give new clout to the sales effort. When the sales manager offered the $200,000 standard for the second time, there were no objections.

Now that we have a firm conviction that planning is an essential skill that is well worth the effort necessary to develop or improve it, in the next chapter we will look at a fact we generally fail to recognize: organizations and their people tend to change predictably, or evolve, and their planning skills must keep step if they are to be effective.

KEY POINTS

1. *Planning: Key to Growth.* We seldom stop to realize the vital importance of planning to the practicing manager. Planning is mandatory for successful growth. When there is failure to plan logically and consistently, people fail to direct their efforts to the opportunities that really matter. Current experience demonstrates that planning skills are vital for small as well as large enterprises. With careful planning, small entrepreneurs can exploit new technologies, better utilize scarce resources, and provide continuing challenge and opportunity for their people.
2. *Plans Create the Future.* Sound plans enable us to influence and shape our mental images of the future. The more we clarify this mental picture through planning, the greater the likelihood of attaining our objectives.
3. *Plans Provide the Framework for the Organization.* Sound organizations are derived from sound plans. Plans establish our desired results and identify the work necessary to accomplish them. Organization determines what work should be done and who can do it most effectively. Few data are available about how to relate plans and organization. However, we can establish the logical connection: plans establish the course of action we will follow; organization is a means of arranging and relating the necessary work.
4. *Plans Guide Delegation.* Success as a manager stems from the ability to delegate responsibilities. Two difficulties arise when you try to delegate. One is that it usually seems easiest to do things yourself. The second is that subordinates often learn to delegate upward more rapidly than you learn to delegate downward. Planning can help you delegate easily and with certainty by identifying what you *must* do yourself and what can best be assigned to

others. Sound plans also define accountability for both methods and results and serve as the basis for the kind of control by exception that will make delegation stick.

5. *Plans Help Motivate People.* People usually work harder and more effectively if they have challenging and demanding objectives. Planning helps motivate people. It provides a tangible picture of the results we want, and when bolstered by performance standards and a system of rewards, it helps to integrate our own objectives with those of the organization as a whole.

6. *Plans Facilitate Communication.* Most communication systems fail to provide information people can use to improve their performance because they do not tap directly into individual responsibilities. Good plans provide a framework for doing this. They can supply people with the vital information they want and need. To communicate, a plan must create understanding.

7. *Plans Are the Basis for Control.* Control is largely ineffective if administered after the fact. The most important aspect of control is that of assessment and regulation while work is in progress. Setting standards to accompany objectives is the first step in control. Programs and schedules which accompany objectives strengthen this aspect and give plans a dual role—determining what to do and ensuring that it is properly done.

QUOTES FROM CHAPTER 2

Significant quotations from this chapter that you will want to consider and discuss in greater detail:

● Marketing planning has improved greatly, so small companies that know how to plan can identify market segments in which they can exert as much muscle as the big corporations and can successfully chip away at specialized markets.

● Sound organizations are derived from sound plans.

● Good plans provide the framework for giving people the information they want.

● Controls often fail because we try to control work after it has been completed. That's much like trying to save money after it has been spent.

THE EVOLUTION OF PLANNING

Progress is not an accident but a necessity.
HERBERT SPENCER

THE CHAPTER IN BRIEF   As we set about developing planning skills, it is important to keep in mind that our need for planning and the way we plan change predictably. When the organization is new and young, people are unsure and inexperienced and they tend to do things in ways they learned elsewhere. This is the natural leadership stage. It calls for informality, flexibility, and a high degree of centralization in planning. As people become competent and confident, they look for more structure and formalization and increasing decentralization. This is the management-leadership stage. If changes are not made at the proper time, the best people will become dissatisfied and leave and planning will become lethargic and ineffective.

LEADERS EVOLVE AND THEIR PLANNING WITH THEM

When we think of good planning, we visualize comprehensive, accurate plans which are largely set by the people who will carry them out and which are decentralized so that managers on the spot can make most of the decisions. This is the ideal promulgated by most of our textbooks, and for many years I subscribed to it. However, I have found that while this is ideal for some organizations at a certain stage in their development, it can be entirely inappropriate at other periods. In fact, the attempt to achieve formalized, inclusive, and detailed plans at the wrong stage may severely handicap growth and success.

In one instance, a brilliant, capable engineer became president of a new company that obtained financing based on a patent he had acquired. With a master of business administration as well as an electrical engineering degree, he determined that good management was a prerequisite. Accordingly, with his immediate team he worked out a beautifully detailed set of strategic plans, together with action plans and budgets. He decentralized authority fast and thoroughly to each operating manager. The business grew quickly, and within a few months the management group had trebled in size. To the president's consternation, the capable, enthusiastic managers he hired were quick to exercise their broad authorities but ignored the careful plans that had been developed. Convinced that participation was the answer, he held a series of meetings and secured their ideas and suggestions, which were promptly built into the plans. But the operating managers were still dedicated to doing their own thing and not to following the plans they had helped develop.

The crisis came when the research manager committed a large sum of money to develop a new product. This had been approved in the 5-year plan but with a lower priority than that of several design improvements vital to immediate customer acceptance. "These new features will make obsolete what we're selling now, and it's my job to get them into production as soon as we can," said the research manager. The sales manager differed vehemently. "We don't know if they'll work, and even if they do, it'll take a year or more to create demand," she said. Both insisted they had been delegated full authority under the company's policy of decentralization.

The president finally solved the problem by taking back the reins. He instituted a daily coordination meeting at which each staff and operating head reviewed current progress and problems and the president made the decisions. Within a year the team had learned to work together. The meetings were stretched to once monthly, and most of the original authority was delegated back to the operating level.

WHY LEADERS EVOLVE

To understand why planning changes predictably, or evolves, we must look to the people who do the planning. Humans evolve physically and mentally. Is it possible they also change predictably in other ways?

In studying the growth and development of enterprises during the past 30 years, I have been struck by the fact that leaders evolve in the way they perform their work as leaders. The needs of followers also change predictably. If this evolution does not take place, both leadership and followership fail.

Suppose you were to organize a new company, or, for that matter, a new department, plant, or club. You would hire or bring in a variety of people with differing backgrounds and training, all uncertain of what is expected of them and at first unable to work as a team. At this stage, you would lay out the ground rules, tell people what was required, check closely on what was being done, and make most of the decisions yourself. Otherwise all would do what they thought best, and your group—and its efforts—would come unglued. In a nutshell, a leader with a new, young, or immature group must adopt a style of leadership characterized by centralized decision making, an organization built around strong personalities, one-way communication, and control by inspection rather than by exception.

Natural Leadership

I have identified this as the natural-leadership stage. "Naturals" in leadership adopt this style intuitively for two reasons. First, during the 4 million or so years of human biological evolution, it has been most successful because it tends to bring results most quickly. Since these results are most rewarding to leaders, they tend to perpetuate this style. The second reason is that our knowledge about leadership and management is late-blooming. Only since World War II have a meaningful number of systematic studies been made to identify leadership styles and traits and to help leaders to change from one style to the other.

I believe there is an evolutionary progression in the way we improve our skills in performing most kinds of work. If you are at all knowledgeable, it is easy for you to tell if a person is a "natural" or a "professional" in designing a house or healing people. A "natural" relies largely upon innate aptitude and personality characteristics to do the work. A "natural" singer vocalizes differently than a trained professional; a self-taught designer has a lower order of skills than a registered architect. As Sammy Snead and many other world-famous golfers discovered early in their careers, a "natural" golfer has much to learn before he or she can compete successfully with the "pros."

The important point is that although you begin as a natural, if you have the necessary aptitudes and personality characteristics, with systematic training you can change predictably or evolve from this natural stage of development to a more mature, competent, and "professional" stage.

If you are a leader with little or no formal training or education in management, you will tend to use the natural-leadership style exclusively because you know no other. If you are a trained, professional manager, you may use the natural-leadership style purposefully when circumstances require it.

During the early stage, most of your planning would be short-range, because you would not have enough facts or commitments to look very far ahead. Because there had been neither time nor opportunity for cohesiveness to develop, you would find it difficult to reach consensus. Simply to get things done, you would supervise much of the planning or do it yourself. And whether you wanted to or not, you would make most of the planning decisions, or you would find the field impregnated with indecision, indirection, and frustration.

The Corridor of Crisis

Eventually the natural leader's scope is outgrown. The signs are clear. People become restless and frustrated when their decisions continue to be made for them. Natural leaders who see themselves as the best salespeople or engineers or surgeons won't permit others to compete and to grow. Emergencies and crises abound because the expedient action of natural leaders meets short-range problems at the expense of long-range, with resulting poor use of resources.

The corridor of crisis is marked by personal discontent and dissatisfaction, increase of costs disproportionate to returns, slow and inadequate action, monolithic and increasingly inefficient organization, and the exodus of the best people. Typically, at this stage in the growth of an enterprise, there is stagnation and decline, a merger with a stronger partner, bankruptcy, or failure.

Management Leadership

Followers who are competent in their work, who are knowledgeable and confident about the overall results to be accomplished, who have enough experience to understand the specific needs and problems of their situation, and who are able to put the needs of the group ahead of their own special interests do not work well under natural leadership.

Because they are knowledgeable and competent, they want to make as many of their own decisions as possible and to understand and accept those they do not make themselves. They want to be kept informed about matters that concern them. They are usually hungry to grow and develop in their jobs and as persons. While they recognize the need for control, they want it to be exceptional, not continual inspection of everything they do. Followers at this stage are outward-directed. They look for satisfaction as much from their membership in the group as from the personal rewards they can take for themselves. I have called this the management-leadership stage. Management leaders are leaders who have learned to act in ways that will satisfy the needs of their followers. Management leaders concentrate on work that will enable them to get results through the group as a whole, working as a team, not through the work they do themselves.

Management leaders have learned to delegate. They build organizations in terms of the work to be done, so that everybody, and not just a few strong personalities, will have a chance to do important work. Management leaders learn to make logical rather than intuitive decisions. They communicate so they understand others and others understand them. And they control by exception.

Accomplishing the changes from natural to management leadership often requires new leaders, because the entrenched natural leaders don't know how to change, or resist making the changes that are necessary.

PLANNING DURING THE NATURAL-LEADERSHIP STAGE

When a company or its individual components are in their early growth stage, they have special characteristics and needs which extend particularly to planning.

Informality

Because markets are untried, people are new, technology is not yet firmly established, and uncertainty prevails as to resources and capabilities, the young organization must be prepared to change direction and methods quickly. It tends to maintain a relatively informal planning structure. While broad, flexible strategic plans are vital, short-term plans are developed almost ad lib in discussions between decision makers, at staff meetings, or in the heat of crises and emergencies. If too much formalization is attempted at this stage, action is stifled and plans end up on permanent file in desk drawers.

Centralization

At this early stage most planning is—and should be—centralized; that is, most planning decisions are made at the top. This ensures coordination and consistency which would not be available if the guiding decisions were made at operating levels. Decentralization of planning is not possible because there does not yet exist an established corporate culture based on tested policies and procedures, a logical organization, and effective controls.

At this stage, managers need guidance and direction in developing their plans. While participation is valuable and should be encouraged, its purpose now should be to secure information, test the practicality of proposed plans, and develop a feeling of emotional ownership.

If you are head of a new company or a new division, or if you are starting a new department, office, or unit, you will tend to be functionally oriented because getting the technical work done is of primary concern. Often you don't have time—or feel you don't—to train others adequately, and as a result, you do much work that others could better be trained to do for you. At this stage, you will find it best to plan rather informally and to centralize your planning. As you and your people gain skill and confidence, you can systematize and decentralize.

To begin with, you will probably develop your own plans and those of the people immediately reporting to you. This is contrary to much current theory; however, you are concerned with how people really act, not with how theories say they *should* act. Make sure the plans express what you want in a clear, logical form. Have the facts in mind so that you can sell the members of your team on the plans you have developed. Discuss the plans with them. Listen carefully to their arguments and suggestions. But at this early stage, you decide what your plans—and theirs—will be.

Flexibility

During the early growth stage, be prepared to change quickly. Since you don't have background or precedents in the new situations that arise, you will need to change your ideas and your plans with care, but without compunction. Although flexibility is vital, you may find that it is hard to come by at this stage. Most of the plans are based on your own ideas and are studded with your decisions. To change may seem to admit of error in your thinking. Often others on your team will see the need for change and will urge it before you are emotionally prepared to abandon your intellectual offspring and to adopt new ideas.

PLANNING DURING THE CORRIDOR OF CRISIS

If you continue to grow and develop as a manager and planner—and many managers do—you will enter into a crisis period in which others on your team have gained competence and confidence. They are ready for more authority, require greater formalization of planning procedures to support this decentralization, and are capable of operating with greater predictability and, hence, stability.

The Need for Change

Continuity and survival depend upon the ability to change at this period. But change will be resisted because people find it difficult to leave the habits they have established. Paradoxically, those who most need change will least want it.

One international engineering and construction company, for example, was founded by an outstanding engineer who staffed his top executive group with fellow engineers. By training and habit, engineers are numbers-oriented. They know the significance and use of quantitative data and rely heavily upon it. Since they understand what numbers convey, engineers tend to minimize narrative or qualitative interpretations. Because of this, a great deal of project planning was done in the field. This was short-term, very specific, and expressed in Program Evaluation Review Technique (PERT) and other charts and tabulations. It was also very successful. But longer-range planning was clearly necessary. The company brought in an outside consultant to launch a new strategic planning program, which was strongly supported by the chief executive.

Overcoming Resistance to Change

Resistance was immediate. Key officers complained of the new planning bureaucracy. Meetings were held but were attended grudgingly. Plans that were submitted tended either to be perfunctory or so loaded with detail that they could be understood only by the originators. Alert to what was occurring, the company struggled with the problem for some 6 years. It was overcome only when basic organization changes were made that replaced several engineers in top executive positions with strong professional managers.

Typical of the planning that underlies successful change is that of Raytheon Co., which grew to its early success through concentration upon electrical engineering. Its technical competence was great, and it gave little attention to formalized management or planning. Its primary customer was the United States government, so it had little concern with systematic marketing. Under professional management today, it has diversified and grown with even greater consistency and success because it sees its first commitment to be the management and marketing of engineering, rather than engineering itself.

A planning orientation toward the chief strengths and interests of the natural leader who starts a company is not necessarily damaging. It may be valuable during the early growth years of the enterprise because it ensures unremitting concern and attention centered on the functions that make for initial success or failure. And there can be little doubt that imperfect plans vigorously pursued by a single-minded advocate will almost always prevail over more complete or logical plans that have divided support.

The Danger Period

When groups mature and their members become more competent, cohesive, and confident, a different style of planning is in order. If the leader does not change, people will leave—usually the best first. What planning is done will remain centralized and grow monolithic and cumbersome as a result. Decision making will slow down at the levels where the action should take place. Costs will increase, and effectiveness will deteriorate.

As a case in point, a large diversified company, today professionally managed, began its existence as a trading company with branches throughout Central and South America. The founder and president, a driving, extremely capable individual, required that he have reports of the previous day's operations from each branch office every morning. They came in, by telegraph, cable, and telephone, from Lima, Cali, and São Paulo.

Since the president spoke Spanish and Portuguese as well as English, this worked very well for a period. Problems were dealt with promptly in their original languages by return telegraph. However, this centralization generated a supporting bureaucracy in the branches. Costs increased and personal dissatisfaction mounted. A steady stream of people left the company—both American expatriates and indigenous supervisors. Some started their own firms, others provided trained talent to competitors.

The crisis occurred when the founder suffered a severe heart attack. The company literally ground to a halt. A consulting firm was called in by the board of directors and worked for 3 years to reorganize, retrain, and decentralize operations.

PLANNING DURING THE MANAGEMENT-LEADERSHIP STAGE

If the corridor of crisis is safely traversed and the enterprise adopts a professional management orientation, delegation, decentralization, and control by exception will be the order of the day. At this stage, new planning requirements parallel those in organization, leadership, and controls. The basic logic which holds is that informed, competent people work best if they are committed to the same overall objectives. They need the greatest possible opportunity to make their own decisions and to do their own work the way they prefer. This is facilitated if several conditions are satisfied.

Decentralization

No plan is any better than our ability to control it. To achieve control requires that we reserve enough authority to measure and evaluate progress and to ensure that corrective action is taken if objectives and standards are not met. This reserved authority must be limited, however. It should be exercised in terms of exceptions, so that each accountable person can make routine corrections while matters that threaten the accomplishment of overall objectives will be brought to the attention of the accountable manager.

Four-Way Communication

Natural leaders tend to tell people what they want and spend little time listening. This can succeed if people are untrained, inexperienced and uncertain, and are looking for direction. However, as groups mature, people increasingly want opportunity to contribute their own ideas, to question what is planned, and to offer help when they have special expertise.

This calls for understanding and acceptance, for communication in four directions. The first is communication downward. Others on the team want to be in on planning from its inception and to be kept informed of new developments as they occur. The second is communication upward. The accountable manager needs to know. Team members need to recognize their responsibility to communicate their own plans, to ask questions, to disagree without being disagreeable, to bring unpleasant matters up tactfully but firmly. If this return flow fails, communication dries up.

Communication on a peer level also is vital. Groups in a staff relationship are part of the team and can offer valuable help in planning if they are brought into the act and kept informed. Finally, outside groups and agencies are vital to the planning effort and must get the information they need to contribute to the plans and their implementation. Since the external environment largely determines how well and in what manner the team can operate best, a return flow of communication is a must.

Formalization

Planning in the early growth stage may be highly informal, mostly verbal and unwritten, but as the organization matures, a formal, logical, and consistent planning structure is necessary. This provides predictability so the various people and groups in the growing enterprise can act with confidence and accuracy. It enables people to learn from one another.

As we set about formalizing our plans, most of us are interested in what others have learned and what they are doing to improve their planning. One way to facilitate formalization is to attempt to capture the knowledge and experience of others by sorting it out and clearly stating whatever conclusions may be reached. In the next chapter, we will discuss one of these areas of general knowledge—the concept of accountability.

KEY POINTS

1. *The Evolution of Planning.* Planning has a natural evolution within an enterprise. Introducing a formalized planning system into an unprepared firm can be as harmful as allowing a firm to outgrow its planning system. The first stage, that of natural leadership, usually culminates in a period of crisis that is supplanted by the management-leadership stage.

2. *The Natural-Leadership Stage of Planning.* The natural-leadership stage is characterized by informality, centralization, and flexibility.

3. *The Corridor of Crisis.* Eventually, as the enterprise grows, there will be a crisis period in which subordinates have gained competence and are ready for more authority. This is a signal of the need for change, for decentralization. Resistance is common during this period—most often those who need change will least want it. If change does not come, however, people will become frustrated and leave.

4. *The Management-Leadership Stage of Planning.* As the enterprise moves to the management-leadership stage, new planning requirements must parallel those in organization, leadership, and controls. Decentralization, four-way communication, and formalization are necessary to provide limits and standards while giving people maximum freedom to use their initiative and creative abilities.

QUOTES FROM CHAPTER 3

Significant quotations from this chapter that you will want to consider and discuss in greater detail:

- If too much formalization of planning is attempted during the natural-leadership stage, action is stifled and plans end up on permanent file in desk drawers.

- Imperfect plans vigorously pursued by a single-minded advocate will almost always prevail over more complete or logical plans that have divided support.

- Team members need to recognize their responsibility to communicate their own plans, to ask questions, to disagree without being disagreeable.

ACCOUNTABILITY FOR PLANNING

There can be no stable and balanced development of the mind, apart from the assumption of responsibility.
JOHN DEWEY

THE CHAPTER IN BRIEF Our plans can be effective only if we have some way of ensuring that they are properly developed and are carried out successfully. This calls for accountability. We establish accountability for both plans and their outcomes by defining the work that must be done, delegating the authority necessary to carry out the plans, securing understanding and agreement, and setting standards to measure both work and results. This accountability cannot be delegated. Differentiation between the accountability of people in line and staff relationships is vital if we are to maintain effective teamwork.

THE CONCEPT OF ACCOUNTABILITY

In performing planning, a few core ideas have evolved that seem to apply everywhere planning is done, and they are generally accepted by practicing managers. In order to deal with these core ideas in a logical fashion, we can separate them out and define and name them. This will provide a convenient basis for securing agreement and improvement. Those who wish can then work within the same framework further to test, refine, and expand these core ideas. To know what generalizations about planning can safely be made will be useful. For convenience we can call these "management concepts" and define them as general ideas in management stated in communicable form. First we will discuss the Concept of Accountability.

THE NEED FOR ACCOUNTABILITY

Managers make things happen in an organization and, conversely, make them not happen. However, when things go wrong, we are most likely to look to the operating levels for corrective action. The chief thrust of quality circles, productivity improvement, and cost reduction is technical and operating personnel. In too many cases, however, the poorest

41

quality work, the lowest productivity, and the highest costs come from managers, not operators.

In a large, diversified processing company, for example, some $500,000 was spent in an attempt to improve the productivity of plant and service employees through work measurement and improvement. No attention, however, was paid to the productivity of managerial personnel, who, per capita, accounted for over 10 times the direct costs of operators. The reason given was that it was impossible to measure management; therefore, there was no basis for evaluating and improving their work.

Since managers commonly are measured by the results they get through others, not what they do themselves, it is difficult to measure their personal effectiveness and productivity. However, this lack of accountability is dangerous. Because of it we find it difficult to identify shortcomings in performance before they reach the crisis stage. And even when results are not what we expect, if we do not know *who* to hold accountable and for *what*, we have little basis for helping the managers concerned to improve.

WHAT IS ACCOUNTABILITY?

There are many different ideas about accountability—all the way from what it means to how it is used. Some insist on individual or unique accountability, others are equally firm that accountability must be shared—joint accountability is the preferred mode. To boil this down to the essentials, we should define accountability in simple, concrete terms and then see how it applies in practice.

We define "accountability" as the obligation to carry out the duties or responsibilities and to exercise the authority of a position in conformance with understood and accepted standards. Here we must define three terms. "Responsibility" is the work assigned to a position. For example, one responsibility of a manager is to prepare an annual plan. "Authority" is the sum of the powers and rights assigned to a position. This makes the marriage. If you have responsibility, you are assigned the work. If you have authority, you have both the right and the ability to make the decisions, spend the money, or move the mountains the work requires. "Performance standards" are the criteria by which the work and results are measured. One standard might be to complete the plan in 3 months; another, at a cost of no more than $73,000.

As an example, suppose you want to install a new word processing unit. Since you do not intend to personally supervise every move that is made, you must be able to hold somebody accountable for installing the word processor for you. But there are many types of word processing units and a variety of ways to install them. To ensure that it is done properly, you will have to agree upon a detailed plan beforehand. By requiring the installation to follow the plan implicitly, you maintain accountability.

Planning can be effective only to the degree we can hold people accountable for doing work and achieving results in an agreed-upon manner. While there is substantial agreement on the need for accountability, the way to establish it is another matter.

ACCOUNTABILITY AND PLANNING

Accountability is a central concept in managerial planning. It may be difficult to hold individuals accountable for parts of the corporate plan, but in managerial planning the idea that individuals, not groups, are accountable is vital. In fact, our business, corporate, financial, marketing, and production plans become useful tools and not display pieces only to the extent we can hold individuals accountable, both for making the plans and for carrying them out.

"A company's President is solely and personally responsible for his firm's success or failure," said Konosuke Matsushita, president of Matsushita Electric Industrial Co. of Japan.* Extended to include every manager in the company, his statement accurately reflects modern attitudes toward accountability. We must be able to hold individuals to account if work is not done or planned results are not secured. Theories of group or team accountability do not hold up in practice, because too much time is required and there is strong likelihood of evasion if we try to hold several people to an obligation for reaching sales objectives or meeting a quality standard.

Planning Accountability Cannot Be Delegated

As a manager, you can delegate to others the work of developing plans for you; you can permit them to make decisions with respect to what goes into plans. However, you cannot hold others accountable for your plans, or for carrying them out, no matter how much they have contributed.

A suburban branch of a metropolitan bank developed a computerized

---

*"A Company's President . . . must not try to pass the buck." Fortune *Magazine*, October 1960, p. 112.

procedure for transferring funds. The savings supervisor of the branch carefully trained a new teller to use the procedure. A few days later the branch manager was confronted by an irate customer whose telephone order to shift a large sum of money had been mishandled. Called to account by the branch manager, the savings supervisor blamed the teller. When this was rejected, she claimed the computer was at fault. "I don't hold the teller or the computer accountable," the branch manager said. "I expect you to find the reason the mistake occurred, to fix it, and to make sure it doesn't happen again."

This holds true at higher as well as lower levels. A manager's plans and their outcomes cannot be delegated. The president usually delegates preparation and implementation of the corporate plan which then becomes the "property" of the planning director or administrative manager. However, no matter how sincere their intent, these individuals can hardly be held accountable either for the content or implementation of the overall plan. As Konosuke Matsushita points out, this can only be the accountability of the president. So also, when we speak of a marketing or finance plan, we usually mean *part* of the plan of the chief executive officer. A division manager's plan may contain manufacturing or operating and marketing or sales components and a plant manager's plan may include production, engineering, and maintenance plans.

Our conclusion: Individuals can be held to account for plans and planning, organizations cannot. The more completely people understand and agree to the plans they are expected to carry out, the better able we are to hold them to account.

IS LINE OR STAFF ACCOUNTABLE?

We have already discussed the problems that arise when staff develops plans that are to be carried out by managers who will be held accountable for results. This is a key issue, for most plans *are* developed by staff. The need is to develop teamwork by identifying the part each plays and ensuring that there is generous credit for all. While the ball-carrier gets the credit for making a touchdown, a good coach knows which players did the passing, blocking, and ran interference to make it possible and sees to it they get full credit.

Managers are accountable for the plans that are developed *for* them by staff. But people in a staff relationship, in turn, have their own accountability for the content and quality of the work they do. For example, if the division manager has a smashing success introducing a new product, the division manager gets full credit. But the corporate advertising department and the advertising agency which developed the advertising plan for the division manager also must get credit for the content and quality of their contribution. A wise division manager who expects to repeat the success will be quick and generous with praise.

Relationships between line and staff are important in planning because staff agencies generally have the specialized knowledge, skill, and time to develop plans for accountable managers. Our understanding of this relationship today is different in many respects from the military usage from which it is derived.

The Line Relationship

"Line" refers to the line of command and accountability and always relates to an objective. If you are obligated to accomplish an objective, you are held to account if you fail or succeed. However, in order to be accountable, you must first agree to accomplish the objective. You must also have the power and right to do what is necessary to achieve it. If you agree to the objective of cutting costs by 10% but are not permitted to consolidate the two positions and buy the improved equipment necessary to accomplish it, the accountability is empty. When you are in a line relationship to any objective, this means that you make final decisions with respect to it. You are always in a line relationship to those who report to you.

Definition of the Line Relationship

This is the command relationship of those persons and positions directly accountable for achieving objectives and therefore vested with the authority needed for that purpose.

The Staff Relationship

"Staff" refers to the relationship you set up when you offer advice and help to others who are accountable for reaching an objective, that is, are in a line relationship to it. Of course, you offer help and advice to a great many people in the organization. Each time you do, you will be most cordially received and your help will be appreciated if you remember how to act in your staff role. (Incidentally, the rules work especially well between husbands and wives, who shift constantly from line to staff in their relationships.)

Definition of the Staff Relationship

This is the relationship of those positions and components accountable for advice and service to those positions and components accountable for direct accomplishment of objectives.

Staff Roles

The use of staff has a long and mixed history. Modern usage tends to make staff groups fully contributing and very important members of the management team. The question of importance almost always arises in the minds of those who do the helping. Many people prefer not to be labeled "staff." However, the question is not one of importance, but of role. Both line and staff have important missions, just as do the surgeon and the anesthetist. Both are vital to success. What is more, all staff positions have line roles and all line roles and all line people are at time staff.

A person is "staff" to another when the primary role is one of providing advice and service, rather than of command. For example, we could have the operating and sales department each collect its own accounts, pay out its own money, make its own financial reports. However, it is much more effective to have one accounting department do this work for both operations and sales. To show this difference in role, we place accounting in the staff role. This placement does not indicate a difference in rank, pay, or importance. It means that the primary, continuing role of accounting is advisory and service, or staff, to the overall key objectives, to the operations and marketing functions, and to the president.

MAKING LINE AND STAFF WORK

Harmonious relationships between line and staff are vital to sound planning, where staff often plays a primary role. Line and staff relationships work best when the person who is accountable for the final result makes the final decisions about how to achieve that result, within limits set by overall policies or agreements. If you are a sales representative, for example, and your objective is to sell 1000 units, you need to be able to make the final decisions about how you will do it, within the limits set by the price book, standard payment, delivery terms, and sales policies. If you are the sales manager or her supervisor, the marketing vice-president, the same holds true. This means that when the sales manager develops her sales budget, she, not the budget manager, decides what goes into it. The marketing director, to whom she reports, approves her budget, not the finance director, to whom the budget manager reports.

It is vital to know how to make effective use of line and staff relationships. When you are accountable for an objective, the likelihood is that you will need specialized advice and help. This may come from your subordinates, your peers, or outsiders. To encourage these people to want to do work for you and to keep their best ideas and suggestions flowing in your direction, you will want to observe certain rules. First, you will be seeking participation. You will get it to the degree you can help other people have an emotional ownership in results that all will work to help achieve. But keep in mind that you are accountable, which means that you make the final decisions. When you've been trying to help other people build their own ideas into what you're doing, it is sometimes difficult to say "no" when they're pressing you to say "yes." Since you are in a line relationship to your own objective, you are accountable for what happens. Explain your stand calmly and reasonably, and make your own decision.

Call on other people when you think they can be helpful. Encourage them to come forward with suggestions when they have specialized knowledge you can use.

HOW TO MAKE ACCOUNTABILITY EFFECTIVE

When you develop a plan, you want to know how you can hold all the people involved accountable for the parts they play. Control is the key. No plan is any better than its controls, that is, the performance standards, the reporting system, and the methods of evaluation and correction you use to make sure the plan is carried out.

The Role of Controls

"Control" is the process of assessing and regulating work as it is being done and when it is completed. When work is completed and the results are in, it is too late to do much about it. At best, if the work is applied or repeated, we can be alert to the causes of deviations and make corrections on the next repetition. However, for one-time programs and projects, it is vital to know when to apply controls for maximum effect.

A television analogy is helpful. An electron gun is used to generate the beam which places a picture on a television screen. The electron gun starts with a heated cathode which emits electrons. This is the point where the action occurs. The beam of electrons is controlled en route to the tube screen. The farther away the controlling devices are located from the electron emitter, the more power is required to achieve a given control, that is, the closer to the action, the easier the control.

A similar situation holds in management control. If we want to control an operation, the best place to start the process is with the people who are doing the work. The more information they have about their work, and the sooner they get it, the more likely they are to exercise effective control.

Who Is Accountable?

We know that our plans are no better than our ability to make sure they are carried out, in other words, to control them. Control, in turn, is dependent upon our ability to hold individuals, not groups, accountable for results. Popular theories of group responsibility and joint or shared accountability offer contrary ideas. However, experience demonstrates that the individuals in a group will tend to dodge or reject accountability. If the group does accept it, it is more difficult to secure corrective action from two or more people than it would be from one. To control with confidence and precision, we should be able to hold individuals accountable for designated results.

As a case in point, Sea Land Service, a subsidiary of R. J. Reynolds Industries, found it difficult to correct marketing problems and sales deviations in the field because plans and budgets followed the customary practice of identifying units and groups. Incentive awards were often disputed because of disagreement about who actually earned the award. Then the company clearly defined the responsibility and authority of each manager and set understood and accepted standards. This established clear-cut accountability. Regional and terminal managers then had individual charters for action, and the confusion was greatly reduced.

In practice, managers cannot inspect everything under their supervision personally. It limits the managers and demotivates their teams. They must hold each person under them to an obligation to do the work and secure agreed-upon results within limits that have been set. Holding individuals accountable is not arbitrary; it is an expression of basic human needs. People want their own territory. Fixing accountability gives them clear-cut duties and rights. It sets limits so that others will not encroach on their work and authority. People who have clearly defined jobs and are supported in making the key decisions quickly develop emotional ownership in what they are doing. This encourages them to protect, enrich, and improve both their work and decisions.

Many planning systems run contrary to these principles by setting up departmental and group plans that are developed from varied inputs but are the clear accountability of nobody. This can be avoided by making each position, and its incumbent, accountable for clearly defined planning responsibilities and authorities within agreed limits.

MEASURE BOTH WORK AND RESULTS

Current emphasis on management by objectives and management by results has much to commend it; however, it is a fallacy to assume that a manager's only concern should be the results secured. By the time results can be measured, the game is over and it is too late to do anything about errors and deviations until the next time around—if there is one.

Since results are always the outcome of work, it is equally important to measure the work done to attain your results. You also want to have standards to measure the work so you can take corrective action before the final whistle blows. Sound plans provide both for the necessary work and the desired results, and they are accompanied by standards that enable you to track both.

This emphasis upon work and results also helps reduce the tendency to measure people and their personalities, not the work they do. You are sure to communicate better if you can say "You are 3 days behind in your schedule, and your costs are off 18%" than if you express it as "You are a slow worker, and you're spending too much money." But this can't be a one-way street. Not only must you reciprocate with *your* help on *their* problems, but you also must give careful consideration to their ideas. You owe every suggestion either an answer or action. And be generous in your acknowledgment and praise. If you neglect to keep people informed about what happens to their suggestions, if you put your own stamp on their ideas and claim them as your own, you'll dry up the well before it can flow.

With this idea of universals in mind, we will next look at three planning principles: the Principle of the Critical Few, the Principle of Resistance to Change, and the Principle of Point of Control.

KEY POINTS

1. *Accountability Is Vital to Sound Planning.* Our plans can only be as effective as our ability to ensure that people do the planning they should and carry out their plans effectively. We secure this accountability by defining the

work to be done and the authority to be delegated and then holding people to an obligation to meet agreed-upon standards.

2. *Accountability Is Unitary.* If we want to control our plans, we must be able to hold individuals accountable both for results and the work necessary to achieve them. Theories of shared or joint accountability usually do not work because people want their own territories to own and develop.

3. *Line and Staff Accountability.* Confusion arises when we try to hold line and staff jointly accountable for plans and their results. The logical way to clarify the situation is to hold each accountable. The person in a line relationship is accountable for the overall results. The person in a staff relationship, who prepares the plans, is accountable for the contents and quality of the plan but not for carrying it out.

4. *Plans Are No Better than Their Controls.* To control effectively, we use performance standards, meaningful reports, and a means of evaluating and correcting deviations from plans. The most effective controls are those that can be applied by the person doing the work. That individual is fully accountable for results.

QUOTES FROM CHAPTER 4

Significant quotations from this chapter that you will want to consider and discuss in greater detail:

- Since managers commonly are measured by the results they get through others, not what they do themselves, it is difficult to measure their personal effectiveness and productivity. However, this lack of accountability is dangerous.

- Theories of group or team accountability do not hold up in practice.

- Individuals can be held to account for plans and planning, organizations cannot.

- When you are in a line relationship to any objective, this means that you make final decisions with respect to it.

- All staff positions have line roles and all line roles and all line people are at times staff.

- No plan is any better than its controls.

- People who have clearly defined jobs and are supported in making the key decisions quickly develop emotional ownership in what they are doing.

- If you neglect to keep people informed about what happens to their suggestions, if you put your own stamp on their ideas and claim them as your own, you'll dry up the well before it can flow.

5

PLANNING PRINCIPLES

It is easier to produce ten volumes of philosophical writing than to put one principle into practice.
LEO TOLSTOY

THE CHAPTER IN BRIEF   Principles are statements of universal cause-and-effect relationships. They are another means of profiting from the experience and knowledge of other managers. The principle of the critical few alerts us in our planning to seek out the few causes that give the greatest results. The principle of resistance to change helps us overcome the greatest obstacle to planning success by making people part of the planning. The principle of point of control puts controls in the hands of the people who carry out the plan.

PRINCIPLES AS PREDICTIVE TOOLS

As in other fields of endeavor, planning has its certainties as well as uncertainties. We have a host of sophisticated tools: mathematical, psychological, and analytical. However, often we become so immersed in these complex methods that we lose sight of the ends we seek. I find that most managers, in fact, soon become impatient with the intricate formulas they try to work out on their computers and calculators and turn the whole lot over to planning staff. In doing so, unfortunately, they also relinquish their proprietary interest in the planning task.

Instead of adding to the complex array of methods we eventually mistrust and ignore, we need to seek the simple truths that underlie human effort. Just as principles have been discovered and defined in other disciplines, so must it be with planning. From observation we know that when certain forces are at work, predictable results tend to follow. For example, if we are planning to reduce inventory levels, we know that only a relatively small number of items will be consistently out of stock, but that these few will give rise to almost all of the complaints. If we center planning on those few, we will be able to keep adequate inventories with greatest certainty and least expense.

We state principles to capture these cause-and-effect relationships in planning. As you become familiar with the principles, you will find them particularly helpful in thinking through alternatives and in reaching planning decisions. First is the principle of the critical few, which is also known as Pareto's law and the 80-20 rule.

51

THE PRINCIPLE OF THE CRITICAL FEW

A hoary truism governs most management action: The squeaking wheel gets the grease. Immediate situations that threaten short-term loss almost always get the largest share of attention and resources. The product line that fails to meet objectives for 7 months is the subject of a dozen management meetings, a staff study, and the attentions of an outside consultant. On the other hand, the product line that becomes an overnight hit gets verbal accolades but no more attention and resources than will enable it to maintain the promising pace it has already set.

The same holds true in other areas. The personnel department plans to use a large share of its budget for companywide programs to reduce absenteeism and to provide counseling for dissatisfied, unhappy employees. It has little money left to keep the high performers motivated and to build skills in those who show aptitude and dedication. Yet even a cursory survey will show that only a few people are chronically absent and a relatively small number are habitually discontented.

The key to success in any undertaking is to use available resources to exploit the greatest opportunities. Our human tendency is to use our resources to solve our most immediate and pressing problems. These solutions generally account for only a small part of the final results. The principle of the critical few helps us to identify the most productive allocation. We can state the principle as follows: *In any given group of occurrences, a small number of causes tend to give rise to the largest proportion of results.*

How It Works

If you toss a coin fairly, the mathematical probability of getting heads or tails is 50% for heads, 50% for tails. But people seem to respond to a different set of probabilities. For example, if you want to identify intelligent people for special training, you can assume that in a group selected at random about 20% will have above-average intelligence, 60% will cluster around the median, and about 20% will have below-average intelligence. If your concern is to plan the most effective use of your sales force, you can anticipate that about 20% of your potential market will produce 80% of your customers. And, almost perversely, if you leave your salespeople to their own devices, they will tend to use about 80% of their time and resources trying to sell to the least profitable 20% of their customers.

This inverse proportion, while it may only approximate 20–80, holds true in most aspects of management. For example, Ducommun, Inc., metals and hardware distributor, finds that some 10% of its customers account for about 65% of its sales. A.C. Nielsen Co. anticipates that 65% of new product introductions will fail while 35% will be successful.

The Marginal Many or the Critical Few?

An important aspect of any plan is to identify the critical few occurrences and to concentrate the largest share of effort and resources on them. Making use of this principle, a Bank of America branch manager in Los Angeles established a formal customer-call program at his branch. Previously, the branch staff had been spending customer contact time on random visits, some of which included marginally profitable accounts. He reversed this by identifying the critical few depositors and borrowers and concentrating on these customers. As he put it, "We have been pleasantly surprised at the additional business that has been obtained from these customers in the way of real estate loans, equipment loans and business savings."*

The principle extends to every aspect of both management and technical work. It can serve as a lever to enable us to get greater returns from the smallest expenditure of effort and resources.

To use this principle, however, we must anticipate several human tendencies. We resist the effort of sorting through the choices available and selecting the most promising. It is much easier to plunge ahead with whatever comes to hand. We must be willing to seek out the leverage points—the critical few causative factors.

When we develop programs for research, for example, we can anticipate that only a few of the projects proposed will have real payout potential; however, our tendency is always to spread available funds over the marginal many rather than concentrating them on the critical few.

Circumventing the Critical Few

A small number of products will generate most sales and profits, yet often we will nurse old and obsolete lines, which, even if they stay in the catalog, require disproportionate effort for paltry returns. In a sales force of any size, a few salespeople will always be the standout per-

*"Management Principles" *Management Magazine,* Bank of America, Vol. 8, No. 7, September 1978, p. 5.

formers and account for the larger part of our sales. Too often, however, we design sales compensation programs which offer proportionately greater rewards to the poorest performers and put a lid on the efforts of the outstanding salespeople.

The principle applies also when you put a new program into effect. You can always anticipate that the large bulk of problems will occur during the initial stages of the project. For example, if you anticipate it will require 18 months to install and debug a new management information system, you can be confident that most of the problems will arise during the first 3 or 4 months. You will tend to staff for this most troublesome period. And this opens the door to one of the greatest sources of waste and inefficiency, for you will be under constant pressure to maintain the same number of people after the program is established, even though 20% or more of them are now redundant.

Anticipating Change in the Critical Few

One caution: The critical few are in constant process of change. The best performers may lose their punch, high-selling product lines fall out of favor, creative people lose their spark. This means that we must be constantly alert for the signals of change. The best way to do this is to watch trends. The critical few rarely drop abruptly out of position; usually they slide back step by step. This can be identified and monitored. Unfortunately, we tend to stick with the loser too long. Because of personal familiarity, reluctance to lose our investment, or sheer inertia, we procrastinate.

Controls can help. Plan to exert 80% control effort during the first 20% of time required to install or carry out any program. This is also true when you hire a new person or retain an outside consultant or specialist. In the beginning, check every day; later, you will check every month. Require frequent reports. Hold meetings often. Make personal inspections.

As soon as matters smooth out, you can ease up, so that by the halfway mark you have decentralized authority to a large degree. You will find that people are not resentful of close control at first because they recognize the need. As you begin to delegate, they will appreciate your trust and the confidence you show in them.

On the other hand, if in the early stages you delegate too much authority and responsibility and maintain minimal controls, you will find that matters soon get out of hand. People will pursue their own special interests, too much money will be spent, the operation will become slack. When you try to correct matters by tightening controls, people will resent your interference and will conclude you have neither trust nor confidence in them.

The Critical Few in Planning Your Time. The principle of the critical few applies especially to planning the use of your own time. One of the most informative exercises you can conduct is to keep a time diary for 5 days. Divide 5 sheets of paper into 30-minute segments. Keep a record of exactly how you spend your time for each segment. If you have a secretary at hand, you might enlist his or her aid. At the end of the week, make a tabulation of the major categories of work, with the time devoted to each. Take the list to each person who reports to you and to the principal staff specialists with whom you work. See how much of the work you have done they would be willing to take over or, in fact, may feel they should be doing. You'll probably find they will lay claim to well over half of what you do. What remain are the critical few.

How can you determine where you should invest your personal time? Most of it should be spent in matters that affect your organization as a whole. Whether it be a section, a department, or the company, everything you do should meet the test: Is this work necessary and important to help my entire group meet its objectives? If the work applies only to individuals, delegate it, for you cannot afford to spend your time doing the work of other people for them.

We know that every plan is a plan for change. Unfortunately, however, when we prepare our plans, we rarely give appropriate consideration to the most vital element in successful change—the people involved. The principle of resistance to change deals with this need.

THE PRINCIPLE OF RESISTANCE TO CHANGE

The history of enterprise is replete with opportunities lost because people resisted change and with futures made by those who seized the occasion. As Machiavelli summarized it: "There is nothing more difficult of success, nor more dangerous to handle, than to initiate a new order of things." The reasons for this resistance are clear enough. We have a basic need for security. This inborn predisposition is threatened by anything that is new and strange. Successful managers are often risk takers. If they expect to bring their people along with them, they must know how to overcome the innate resistance to change that is present. The following statement of the principle summarizes the situation: *The greater the departure of planned changes from accepted ways, the greater the potential resistance by the people involved.*

We tend to resist change because we fear and distrust people and things with which we are unfamiliar and which may threaten our security. It follows that the more we can help our people to understand changes and what they involve, the more familiar they will become and the less opposition there will be.

How to Overcome Resistance

This familiarity is not difficult to achieve. Two key words govern it: communication and participation. A midwestern warehousing chain, for example, planned to change from one to three shifts to better utilize capital equipment and meet delivery schedules. When the change was proposed, however, resistance was so universal a strike was threatened. The company retreated and developed a new plan which provided for overcoming resistance to change.

A task force of warehouse employees was appointed and asked to study the advantages and disadvantages of the change in shifts. The task force determined that substantial savings would be possible; however, fewer day-shift operators would be needed and some would have to change to less desirable hours. The company offered to share half the savings in the form of shift premiums. A series of employee meetings was conducted, the advantages and disadvantages were discussed, and employees were asked for their recommendations. A clear majority was in favor, so the change was successfully introduced.

Communication and participation will not occur automatically; they must be built into the plan. This means that an early step in any plan should involve telling those concerned what the plan is, what the benefits to them will be, and what will happen. Equally important is to provide for involvement by the people concerned. The more they participate in the decisions that are made, the greater the emotional ownership they will develop and the better their support. Securing communication and participation requires time, and this should become part of every schedule that is developed.

THE PRINCIPLE OF POINT OF CONTROL

The principle of point of control can be stated as follows: *The greatest potential for control tends to exist at the point where the action takes place.* As a case in point, in a Pittsburgh company, reports of plant variances were sent directly to the division manager, who analyzed them and then sent them back with directives written and underlined in red. This gave rise to continuing explanation and rationalization through eight organization levels. A new division manager developed objectives, programs, schedules, and budgets at the supervisory level and provided the supervisors with performance reports. As a result, the total number of reports decreased, unnecessary coordination was eliminated, and operating control became more effective than it had ever been in the past.

This brings home the conclusion that we cannot achieve adequate controls without accurate objectives, programs, schedules, and budgets. We should make sure that our plans are developed with the participation of the people who will actually be doing the work. Once we have their approval, we can hold them accountable for control based on these plans. When variances occur, our people will then be able to identify why they have occurred and to take effective corrective action.

We have looked at some of the factors necessary to formalization of planning. In the next chapter, we will further the process by developing a logical structure of planning.

KEY POINTS

1. *Principles: A Means of Capturing Universals.* One way to distill the essentials of any field of knowledge is to identify those cause-and-effect relationships—or principles—that will provide continuing guidance. We define several principles that apply wherever planning work is done.
2. *The Principle of the Critical Few. In any given group of occurrences, a small number of causes tend to give rise to the largest portion of results.* Keeping this in mind, managers can use available resources to exploit the greatest opportunities. A small number of products often generate most sales and profits—these are the critical few.
3. *Changes in the Critical Few.* The critical few are in constant process of change. Controls can help us identify and monitor these changes. A large degree of control at the beginning of a new program is necessary to keep the operation tight—later, responsibility can more easily be delegated.
4. *The Principle of Resistance to Change. The greater the departure of planned changes from accepted ways, the greater the potential resistance by the people involved.* Greater understanding of change results in greater emotional ownership of the plan and, hence, less opposition.
5. *The Principle of Point of Control. The greatest potential for control tends to exist at the point where the action takes place.*

QUOTES FROM CHAPTER 5

Significant quotations from this chapter that you will want to consider and discuss in greater detail:

- A small number of products will generate most sales and profits, yet often we will nurse old and obsolete lines, which . . . require disproportionate effort for paltry returns.

- When we prepare our plans, we rarely give appropriate consideration to the most vital element—the people involved.

THE STRUCTURE OF PLANNING

It is awkward to carry uncoined gold: that's what a thinker does who has no formulas.
FRIEDRICH NIETZSCHE

THE CHAPTER IN BRIEF   With a foundation of basic concepts, principles, and defined terms, we can now look to the development of a logical structure of planning. Our first need is to set up a scheme of classification so we will have an orderly and logical way of assembling our data. We will discuss the Concept of Work Classification as a basis for classifying the work of management and planning. We will find it also provides an integrating logic for developing our planning, control, and organization structures.

NEED FOR A PLANNING STRUCTURE

Everywhere we see the need for structure, for formulas. The human body has flexibility; its tissues and organs mesh with integrity; and it has the ability to grow harmoniously because of its supporting and limiting skeleton. Planning also must have a structure. By this we mean a framework into which all parts of the planning process will fit.

Every company that plans of necessity has developed some kind of planning structure. Some are logical and integrated. We can learn much from them. However, I found that most planning structures have been built rather haphazardly. From the experience of companies that have developed effective planning structures, it is clear than an orderly, logical framework offers many advantages. It will facilitate the coordination of plans at different levels and among positions on the same level. If the logic of the structure is consistent, it will accommodate the various types of plans we require and thus avoid the territorial prerogatives and compartmentation that blunt much current planning effort.

In seeking leads for such a structure, I could find no clear rationale which looked at planning as a whole rather than in terms of its individual parts. As I talked to planners, it became obvious that most were uneasily wedded to the planning system that already existed in their companies. As we have seen, most of these derived originally from the budgetary process and conformed to the technical demands of accounting rather than the creative requirements of management.

The planning structure we develop should help each individual, each group, and the enterprise as a whole to proceed in unison toward the same ends. To be useful, such a process not only must satisfy the negative criteria of avoiding overlap and duplication of effort; it must also contribute positive attributes of encouraging proper scope and timing. It should facilitate coordination of plans at different levels and among positions on the same level.

THE CONCEPT OF WORK CLASSIFICATION

Planning cannot stand by itself. Since it both is part of and overreaches all of management, the planning structure will be part of the management structure. The first step in developing an orderly, logical planning and management structure is to find means of sorting, categorizing, and defining the information we use in planning and of establishing a consistent terminology based on it. This calls for a system of classification.

Benefits of Work Classification

Other sciences and disciplines have had similar problems in their formative stages. For example, from the days of Aristotle, attempts were made to develop an orderly, logical classification of the million or more different types of plants and animals. For lack of such a taxonomy, early scientists could not communicate accurately or build upon knowledge that had been accumulated by others. The problem was solved only after Linnaeus developed a classification based on logical analysis, identification, and definition of the different types of plants and animals.

Since a first requirement of measurement is that anything that is to be measured must first be identified and defined, a logical classification of work would enable managers to measure and evaluate their performance and results more precisely. It would also facilitate exchange of information about better methods that lead to improved management results. A standardized classification of management work would be a valuable aid to management education for it would help identify the logical sequence of subjects which should be learned to master any one field or management as a whole.

Definitions

We can define "work classification" as the logical arrangement of different kinds of work in groupings according to recognized criteria.

The classification must be logical so it can be replicated by others in precisely the same manner and with similar results. If we can establish criteria by which to evaluate the groupings, we will have a means of determining whether they are valid.

Definition of Work. The term "work" needs definition. It comes from a Greek word meaning "to do," but, while usage varies, the definition in terms of mechanics is most common. This specifies that work is the transfer of energy by a force acting against a resistance or body so that displacement occurs. Work thus is a form of energy that can be converted into other forms of energy. We rarely consider the many ways in which transfers of energy can occur, but it is clear we also might consider electrical, chemical, human, and even genetic work. Since our concern now is human work, we will concentrate on it.

For our purpose we look upon human work as the exertion of mental and physical effort to achieve an objective. The energy used in human work may be mental or physical. It is purposeful in that it is intended to achieve results; otherwise, it is not human work any more than a drive wheel at rest is mechanical work.

The Classification Logic

With these considerations in mind, we now need to state a logic on which we can base our classification of work, a conceptual framework into which we can fit all the different kinds of human work, hopefully in comfortable companionship with one another. As criteria, we can establish that the work categories must be logically related through some common integrating factor. They should be discrete, in that each should have clearly identifiable beginning and end points. There should be little or no overlap or duplication in the categories of work. Taken together, they should form an interrelated whole, but each should be clearly definable as a separate entity.

Human Needs Are the Engine. If we are to classify the different kinds of human work, we should understand why people work in the first place. The answer is clear: because they want something. We work to satisfy needs, wants, and desires. These needs are of two kinds: those which are with us when we first enter the world, which we can call "genetic needs," and those which we learn or acquire after birth, which we can call "cultural needs." Needs are the engine that drive all human action: the need to fill our stomachs, to find relief from frustration, to conquer the world.

Needs Are Satisfied by Results. Needs prompt action. We are hungry, we eat. The work of eating does not truly satisfy our need, however. Our hunger need is satisfied when we ingest the product of the eating, the nutrients necessary to remain alive and active. Needs are satisfied by results, not by work. This distinction is so simple it is often overlooked. Yet it is vital to our understanding of the logic of the planning process.

Results Are the Outcome of Work. Results occur because physical and mental effort have been expended. If we see a result, for example, a piece of advertising literature or a new computer installation, we can readily determine what work was necessary to produce it. This distinction is important because the common tendency of planners is to confuse results with the work necessary to accomplish them. Another factor differentiating work from results is that results of themselves do not consume resources. For example, the new advertising brochure is an end point; it is the work that goes into it that uses materials, human effort, and other resources. Results then, are clearly different from work, and results are always the outcome of work.

Work Leads to Results. The reverse is also true. If mental and physical effort are being expended purposefully, the intention is to produce a result of some kind. We may not get from the work the result we expected, but the intention is there. If we observe work being done and we are familiar with the operation, we know what result can be expected. For example, if we see typing work being done, we know a definite type of communication will result.

This interaction between work and results is simple, but it is not simplistic. It is a powerful logic that will help us develop structures for planning, organization, and controls. We show it in Figure 6-1.

From the figure, we can see that needs prompt both work and results. To put it another way, since objectives are predetermined results and organization is the arrangement of work, we can say that we accomplish objectives through organization. The figure shows standards, which are the basis for controls and are derived from the same logic that will yield our plans and organization. We will discuss these ideas as we proceed with the concept of work classification.

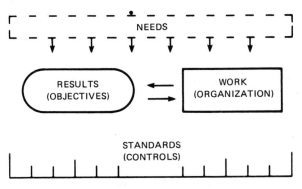

FIGURE 6-1 The Logic of Work and Results

Statement of Concept. We can state the concept of work classification as follows: *Work can be arranged logically by dividing it into the categories and subcategories necessary to achieve its objectives.* This implies that the work done by humans can be divided into logical categories by defining the objectives to be achieved and then determining the categories of work necessary to achieve those objectives. Each category of work can be divided into subcategories, following the same logic.

The Classification Nomenclature

To provide names for the different categories of plants and animals, we use a nomenclature with such terms as "family," "genus," and "species." We also need a nomenclature to identify the different categories of human work. Since there is presently no classification nomenclature or taxonomy, I have proposed that we use the following, with the acronym COFASE:

Class

Order

Function

Activity

Segment

Element

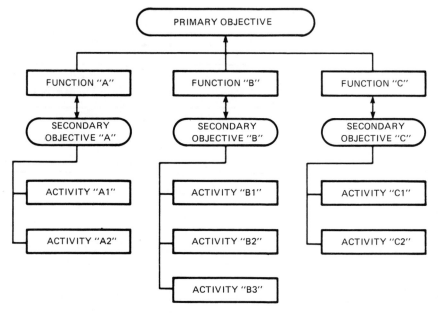

FIGURE 6-2   The Classification Logic

The classification logic is shown schematically in Figure 6-2. Here we see the *functions* derived from the primary objective and the *activities* derived from the secondary objective. This can be continued through all levels to the *elements*. If we wish, we can begin with *class* or *order* rather than *function*.

As an example of the use of the concept of work classification, we will now look at the classification of the class of human work.

THE CLASSIFICATION OF HUMAN WORK

If we want to divide the *class* of human work into its *orders*, we begin with the objective. As we have seen, the objective of human work is to satisfy genetic and cultural needs. Again following our concept, to determine the orders into which the class of human work logically divides, we ask ourselves: What are the primary categories of physical and mental effort people exert so that they can satisfy their genetic and cultural needs?

The Orders of Human Work

Using the classification logic, I have been able to identify two orders of human work, namely, technical and management. One is work that is applied directly to resources; for example, a carpenter works directly on the building being constructed, a surgeon operates directly on the patient, a salesperson appeals directly to a customer. Since this work has a purpose, is of a particular kind, and is done by an individual, we call it "technical work." We can define the Order of Technical Work as *the physical and mental effort exerted by individuals to secure results through their own efforts, rather than through the efforts of other people.*

A second order of human work is the physical and mental effort a person in a leadership position exerts so as to secure results from resources through and with other people. This I call "management work." Project supervisors build houses by supervising the technical work of carpenters, masons, electricians, and plumbers. Supervisors are managing while they plan, organize, lead, and control the work of the technical specialists. They perform technical work when they do carpentry, plumbing, or masonry work.

We can define the Order of Management Work as *the physical and mental effort exerted by individuals in leadership positions to secure results through the efforts of other people.*

The Functions of Management Work

Our concern now is to break down management work and technical work into their functions. We will begin this work analysis with management work, as shown in Figure 6-3.

As we have seen, to develop a logical classification, we must first determine the objective. We know that the objective of all managers is to perform that work which will enable them to get effective results through other people. This means that they do not do the same work as their followers. Managers are leaders, and as such, they have a unique organizational position which enables them to perform certain work which their followers cannot perform for themselves.*

---

*For a more complete analysis of the position and evolution of leaders and managers see Louis A. Allen, *Professional Management: New Concepts and Proven Practices*, McGraw-Hill Book Company, New York, 1973.

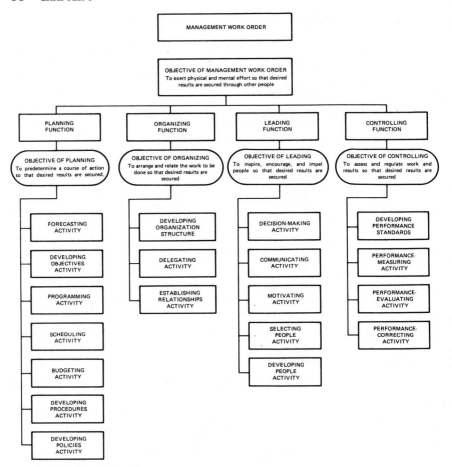

FIGURE 6-3   Classification of the Management Work Order

The Management Functions. Following this logic, we can conclude that leaders have a unique vantage point that enables them to perform four kinds of work most effectively for the groups they lead.

1. Before a group can act effectively, it must determine where it wants to go and how best to get there. The leader must see to it that a course of action is determined in advance which is understood and agreed to by all who will work to accomplish it. We can define this management function, as predetermining a course of action. A convenient semantic label is "planning."

2. People working together tend to overlap and duplicate the tasks they perform, so time, effort, and resources are wasted. The leader must ensure that each person has a clear-cut area of work that does not overlap others and that all members of the team know how to work effectively together. This function is arranging and relating the work to be performed. We call this function "organizing."

3. Work gets done and results are secured only to the extent the people involved are willing and able to work hard and productively. This module of work is influencing people to take effective action. The term "leading" is appropriate for this function.

4. Finally it is necessary to check to make sure the work is being done properly and the desired results are being secured and, if not, to rectify matters. This function is assessing and regulating the work in progress and the results secured. "Controlling" is an acceptable term for this function.

Since work done by humans to secure results through other people is virtually the same wherever it is performed, we find that the breakdown of the management-work order into its functions is much the same in all countries and cultures.

The four management functions are interrelated. We cannot plan effectively without also controlling, leading, and organizing. No control can be any better than the plan which it measures. Organizing is vitalized by people, and people are most effective—for themselves and their enterprises—when they work within the limits of plans, organization, and controls.

Activities of Work

Each function can be further subdivided. Management *functions* subdivide into *activities* which are universal. Here are the activities of the management functions:

Planning Activities:

1. Estimating and predicting future conditions and events: Forecasting

2. Determining the results to be accomplished: Developing Objectives

3. Determining the action steps necessary to achieve desired results: Programming

4. Determining the time sequence for action steps: Scheduling

5. Determining resources required to carry out action steps and achieve results: Budgeting

6. Standardizing work that must be performed in the same way: Developing Procedures

7. Establishing standing decisions to apply to repetitive problems and questions of overall importance: Developing Policies

Organizing Activities:

1. Identifying the work that must be performed and arranging it in logical groups: Developing Organization Structure

2. Assigning to others the work they must do and the right to make the necessary decisions, and creating an obligation to do the work and make the decisions in terms of agreed-upon standards: Delegating

3. Establishing the conditions necessary for people to work cooperatively and harmoniously together: Developing Relationships

Leading Activities:

1. Arriving at conclusions and judgments necessary for people to act: Decision Making

2. Creating understanding among the people involved: Communicating

3. Inspiring, encouraging, and impelling people to act: Motivating

4. Finding the right people: Selecting People

5. Helping people develop their knowledge, attitudes, and skills: Developing People

Controlling Activities:

1. Establishing the criteria against which work and results will be judged: Developing Performance Standards

2. Recording what has been done and reporting it to those who need to know: Measuring Performance

3. Determining how well work has been done and results achieved by comparing them with the standards established: Evaluating Performance

4. Rectifying mistakes and improving performance: Correcting Performance

For convenience we show the breakdown of the management functions and activities only in Figure 6-4.

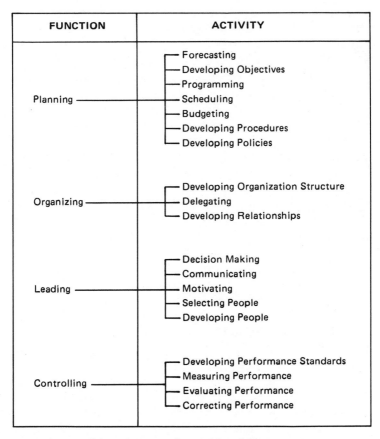

FUNCTION	ACTIVITY
Planning	Forecasting Developing Objectives Programming Scheduling Budgeting Developing Procedures Developing Policies
Organizing	Developing Organization Structure Delegating Developing Relationships
Leading	Decision Making Communicating Motivating Selecting People Developing People
Controlling	Developing Performance Standards Measuring Performance Evaluating Performance Correcting Performance

FIGURE 6-4   The Functions and Activities of Management

The Functions of Technical Work

Management work cannot exist of itself; it must be planning, leading, organizing, and controlling other work. A manager works so that he or she may help others. A person operating an extrusion press produces toothpaste tubes which are end products of value in themselves; a teacher helping a student master calculus helps produce a mathematical skill which also has its own intrinsic value. On the other hand, a manager who does the work necessary to plan, organize, lead, and control the efforts of a dozen extrusion press operations or one who manages the teaching faculty of the university works so that others may achieve the end result. Work applied directly to resources is the order of technical work.

Variability of Technical Work. The order of technical work does not subdivide into functions in the consistent pattern that is true of management work. Some functions of technical work, especially those in formalized sciences or professions, can be classified in near-universal terms wherever practiced. For example, the medical services function will have similar activities, such as surgery, obstetrics, pediatrics, radiology, pathology, and pharmacology, in virtually every part of the world. However, the classification of most functions of technical work varies from one country to another and even among different types of enterprises or within the same enterprise in the same country. As a case in point, subdivision of the Marketing Function of Technical Work depends upon such factors as technology and culture; for example, market research, advertising, market forecasting, sales service, and distribution are common activities of the marketing function in the United States, but the breakdown is quite different in Russia and England. Again, the Purchasing Function of Technical Work will tend to have different activities in a city school system compared to those in a steel mill or a religious institution. The Research Function of Technical Work will have a different breakdown in governmental health-care services contrasted to that in a university, a large chemical company, or a research institution. In fact, the classification of technical functions may vary, even within different parts of the same organization. For example, the Buying Function in a large merchandising group will have different activities in the shoe, ladies' ready-to-wear, and men's haberdashery departments of the same group.

Much of this variation in technical work categories is haphazard and even illogical. The work has been grouped in terms of the strong personalities of outstanding individuals and continues to be viable only because of the compensating strengths of the people involved. A major

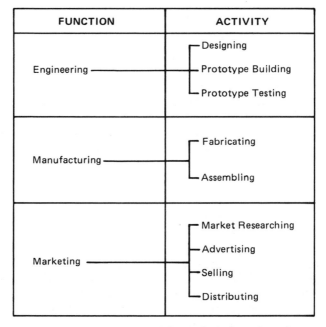

FUNCTION	ACTIVITY
Engineering	Designing Prototype Building Prototype Testing
Manufacturing	Fabricating Assembling
Marketing	Market Researching Advertising Selling Distributing

FIGURE 6-5 Classification of the Technical Work Order

opportunity for improved efficiency, reduced costs, and more human use of human beings lies in recognizing the essential logic of these work processes and in establishing a rational pattern through proper classification. Since technical work does not follow a standardized format, the work included in each category must be developed for each enterprise. This can be accomplished by following the technique used to classify management work.

A typical classification of the technical work order into functions and activities is shown in Figure 6-5.

DEVELOPING THE BASIC PLANNING STRUCTURE

Following the logic we have established, we can now develop a framework for our plans. To be most useful, this structure should be unitary; that is, it should be directed toward one overall result. For this reason, it will have vertical traceability. Since it must provide for all the individual managerial positions in the organization, the planning structure will be hierarchical, with levels corresponding to the organization structure.

The Logic of the Planning Structure

Following the classification logic we developed, we can establish a hierarchy of continuing objectives by using continuing work categories as the bridge, as shown in Figure 6-6.

Our primary continuing objective, which we will call the Key Objective, states the overall results the organization as a whole will commit itself to use its resources to accomplish.

To accomplish the primary objective, we must perform the necessary primary continuing categories of work.

The results that will be the outcome of the work performed in the individual primary work categories will be the secondary continuing objectives. Since they identify the critical few areas in which results must be achieved, we call these Critical Objectives.

Developing the Organization Structure. We develop an organization structure by arranging and relating the work to be performed. The framework of this structure is logically composed of the primary categories and subcategories of work that must be done on a continuing basis. We have already identified these in the functions and activities developed in the work classification.

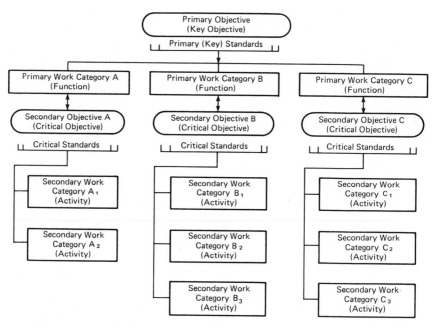

FIGURE 6-6   The Logic Translated to Planning, Organization, and Control Structures

The basic categories of work can be arranged in different combinations. The two primary choices are functional and divisional organization structures. However, no matter how complex the structure becomes, it will always have the building blocks of the primary work categories.

Deriving the Control Structure.

Since performance standards are criteria by which we measure the work done and the results secured, we can most readily derive performance standards from the objectives we have already defined.

As we can see in Figure 6-6, primary or Key Standards can be derived from the key objective. These standards will give us overall measures of progress. Since the objectives hierarchy cascades without overlap or duplication, this will also be true of the standards hierarchy. Standards, of course, are the basis for measurement, evaluation, and performance correction, so we extend the standards hierarchy to form a control structure.

A Real-Life Example. We can see how this logic applies in the development of integrated planning, control, and organization structures for a personal-transportation company, as shown in Figure 6-7.

Here the key objective establishes the purpose and direction for the enterprise as a whole. The key standards provide measures for success in meeting the key objectives. The secondary or critical objectives state the implementing results that must be accomplished to meet the key objective. The Critical Standards in turn provide measures for the critical objectives.

Cascade of Objectives and Standards. The key and critical objectives and standards can be cascaded to lower organizational levels because they have been developed in parallel with the hierarchy of work categories of the organization structure. This cascade is particularly valuable because it facilitates integration of the total planning, controlling, and organization structures and also serves as a communication channel for vital operating information that applies to all levels.

TIME IN THE PLANNING STRUCTURE

Time is a structural dimension in all planning. While time is a continuum, we must break it into chunks if we wish to measure it. We can

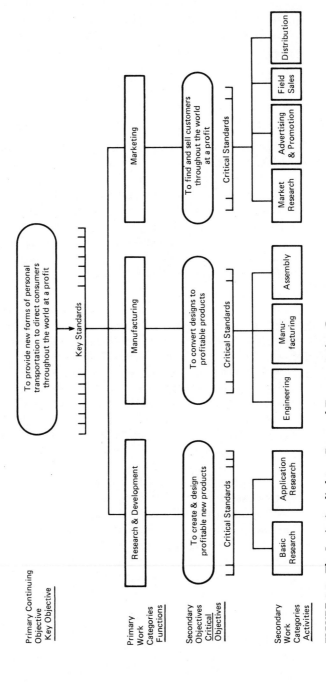

FIGURE 6-7 The Logic Applied to a Personal Transportation Company

have a different plan for the major time categories, that is, daily, monthly, annual, or 10-year plans. These in turn can be conveniently grouped into short- and long-term plans. Thus the strategic plan is long-range, and the operating plan short-range.

The nature of the long- and short-range plans varies with their predictability. We know with a reasonable degree of certainty what will happen today and tomorrow, but as we look beyond this, we become less certain. For this reason the strategic plan is designed to provide overall guidance. It is broad, general, and difficult to measure. The short-range plan is more sharply focused, specific, and highly measurable.

The Periscope Syndrome

The chief shortcoming in the long/short range categorization is that it encourages us to regard planning as an intermittent, sporadic process, in which we stop periodically to raise the periscope and look ahead, jotting down our plans to cover the situation fleetingly revealed. This proclivity stems from the budgeting antecedents of most planning processes. Budgets, traditionally, have been developed annually. New sightings have been taken quarterly or, at best, monthly. In the interim, the hatch has been tightly closed and the budget has been carefully followed without much regard for what has been going on outside.

Bridging the Gap

We need a better means of bridging the time gap between strategic and tactical, long- and short-range plans. In our planning, we must be able to scan the horizon one minute and then focus on the very near future in the next. This bifocal accommodation is difficult; but effective planning must be systematic thinking about the future, and it must take place continuously. Every decision or problem has implications for the future, and all become raw material for the building of plans. While it is true that specific projects must have definite completion times and hence will be periodic, we need an overall set of decisions and objectives that will enable us to maintain the consistency and integration we require.

How can we avoid this discontinuity in time? To bridge the gap between present and future, I have found it most helpful to regard time as what it is—continuing—and to develop continuing plans to cover it. These continuing plans cover time from this moment to as far into the future as we can project our thoughts and imagination.

Since we must also have plans that will be carried out within specific time limits, beneath the umbrella of continuing plans we develop time-limited plans, which will enable us to accomplish our continuing plans. The time-limited plans in turn can be divided into long- and short-range plans.

Continuing Plans

Continuing plans are those that remain in effect until they are changed. They are ongoing, and they apply equally to the present and the future. If they are to serve their purpose well, continuing plans must not only provide integration of time but must also furnish continuous coverage from top to bottom within the organization. Ideally, there should be no gaps in the planning network from the first-line supervisor to the chief executive officer.

Time-Limited Plans

While time is continuing, most of our projects and tasks have time limits. For example, we expect to complete the new building in 2 years, to introduce a training program by January 1, to spend no more than 3 weeks debugging the computer program. Time-limited plans are those which are intended to be completed within a specified time period.

Time-limited plans are the workhorses of the planning effort, for we expect them to carry most of the burden of planning our everyday work. Depending on the need, they may extend from 1 day or less to 50 years or more. For example, replacement of a faulty motor may require a plan covering 4 hours, while planning, gaining approval for, and building a new hydroelectric dam may require 40 or 50 years of sustained effort. To cover this spread, we divide time-limited plans into long- and short-range.

Long-Range Plans. A long-range plan extends as far ahead as it is possible to specify the desired end results. This usually means as far ahead as we are able to make definite commitments of funds. The time period of long-range plans is usually more than 1 year in the future. Long-range plans are intended as guidelines; they provide a set of constraints within which we can develop with confidence our short-range plans with their specific commitments to action.

The time period of long-range plans varies with the enterprise. Many planners project a period at least as far ahead as will be required to secure the desired economic return from the investment in resources. As a simple example, if new data processing equipment is installed, the plan for its use should extend over the number years required to justify the investment.

Long-range plans often put a different perspective on short-term decisions. For example, if the data processing equipment is likely to be outmoded when it is only half paid for, we will want to shorten the payout period or devise some other means of securing adequate return on our investment.

Short-Range Plans. A short-range plan specifies what resources will be committed and what actions will be taken in the immediate future. The short-range plan usually covers 1 year or less. This provides a set of time intervals paralleling the calendar or fiscal year. Because it is intended to be implemented rather than to provide guidelines, the short-range plan will be more detailed and specific than the long-range plan.

The short-range plan sets in motion a series of events: a program to be carried out, schedules to be met, budgets to direct resource expenditures. Because of this action commitment, short-range plans are more precise than long-range plans. Generally they are also more difficult and costly to change.

Linking Long- and Short-Range Plans. You will need to establish a solid link between your short-range and long-range plans, or your short-range planning will tend to eat up the long-range. In other words, you will complete one short-range plan only to launch into another, and long-range plans will stay in the file drawer.

The common way to avoid this problem is by planning on a sliding basis. This method requires that you review long-range plans at least once or twice a year. At each review, you extend the long-range plan for the length of the review period. For example, if you review 5-year plans every 6 months, then every 6 months you must project the forecasts, objectives, programs, and budgets an additional 6 months, at the same time making short-range plans for the immediate future in light of your projections.

This method results in continuous coverage and ensures smooth transitions from one planning phase to the next. Of course, you don't have to wait until an appointed time to review long-range plans. This can be done at any time they might be significantly affected by new short-range plans.

In the next chapter, we will put the logic of planning to work. We will use it to develop an integrated set of objectives and standards we call a Position Charter, and we will relate this to Position Plans and Enterprise Plans.

KEY POINTS

1. *Need for a Planning Structure.* A logical planning structure will have great value in providing a common framework for all the planning work we do. Since planning is part of management, this logic can also help to integrate planning with the other components of management.

2. *The Concept of Work Classification.* The logic of work classification is the basis for developing a planning structure because our first need is to sort out and label the various parts of planning. Work classification is the logical arrangement of work into various groupings according to standard criteria. Since work always leads to results or objectives, a logical arrangement can be derived by analyzing the work and dividing work into categories and subcategories necessary to achieve its objectives.

3. *What Is Human Work?* Using work analysis, we can divide human work into two major subcategories—technical work and mangement work. The two are distinct in that technical work is the effort exerted by individuals to secure results through their own efforts, while management work is the effort exerted by individuals in leadership positions to secure results through the efforts of others.

4. *The Management Function and Activities.* Following the classification logic, each management function can be further subdivided into activities. Planning breaks down into forecasting, developing objectives, programming, scheduling, budgeting, developing procedures, and developing policies. Organizing is divided into developing organization structure, delegating, and developing relationships. Leading is made up of decision making, communicating, motivating, selecting, and developing people. Controlling breaks down into developing performance standards, measuring performance, evaluating performance, and correcting performance.

5. *Technical Work Order.* Technical functions are analyzed in the same manner as management. However, since technical work tends to vary with the technology, the conditions, and culture, the technical functions differ in their categories and subcategories.

6. *Integrating the Logic.* The classification logic provides a basis for integration of the planning structure through the hierarchy of results and objectives. It provides a bridge to the organization structure in the hierarchy of work. It enables us to develop a control structure by deriving it from the performance standards that are developed to measure results and work.

7. *Bridging the Time Gap.* To avoid the artificial separation of plans by time periods, we can prepare continuing and time-limited plans. Continuing plans provide ongoing coverage, with revision and updating as necessary. Time-limited plans cover specified time periods, such as 1, 10, or 50 years. Time-limited plans can be divided into short-range and long-range.

QUOTES FROM CHAPTER 6

Significant quotations from this chapter that you will want to consider and discuss in greater detail:

- Needs are satisfied by results, not by work.

- Managers are leaders, and as such, they have a unique organizational position which enables them to perform certain work which their followers cannot perform for themselves.

- The planning structure will be hierarchical, with levels corresponding to the organization structure.

- The key and critical objectives and standards can be cascaded to lower organizational levels because they have been developed in parallel with the hierarchy of work categories of the organization structure.

- Every decision or problem has implications for the future, and all become raw material for the building of plans.

THE ENTERPRISE PLAN

If we could first know where we are and whither we are tending, we could better judge what to do and how to do it.
ABRAHAM LINCOLN

THE CHAPTER IN BRIEF   The plethora of plans that is available is characterized more by semantic differences than functional uniqueness. Two types of plans will satisfy most requirements: position plans and enterprise plans. Position plans cover the work and results for which managers are accountable. An enterprise plan encompasses the external and internal planning needs of the enterprise as a whole. The chief executive officer's position plan becomes the enterprise plan by adding to it the sectional plans necessary to provide the required coverage. Primary issues in developing the enterprise plan are planning responsibilities and roles and the sequence and timing of plans. The success of planning depends largely on clear specification of what planning work is to be done by each organization level and how people will work together as a team. The responsibility and role of specialized staff is often nebulous and needs to be carefully defined. The sequence of planning follows the logic of the planning classification. Planning schedules should be developed to ensure that time is provided for both top-down cascading and bottom-up understanding and acceptance of plans.

WHAT TYPES OF PLANS ARE NEEDED?

We have now developed the logic for a planning structure: the hierarchy of needs, results, and work that enables us to predetermine the courses of action we can follow in the future with confidence and success. We have discussed the timing and requirements of the structure. Now we come to sharper focus on the types of plans that we can develop within this logical framework.

While the planning professional will probably prefer an array of sophisticated plans that can be fine tuned for any set of conditions, most managers will find that their requirements can be satisfied with two types of plans: position plans and enterprise plans. Both originate in the chief executive officer's plan, whose position plan is necessarily the strategic and tactical plan for the enterprise as a whole. We show this in Figure 7-1.

In the figure, we begin with the initial planning input from the pri-

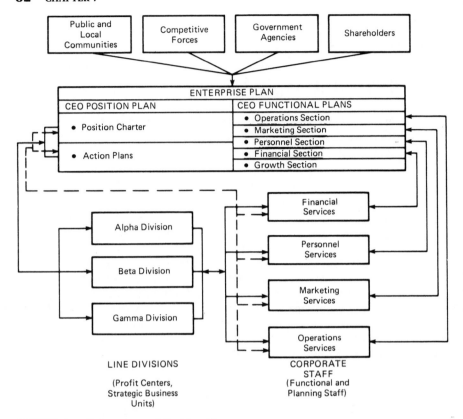

FIGURE 7-1   Enterprise and Position Plans

mary external publics: national and local communities, competitive forces, governmental agencies, and shareholders. Within the limits set by these groups, the enterprise plan contains the chief executive officer's position plan, which consists of the Position Charter and Action Plans. These are cascaded both to the line divisions and corporate staff. The functional sections of the enterprise plan are developed for the chief executive officer by the corporate staff.

I emphasize that these plans are developed *for* the chief executive officer because they must not only be his accountability, he must also fully understand and be deeply committed to them. The functional plans are part of the chief executive officer's enterprise plan and not the plans of the corporate staff groups. Each of the latter has its own position plan, consisting of position charters and action plans.

THE POSITION PLAN

A position plan covers that part of the total organization for which a manager is accountable. It is not limited to his or her personal responsibility and authority. Thus the division manager's position plan covers the results to be secured, the standards to be met, and the work to be done by the division as a whole. A section supervisor's position plan is the supervisor's part of the division plan to be implemented with and through all the people of the section.

Position plans provide for both continuing and time-limited coverage. This is accomplished through the position charter and action plan, as shown in Figure 7-2, the position planning logic diagram.

Parts of the Position Plan

Preliminary to the development of the position plan, forecasts are made to scan the future environment and to arrive at assumptions which will provide guidelines and boundaries for the plan itself. The position charter is made up of key and critical objectives, accompanied by standards, and key strategies.

The key objective is the overall, primary, continuing objective which determines the purpose and nature of the enterprise and its components. It specifies why the enterprise or component exists. The key standards provide criteria for measuring success—or lack of it—in achieving the key objective. Key strategies define the general approach that will be followed to achieve the key objective and to meet the key standards.

Critical objectives state the most important, continuing results that must be accomplished to attain the key objectives, while critical standards are criteria for measuring the critical objectives.

Unique Features of Position Plans

The position charter brings together in one place several planning elements and places them in logical relationship to one another so they can be cascaded. The key objective is the equivalent of the Mission or Scope Statement or Business Definition; critical objectives cover much the same ground as Functional Objectives. Mission or scope statements and functional objectives often are not developed systematically or are isolated as separate programs. In the position charter, the standards are brought into direct relationship with the results they are intended to measure so that they form an organic whole.

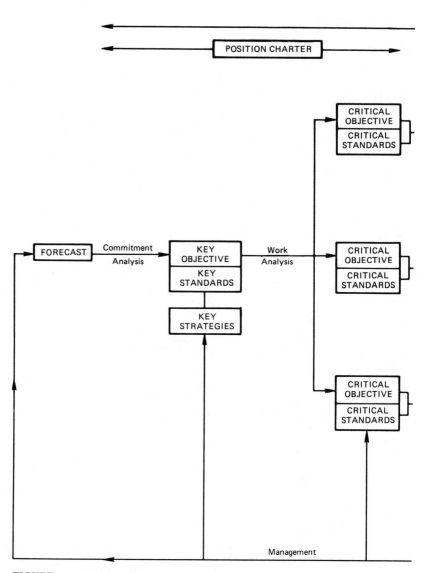

FIGURE 7-2   Position Planning Logic Diagram

84

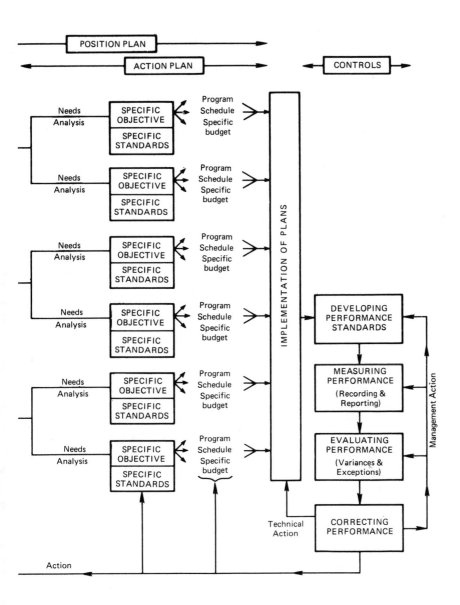

85

Action plans encompass much the same elements as the MBO program and operational plans. However, they have the unique advantage of being derived directly from the continuing plans of each position, so that they systematically identify both deficiencies and opportunities and provide for positive action. The position plan will be described in detail in later chapters.

THE ENTERPRISE PLAN

The enterprise plan is the course of action to be followed by the enterprise as a whole in relation to the publics it must satisfy: shareholders, national and local government agencies, the public, and employees. Enterprise plans are also called corporate, strategic, and long-range plans. To arrive at a useful understanding, we should first come to some agreement on the nature of the enterprise plan and the terminology we will use to describe it.

The Nature of the Enterprise Plan

If you are concerned about developing an overall enterprise plan, you may be approaching the matter from one of several different viewpoints. If you are the chief executive officer and you are fortunate enough to have a seasoned and competent staff planner or planning staff, you probably already have an enterprise plan in place or in process. Your concern may be to check what you have and to find new ideas to consider and eventually to test.

Possibly you are a chief executive who is vaguely dissatisfied with the planning system in effect because it generates a great deal of paper but, somehow, doesn't bring you to the formulations you need. You may be manager of a division, subsidiary, strategic-planning unit, or other type of profit center so that, in effect, you are chief executive officer for your own component and your interests parallel those of the chief executive officer.

Parts that Make Up a Whole. You will probably agree that an enterprise plan cannot be one plan for all parts of the enterprise. It must be an assemblage of self-sufficient planning modules which when put together form the grand design, but each of which must be able to carry its own share of the total burden.

Enterprise plans for the small, young, and functionally organized firm differ from those of the large, divisionalized company in the relative independence of their primary organization components. A small, young company is like a football team or an orchestra. In the functional structure, no move can be made successfully unless every member moves in unison, carrying out a precisely defined role. This is why at this stage a firm, demanding team leader or orchestra conductor is usually more successful than a compliant, relaxed type.

The enterprise plan for the large divisionalized enterprise is more like a fleet of ships. It is an assemblage made up of relatively self-sufficient components which are held in beneficial association by a desire to share common sources and rewards. Within this flotilla of plans, managers can chart their own courses, following the same bearings and moving within common constraints, but with enough freedom to veer off and investigate bays and islets that may offer special opportunities.

Clarifying the Terminology

A name is a label that identifies the medicine in the bottle, and the names we use for planning sometimes lead us to gulp paregoric when we really need a tonic. As we have seen, "strategy" is one culprit, and this is particularly true when we apply it to the enterprise plan.

We will better match label and medication if we substitute for the term "strategy," the more accurate designation "continuing plan." For "tactics" or "operational plans" we will do better with "long- and short-range plans." I suggest this with some temerity. However, more precise terminology will enable us to describe and understand much more clearly what actually happens as managers complete their part of the enterprise plan, of which strategies are only a part.

The chief executive officer is primarily concerned with preparing continuing plans that will chart the course of the enterprise as a whole and with developing standards that will provide prompt and accurate intelligence about deviations and deficiencies from the established course. These continuing plans apply to all the ships in the flotilla. They are communicated to all ranks and reconciled so that, when finally approved, they provide operating instructions within which each unit can proceed with confidence.

Continuing plans must be implemented, and their execution lies in the hands of the ship captains—the division and department heads. Each has a position plan for navigating and operating his or her own ship but also follows the charts that show the course for the fleet as a whole.

Parts of the Enterprise Plan

As we have seen, the enterprise plan is built around the nucleus of the chief executive officer's position plan, which contains the continuing objectives, strategies, and standards for the enterprise as a whole. It is roughly equivalent to what is often called the strategic plan. As we have noted, it has the advantage of bringing standards into a logical relationship with the activities they measure. The enterprise plan includes, in addition, those planning documents necessary to encompass the needs of the groups to whom the chief executive officer is accountable.

The accountability of the chief executive extends beyond his or her position plan. The added scope required is provided by functional plans. Most of these are developed *for* the chief executive by the appropriate staff technical functions. Some may require outside help. Although they must be developed to fit the needs of each enterprise, the sections of the enterprise plan indicated in Figure 7-1 are typical. They are outlined below.

Financial Section. We often think of the Financial Plan as a discrete document, with its own form and purpose. To be most effective, however, we should regard it as an integral part of the chief executive officer's enterprise plan, developed *for* the chief executive by the staff finance group. The chief financial officer plans for his or her own area of accountability in the position plan, but this is separate from the financial component of the enterprise plan.

The financial component of the chief executive's enterprise plan will make provision for converting the materials, tools, facilities, and time of people used in the plans into monetary terms. This is accomplished through the accounting system.

Human Resources Section. As is true of other aspects, the chief executive is accountable for making most effective use of the human resources of the enterprise. This is exemplified in the human resources section of the corporate plan, which is prepared by the human resources or personnel staff function.

This plan must envisage the short- and long-term needs of the enterprise for people: how to attract and hold them and what methods to use to motivate, compensate, and develop them.

Planning for people on a corporate basis is usually left to the personnel function, but most chief executives will acknowledge that it should be their most important responsibility. A properly balanced Human Resources Plan will forecast personnel needs in keeping with long-term growth plans. It will make provision for developing people internally and for selecting and hiring them from outside sources.

Compensation is always an important element. Maintaining balance and equity requires plans for systematic job evaluation and maintenance of properly related salary ranges. Incentives and bonus payments, fringes, and benefits are part of the total compensation package. If they are not planned on an overall basis, waste and dissatisfaction result.

Harmonious relationships with labor unions and other types of employee representation also must be planned, or they will deteriorate into continuing skirmishing that is equally damaging to both management and unions.

Marketing Section. "Marketing" refers to the process of determining customer needs, advertising and promoting the benefits and features of the products or services offered, persuading customers to buy, and following up to ensure satisfaction and referral. Marketing may also include physical distribution of the product to the customer. The marketing component of the enterprise plan is normally called the Marketing Plan.

Growth Section. This is often called the Development Plan. Although it has different interpretations, today it generally represents the plan for growth beyond the normal expansion of operations already in place. For a business enterprise, growth centers on the internal development or external acquisition of new products and new markets. Internal growth occurs largely through research and development that leads to new products or to improved versions of existing ones.

The growth plan includes the plan for diversification. This may be internal through research and development or external through acquisition. Thus the Research and Development and Acquisition Plans may be subsets of the diversification plan. Since it may be necessary to dispose of operations that do not fit or are unsuccessful, the divestment plan may also be part of the growth plan.

The Critical Responsibilities of Enterprise Planning

Designing an enterprise-planning system is not a matter of drawing flowcharts, preparing procedures, and planning timetables. The planning documents are a record of the thinking that has taken place, but this written record will have a short life unless we think through conceptually several vital aspects of enterprise planning. These include planning responsibilities and roles and the sequence and timing of plans.

These concerns apply to the four principals: the chief executive officer, the specialized staff groups, the divisional manager, and the

	OBJECTIVES	STANDARDS	ACTION PLANS
Chief Executive Officer	State results to be achieved to satisfy needs of stockholders, government, society, employees, customers. Establish priorities for resource utilization.	Establish level of excellence for the enterprise as a whole in terms that can be cascaded to lower levels.	Specify long- and short-range action necessary to achieve objectives and meet standards. Delegate to line and staff heads.
Specialized Staff Heads	Develop forecasts, analyze past results, and reconcile proposed objectives with needs of line operating heads and the chief executive officer.	Develop quantifiable measures that represent most effective use of available resources. Secure agreement on standards and ensure that there is continuing reporting, evaluation, and improvement in terms of these standards.	Work with line operating heads to translate broad action statements of the chief executive into specific objectives and standards that will ensure attainment of overall objectives and provide basis for feedback and control.
Line Operating Heads—Divisional Level	Review corporate objectives with specialized staff, reconcile with divisional resources and priorities and recommend final statement of enterprise objectives to chief executive.	Determine what is reasonable and achievable with participation of managers to the lowest operating level. Clarify and reconcile these with specialized staff and secure agreement of CEO.	Develop action plans with participation of accountable managers. Delegate implementation. Maintain control by exception. Ensure prompt, generous rewards for achievement. Closely monitor substandard performance.

FIGURE 7-3 The Primary Planning Responsibilities

90

functional managers who report to the divisional manager. If the enterprise still is functional and has not divisionalized, the functional managers will be reporting to the chief executive officer rather than the division manager. We will look at these responsibilities in turn. They are summarized in Figure 7-3.

The Chief Executive Officer's Responsibility and Role

Using all the skilled help he or she can muster, the chief executive must lay out the strategic direction in which the enterprise is to move. This is a complex undertaking. Whether the governing body is a board of directors or a board of trustees, the chief executive has the initial task of identifying the expectations of its members and developing plans that will satisfy them. This calls for analysis of the financial and operating history and capabilities of the enterprise. It demands assessment of the corollary expectations of all the audiences to which it is subject.

Board members may contribute to the development of overall objectives, standards, and strategies, but the board functions more effectively if it maintains the role of review, analysis, and approval. I have found that the more deeply involved board members become in developing specific plans, the more likely they are to protect and nourish their brainchildren rather than to maintain the objective viewpoint of a noninvolved expert.

Short-Range Planning. The chief executive officer must ensure that short- as well as long-range action is initiated and maintained so that the overall objectives and standards will be met. This is accomplished through the long-range and short-range action plans. The chief executive officer coordinates strategic programming efforts and integrates these into a cohesive, purposeful whole as the enterprise moves to accomplish its strategic objectives. These strategic programs may be stated as action plans, which are delegated in successively greater detail. They also become more measurable as they are cascaded to the point where they are finally carried out.

Planning Relationships. The chief executive has responsibility and authority for initiating the overall planning process and for approving the contents of the enterprise plan. At times the chief executive officer may seek to delegate this authority to specialized staff groups, especially to the planning head, but invariably this turns out to be a mistake. No matter how capable the planner, it is the leader who must lead.

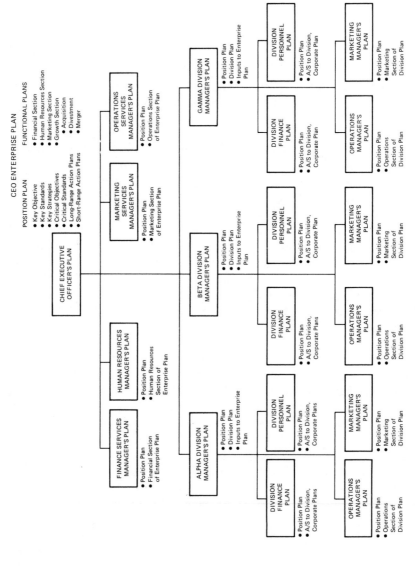

FIGURE 7-4 The Primary Planning Relationships

The planning relationships of the primary levels are shown in Figure 7-4. Here the significant roles for objectives, standards, and action plans are summarized.

Measuring Results. The chief executive officer and knowledgeable boards of directors insist on measurable standards for the enterprise as a whole so that overall progress and results can be monitored and evaluated at reasonably close intervals, in some cases monthly but at least quarterly. The favored measuring stick of the past was profitability. However, this is no longer considered adequate by itself, and there is a general move to identify and define standards in the critical few aspects of performance. John H. Bryan, Jr., chief executive officer of Consolidated Foods Corporation, puts it well. He says: "It is essential that we evaluate our people against consistent, high standards on the basis of performance and measurable achievement."

Specialized Staff Responsibility and Role

The role of specialized staff is changing in today's fast-moving, intensely competitive, and increasingly technological environment. In the past, specialized staff heads often served as surrogates in their areas of expertise for the chief executive. Now they have adopted the role of skilled internal consultants who have the objectivity and the interpersonal skills necessary to negotiate and reconcile the primary objectives and standards with the two principals directly accountable for their accomplishment—the chief executive and the division heads. It is for this reason that the specialized staff groups are shown as "services" in Figure 7-4. Their role is to serve—to advise, to counsel, and to do things for other groups that these people do not have the knowledge or specialized skills to do for themselves.

Each specialized staff group develops its functional section for the enterprise plan. It also guides and coordinates the contributions of the divisions to the enterprise plan. As companies grow, the specialized expertise and counsel necessary will probably demand a separate group to specialize in planning as a function.

Specialized staff groups probe and evaluate the likely shape and characteristics of the future environment for their functions and help the line principals to agree upon assumptions that will govern the resource-commitment process. This advisory and service role is maintained in the initiation and development of all aspects of enterprise and divisional plans and in the cascading of them to lower levels. But today there is more general recognition that the plans are owned by the people who will carry them out. Staff counsels and advises and is accountable for the content and quality of the advice and service it provides but not for the final results. Authorities are delegated in this context.

A critical gap in most planning systems is the one between the enterprise plan and the operating plans developed at lower levels to guide day-to-day activities. As shown in Figure 7-4, specialized staff can first fill that gap by translating the broad action statements of the chief executive, which the staff groups helped develop, into specific objectives and standards that will ensure attainment of overall objectives and will also provide the basis for feedback and control.

Divisional Level Responsibility and Role

The most certain and precise knowledge of deficiencies and opportunities lies at the level of the line operating heads—usually the division or department manager. It is here that plans must be developed that will trigger the action that leads to success or failure. This is probably the most difficult and demanding part of the line operating head's job— and that is why it is so often abdicated in favor of the specialized staff groups.

What Comes First? The relationship between division and chief executive officer is most complex, for it is easy for either party to misconstrue or overstep. The divisional profit center is rewarded in terms of its success and too often that is not related meaningfully to the overall success of the enterprise as a whole. When this is the case, a vital requirement at the line operating level is to develop objectives and standards that contribute to those of the enterprise but do not benefit the division at the expense of corporate success. While trade-offs among divisions are feasible and necessary, the governing factor always has to be "what is best for the enterprise as a whole?"

Who Is Accountable? An inviolable rule in today's divisionalized, decentralized enterprise is that the profit center managers who are expected to achieve final results and meet overall standards must agree to what is required of them before they can be held accountable. Rarely today do we see a board of directors or chief executive officer unilaterally determining what they would *like* to accomplish and thrusting this down the throats of those who are to bear the burden. As Peter Haas, chief executive officer of Levi Strauss & Co., puts it, "The chief executive can best manage by persuasion and consensus."

This consensus extends to all aspects of divisional operations that impact upon other divisions or the enterprise as a whole. Since divisionalization can be effective only if there is commensurate decentralization, division managers are generally delegated the responsibility and authority necessary to hold them accountable for the profitability of their divisions.

The Portfolio Concept. Overdecentralization of authority poses dangers which are epitomized in the portfolio concept of managing divisionalized enterprises. This looks upon the divisions as a collection of businesses, often unrelated, which are run much like the subsidiaries of a holding company or the primary investments of an investment fund. Several decades of overdiversification have brought the lesson home, and today there is a general tendency to make the whole enterprise greater than the sum of its divisions by exploiting the potential synergy of complementary products, shared technology, and common sources of supply.

Measuring Divisional Success. While divisional heads must be in agreement on the obligations they undertake, they have neither the objectivity nor the perspective to make unilateral decisions for their own components. A particular area of concern is the performance standards that will measure divisional performance. These are frequently the basis for incentive awards for the divisional head and his or her key managers and become increasingly significant as the potential reward increases. Again consensus becomes the mode of choice. The example set by successful Japanese companies which spend a great deal of time and effort to arrive at understanding and agreement has prompted a similar effort by many U.S. firms.

The driving force of any set of plans is the document that prompts day-to-day action. Divisional action plans are largely derived from corporate plans, although a significant number may have local origin. The specific standards of the action plan become the basis for control and provide for rapid, precise identification of both deficiencies and unusual accomplishment.

The Sequence of Planning

What sequence of steps should be followed in developing the enterprise plan? Several different approaches are in current use, ranging from the simple, straightforward, small-company measures taken by Measurex to the complex, iterative process necessary for the multidivision, decentralized planning needs of General Electric.

Once we have established the logic of the planning process and sorted out the terminology, the sequence of steps to be followed for enterprise planning becomes almost as clear-cut as that for position planning. It is logical, for example, to forecast before we set objectives and to determine our strategies before we go to action plans. The same rationale holds for small companies as for large. In the large, mature company, many more committees will be involved, planning decisions will tend to be decentralized and participatory, and the planning system itself will be much more complicated.

A large company instituting formalized planning will encounter many of the same problems as the small company and will want to begin with a simple, spare approach that can be elaborated with experience and with the development of managerial planning skills. Division and functional managers who do not have the support of an enterprise planning system will find that the basic sequence provides a useful guide.

Plan the Planning System. Planning involves a great deal of managerial time, no matter how simple and straightforward it may be. Since many people are involved, coordination is vital. There is nothing more demoralizing than to ask your managers to prepare forecasts, objectives, or strategies, to receive a flood of paper in return, and then to realize that they didn't quite know what you meant or that they really didn't know how to do what you wanted. The best way to avoid this fatal pitfall is to design the planning system you intend to use, test it out on one unit or department, identify and correct the deficiencies, and then extend it to wider use.

Always develop procedures to cover the planning work that must be done. Be certain that each person who is expected to plan is trained to use the planning approach. At least annually, conduct a survey of the managers who prepare plans so that you can spot deficiencies early and correct them.

Carefully weigh your need for planning staff. One capable staff planner with an efficient secretary can provide a surprising amount of advice and service if accountable managers are required to develop their own plans. Anticipate that requests to add to planning staff will begin at once and mount in intensity as the planning cycle grinds on. Resist them. A continuing danger in any planning system is to focus so sharply on current and short-term problems that funds are largely concentrated on immediate needs and contingencies. Money is not spent now that will ensure improvement and growth in the years ahead. One reason for this is that the implementation plans for long-range development fail because they are related to the short-term tactical plans and come into operation only when the long-term opportunity has become a short-term problem or crisis. To be most useful, the short-range or annual action plan should be a snapshot of 1 year of the long-range plan. This means that each manager becomes both a strategic and a tactical planner. Long-range planning is as much a responsibility of operating management as it is of the top executive level. To proceed otherwise is to maintain an artificial barrier between the past and present and the future.

With the planning system in place, you can look to a planning cycle similar to that in Figure 7-5. The primary phases of the long- and short-range plan are shown as they are implemented during a calendar year.

Forecast Future Environment. External economic, political, demographic, and competitive factors exert continuing pressure on the enterprise and mold it to a rough approximation of the form it will finally assume. The large company will often have specialized staff experts who will generate these forecasts or will work with outside professionals. As we noted earlier, this work can be done *for* managers; however, the process of evaluating data and applying it to the internal situation cannot be delegated safely.

Forecasting applies to the enterprise as a whole and to each of its components. While it is impossible to predict accurately what will happen in the future, it is entirely feasible to identify and extrapolate trends and to develop the ranges within which events will probably occur.

Since forecasting provides the background data for both long- and short-range plans, as we see in Figure 7-5, the process starts at the chief executive level and is cascaded.

Your forecasts will give an overview of developing trends in the vital factors affecting your area of accountability. These may range from technology to human resources and markets, depending on your position. Forecasts will provide an assessment of your competition, shifts in markets and product demand, and the opportunities and threats that you can anticipate. These estimates and predictions will be consolidated into a set of assumptions upon which your subsequent planning will rest.

Revise Position Charter. It may require several attempts to develop and secure agreement on your position charter. After the initial preparation, it is revised and updated at regular intervals, usually twice annually.

The first input is from the position charter of your superior. This usually leads to review of key objectives and standards and updating of the strategy statements. Again we note that since these are contained

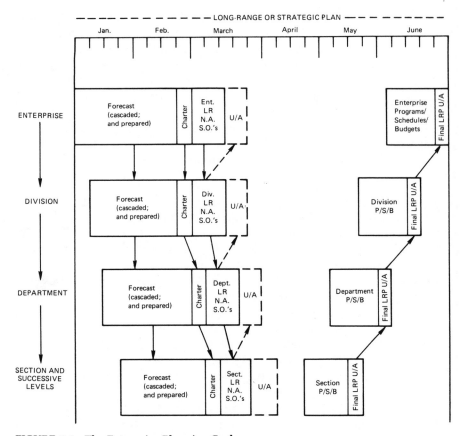

FIGURE 7-5   The Enterprise Planning Cycle

in one document and are revised in logical relationship to one another, the process is much simpler than in separate development of objectives, strategies, and standards.

The chief executive's key objective sets up limits within which the enterprise as a whole will operate. Each manager then develops a supporting structure within these limits. Forecast assumptions provide the raw material from which the market, product, and other commitments are fashioned.

Revision Triggers Change. Key strategies are developed to force analysis of the options available to achieve the key objective. Key and critical standards set criteria for performance over the long-range future. This encourages managers to lift their sights beyond today and to develop measures that will ensure survival and success.

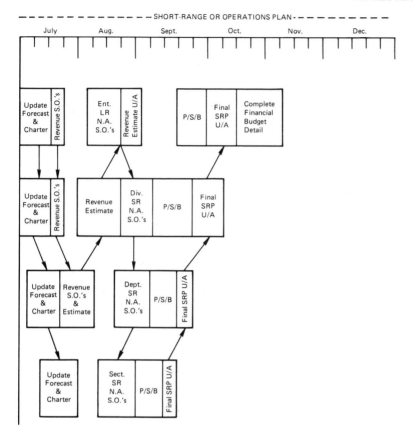

The annual revision of the position charter is not a perfunctory modification of a few words or phrases. It is intended to trigger fundamental changes in the enterprise's approach to its future and to subject these ideas to review, enrichment, and reconciliation at every level.

The key objectives and standards of the position charter also provide the basis for developing the controls that will be used to measure the accomplishment of your plans. You will want to quantify your key and critical standards whenever possible to facilitate reporting and evaluation.

Cascading the Charter. The cascade of the position charter proceeds in waves. At an earlier stage I believed that this movement should proceed from the bottom up, but in light of experience I am convinced that the process should begin at the top. The first statement, or revision, of the key objectives, standards, and strategies is a tentative document which sets forth the conclusions of the chief executive. These statements have the advice and counsel of the specialized staff groups and the initial inputs of divisional managers and staffs. However, this first pass is from the enterprise point of view. It expresses as much the hopes and expectations of the president and board as it does the true capabilities of the divisions to deliver the goods.

The next wave of the cascade involves securing the commitment of the divisions. This begins with assessing capabilities and resources and securing participation of the functional departments to the extent necessary to prove out the initial proposal. Even after commitment is secured, there is always the implicit understanding that if the development of programs, schedules, and specific budgets casts a different light, the whole matter may be brought up for renegotiation.

Develop Specific Objectives. You will assess your current performance compared to your key and critical objectives and determine the needs that must be met to achieve the results you want. This may involve correcting deficiencies or taking advantage of opportunities. You consider each key and critical objective and standard separately. This includes determining how you are currently expending your resources.

The needs analysis will focus on the areas in which you must achieve specific results to overcome deficiencies and to highlight new opportunities. You write a specific objective which describes the activity that will satisfy the need you have identified.

For each specific objective, you develop specific standards that clearly define the level and type of performance that is expected. These standards should describe the condition that will exist when the objective is achieved. They will be quantified and measurable.

This approach has a unique advantage in that it provides a method for systematic assessment and assignment of priorities for long-range action plans that will achieve the key objectives and strategies. Each critical objective and its attendant analysis of needs will generate several long-range action plans. To illustrate, if a critical objective for the consulting firm we have used as an example earlier is to maintain market leadership in management education programs, we might have long-range action plans for developing behavior-modeling programs, initiating counseling services, increasing market staff, and entering non-English–language markets.

These action plans might extend as much as 5 to 8 years in the future. Each has its own specific standards and specific budget and is accompanied by a value analysis so that we can assign priorities in terms of the funds available.

Many of the steps in the long-range action plan will be translated directly into short-range action plans. As these are cascaded, they become more detailed and eventually become part of the day-to-day work planning of the components to which they pertain.

Another advantage of the position-planning approach is that the action plans can be used to bridge two or more operating components. The specific objectives, program steps, schedules, and budgets all become part of this process, resulting in a matrix in which all except the accountable manager become staff and provide advice and service in achieving the principal's specific objective. However, since each contribution is the subject of its own action plan, the roles are clear, there is no question as to reporting relationships, and control is integrated with the plans.

Secure Understanding and Acceptance. As a manager, you develop objectives and standards that apply primarily to other people. As important as the accuracy of the work itself is understanding and acceptance on the part of the people who will be expected to perform it. This begins with your superior. Since the work you do must support your superior's objectives, you will want to get understanding and acceptance of your specific objectives and specific standards before developing the rest of your plan.

You will also want to get the understanding and acceptance of your subordinates for the specific objectives and standards you cascade to them. You can assume that you and your people will be coming from different directions and that what you see as a reasonable and challenging objective or standard may appear quite different to the person accountable for achieving it.

This cascade from the long-range action plan of the chief executive officer to the vice-president of marketing and the manager of market research is shown in Figure 7-6. The time frame is also shown schematically.

Develop Program, Schedules, and Specific Budgets. After you have reached agreement on the specific objectives and standards, you can develop the remainder of your action plans with a good deal of latitude.

Long-range action plans will contain programs, schedules, and budgets with long time spans, while short-range ones will be much more specific. You calculate costs for each program step to arrive at your specific budget.

To avoid awkward allocation of fixed and overhead expenses, it is generally best to charge only direct and variable costs, while overhead costs are collected for the entire component. You may also find that

PROGRAM STEPS	1984	1985	1986	1987	1988
CHIEF EXECUTIVE OFFICER PROGRAM STEP					
Establish Business in West Germany					X
V.P. MARKETING PROGRAM STEP					
Research West German Market	X				
Select West German Associates		X			
Translate Selected Programs					
Generate $200,000/Yr. Revenue			X		
Select Office Site			X		
Open Office				X	
Staff Office				X	
MANAGER, MARKET RESEARCH					
Identify West German Potential	X				
Evaluate Competition	X				
Define Market Segments	X				
Quantify Initial Targets	X				

FIGURE 7-6   Cascade of Specific Objectives and Program Steps

some costs cannot be assigned to individual steps. Add these to the totals below the last program step.

Short-range action plans will cover enough ground to have predictive value for the next year. Since the amount of revenue sets limits for action plans and the financial budget, specific objectives for short-range revenue generation are developed and validated by repetitive assessment at each management level directly involved. Isolation of revenue estimates and agreement on them independent of the budgeting process gives them an objectivity not obtainable when they may be influenced by a companion desire to justify expenditures for preferred projects.

The development of the long- and short-range action plans and the negotiation and reconciliation that must take place from both directions consume the most time. However, this involves a rigorous assessment of current experience as exemplified by success in achieving objectives and standards, so it is worth the time necessary to do it right.

Specific budgets are developed as part of the short- and long-range action plans. As shown in Figure 7-5, these become inputs to the detailed financial budget, which is completed in the final quarter of a fiscal year. This sequence and timing of the budget follows the logic both of zero-based budgeting and PERT/cost. It requires that a careful determination be made of the work that is to be done, the results that are to be achieved, and the value of the results.

If you wish, you can calculate the benefits or value to be derived from completion of the action plan and show these on the action plan form. The benefits must be measurable so that you can compare them to costs and use them to evaluate the priority and worth of the action plan.

There are many ways to show benefits or value. You may want to consider improved revenues, reduced expenses, increased productivity, or improved efficiency. Avoidance of costs, penalties, or losses is also quantifiable.

Timing of the Planning Sequence

Since the planning cycle involves a series of iterative activities, all of which must be completed before the new planning year ensues, the planning schedule is generally best developed to cover a full 12-month period.

As shown in Figure 7-5, long-range forecasting is done early and can be cascaded from top to bottom in the first 2 months of a fiscal year. Updating of charters can generally be accomplished with some dispatch, since only a few aspects will probably need revision. For the same reason, the cascading of charters will probably only require 2 or 3 weeks.

Since position charters are the baseline for both the needs analysis and action plans, a more detailed examination and final understanding and acceptance are scheduled for the beginning of the second half of the year so that the data are available before a final determination is made of how funds are to be spent.

Planning cycles will vary widely for different enterprises. The suggestions in this chapter are centered on areas of general concern and are intended only to show the relationship of the position plan and the enterprise plan and the part each plays in the planning process.

In the next chapter, we will look at the initial steps we follow in developing a position plan. We will first examine in detail the process of Commitment Analysis and, later, the development of the Purpose Commitment. These define the type of enterprise we commit ourselves to build and the purpose it serves.

KEY POINTS

1. *Two Types of Plans.* Position plans define the planning accountabilities of individual managers; the enterprise plan establishes the course of action to

be followed by the enterprise as a whole. Since the chief executive officer is accountable for the organization as a whole, the CEO's position plan is the primary component of the enterprise plan.

2. *The Position Plan.* Parts of the position plan are developed within a framework set by the forecast. The position plan contains the key objective, which is the overall, continuing objective. This is supported by key standards, which provide criteria for measuring achievement of the key objective. Key strategies specify the general approach to be followed in achieving the objective and meeting the standards.

3. *The Enterprise Plan.* While the CEO's position plan is the nucleus, the enterprise plan also contains planning sections which cover aspects of the CEO's accountability beyond the position charter. These include the finance section, human resources section, marketing section, and growth section.

4. *Planning Responsibilities and Roles.* Definition of the planning work to be done and clarification of the relationship necessary for effective teamwork are vital to successful planning. Relationships and roles are specified for the chief executive, the specialized staff groups, and the line operating heads.

5. *The Chief Executive's Role.* The chief executive works with the board and the managers to set the course for the enterprise. Long- and short-range plans must be developed and relationships must be clarified among the people who will work as a team to prepare the plan and carry it out.

6. *The Specialized Staff Role.* Although circumstances and people tend to push staff into a command role, the most effective continuing relationship is advice and service. Staff groups play a key role in developing functional plans for operating managers. They also are best placed to interpret and coordinate the requirements of the chief executive with the capabilities of the line functions and departments.

7. *Divisional Manager's Role.* As accountability for end results is vested in the divisional manager, so also must be the obligation to plan for those results. When divisions are profit centers, there is a temptation to place the interests of the division ahead of the organization as a whole. This is especially true if compensation is dependent on performance. However, objectives and standards should be designed to establish and measure both long- and short-term performance and to give corporate results priority over those of the divisions.

8. *The Planning Sequence.* Position planning provides for the establishment of both continuing and time-limited plans at the top level and the subsequent systematic cascade to all parts of the organization. The position charter sets the framework. Long-range action plans then specify projects that will be carried out over a number or years. Action plans can be given priorities by determining the benefit or value to be derived from each and comparing that to the cost of carrying each out.

9. *Timing of the Enterprise Plan.* Since the plan must be completed before the end of the year, preparation begins in the first quarter and proceeds through a 9- or 10-month period. Position charters are revised and updated to provide new challenges and to open doors for innovation. Action plans then serve as the implements to carry out the intent of the position charters. Financial

budgets are developed as the final step, to test feasibility in terms of the funds available.

QUOTES FROM CHAPTER 7

Significant quotations from this chapter that you will want to consider and discuss in greater detail:

- Most managers will find that their requirements can be satisfied with two types of plans: position plans and enterprise plans.
- Enterprise plans for the small, young, and functionally organized firm differ from those of the large, divisionalized company.
- The more deeply involved board members become in developing specific plans, the more likely they are to protect and nourish their brainchildren.
- The driving force of any set of plans is the document that prompts day-to-day action.
- One capable staff planner with an efficient secretary can provide a surprising amount of advice and service.

THE POSITION PLAN

To have a growth-oriented work environment, everyone will have the same managerial objectives and will identify with them no matter where they are in the organization or in the hierarchy.
ABRAHAM MASLOW

THE CHAPTER IN BRIEF   Position plans provide a logical grouping of responsibilities. They are made up of continuing plans, contained in position charters, and time-limited plans, in the form of action plans. Position forecasts set the stage. Commitments are made as to type and purpose of enterprise, the products and services it will provide, and to whom they will be provided. A commitment is also made as to the scope of operations. Put together, these commitments form the key objective. Following the classification logic, a work analysis is then completed, and this yields the critical objectives, which are statements of the most important results that must be accomplished to achieve the key objective. Key standards and key strategies may be derived from the key objective; and critical standards, from the critical objective. Action plans are made up of specific objectives, programs, schedules, and specific budgets. This position plan is cascaded from top to bottom and reconciled from bottom to top. Controls are derived from key, critical, and and specific standards.

WHAT IS A POSITION PLAN?

Plans are made for and by people; organizations do not plan, the people in them do. Although we speak of strategic, operational, marketing, and financial plans as if each had a separate identity and existence, in fact every plan is a position document which is the obligation of an individual manager.

We define a "position" as a set of related and continuing accountabilities in an organization that one suitably qualified person can maintain. For example, if the controller, treasurer, and audit departments report to the finance manager, the position of finance manager is accountable for all three. Even though different people march in and out of these positions, we would expect the accountabilities to remain unchanged until purposefully modified.

107

ADVANTAGES OF POSITION PLANNING

Developing plans for positions rather than for individuals or enterprises has advantages. Position accountability greatly simplifies the task of clearly identifying responsibility and authority for each of the plans required. It also provides for logical grouping of components of each plan under the manager who is organizationally accountable. This avoids the fragmentation of planning and diffusion of effort that occur with generic accountability.

An important distinction is that managers are not planning for their own work but for their total accountabilities. Thus, the chief executive's plan is not the course of action he or she personally intends to carry out; rather, it is the course of action that will be carried out by the team under his or her leadership. In other words, the CEO's plan includes the objectives he or she will accomplish through the managers of research and development, manufacturing, marketing, finance, and human resources.

Through this summary display of objectives for the manager's team, the position plan delineates responsibility, provides a basis for measuring performance, and minimizes overlap and duplication of effort. It provides the further advantage of automatically integrating the subsidiary plans for all positions derived from the objectives already set forth.

When we think in terms of positions, we can consider the total task and what needs to be done to accomplish it. We can balance and relate the different kinds of work for which the position is accountable and make sure there are neither gaps nor duplication of effort.

Since these thus become ideal positions, we are unlikely to find the ideal people necessary to implement them perfectly. However, we can readily determine the gaps between people and their positions and either help the position incumbents to grow or provide necessary support.

COMPONENTS OF THE POSITION PLAN

In keeping with the classification of work we have developed, we would expect the plan for each position to be made up of the appropriate activities of the function of planning. These can be placed most conveniently in two groups based on the time spans involved. We consolidate our continuing plans in a document we call the position charter and our time-limited plans in another, related set of documents, our action plans. We will look at these from an overall perspective in this chapter, then discuss them in detail in following chapters. The contents and flow of position planning and its constituent position charter and action plans are shown in Figure 7-2. The diagram has been expanded to show the relationship of all the planning and controlling activities. The position charter is the foundation of the system.

The components of the position plan are identified in Figure 7-2. As we have seen, key, critical, and specific standards are segments of the activity of control, but we show them in their companion role with the objectives from which they are derived.

You will find a close-up of the position plan in Figure 8-1. Here you will see that the logic for the various parts is specified and a breakdown of the elements of work is provided.

We will next examine the Position Forecast and the various parts of the position charter.

THE POSITION FORECAST

Your primary concern in position forecasting is to estimate and predict the characteristics of the environment in which you will be operating. On the basis of these estimates and predictions, you can make assumptions about the future. In keeping with the principle of the critical few, you will want to concentrate on those vital areas that will most influence your future success.

If you are the chief executive officer, you and your staff will develop the enterprise forecast. Here you will make assumptions about such factors as the type of enterprise yours is to become, its purpose, the products and services to be offered, the customers or clients on whom the marketing effort will be centered, and the scope of operations.

If you head a division or strategic business unit, your forecast will become a primary report to the enterprise forecast. If you manage a department or other functional component, your superior's forecast will probably be cascaded to you, and you will contribute to its functional content.

There are many alternatives in forecasting. If you have already prepared a forecast for the strategic plan, the pertinent elements of that forecast can be expanded and made current for your position plan. Possibly there is no enterprise forecast, and you are not in a forecast cascade. You can then initiate your own forecast by digging out the data you need from other units, securing advice and help from the appropriate staff departments, and arriving at assumptions which you can check out with your superior.

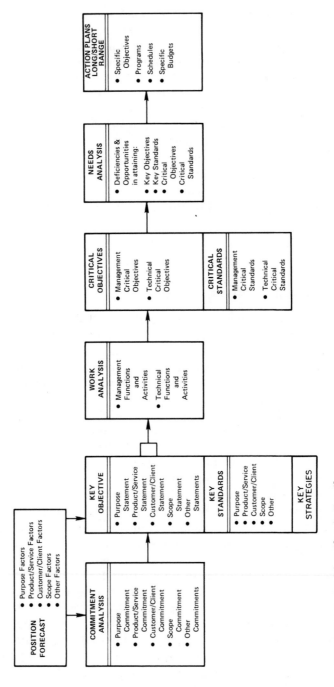

FIGURE 8-1 Position Plan in Detail

If you do not already have a format for preparing your forecasts, here are helpful guidelines:

1. *Identify the Critical Few Areas to Forecast.* You can obtain these from your position charter. You will already have identified the most import commitments you must make; you can now use these as guidelines for collecting and evaluating forecast data. Review each commitment in your key objective and your key standards. Answers to questions such as the following will provide the information you need.

   a. *Purpose.* How successful have you been in achieving your purpose and meeting your standards? Look back as far as you can to identify trends or distinctive cycles or movements. What kinds of assumptions about the future must you make to meet your standards in such areas as sales volume, prices, costs, competition, technology? What are the external and internal threats and opportunities?

   b. *Product/Service.* What categories of products or services have you provided to customers or clients, both external and internal? How successful have you been? What changes will occur in the future?

   c. *Customer/Client.* What categories of customers or clients have you served, both externally and internally? What categories should you serve in the future? What influences will cause the customer/client categories to change? To what degree can you control these influences?

   d. *Scope.* What considerations will influence the geographic and other areas in which you serve internal and external customers or clients? What changes will probably occur? When?

2. *State the Range of Possibilities.* A "forecast" is an estimate or prediction. It indicates what we think will probably occur. It is unlike an "objective," which is a result we will *cause* to occur by use of resources. For this reason, it is good to select a range of reasonable possibilities for your forecast. These can indicate the pessimistic, optimistic, and most likely cases. For example, you may anticipate that market demand will increase an additional 20% each year for the foreseeable future if everything goes right that should go right, will increase only 4% if everything goes wrong, and

will increase 12% if some things go right and some things go wrong, which is the most likely case.

An Example of a Position Forecast

The following is a simplified, summary example of the use of forecasting in position planning. Suppose you decide to start a consulting firm. You study the market and current available services and conclude that over the next 10 years enterprises will need skilled, specialized help in improving the way they manage. The conventional problem-solving approach to consulting will be inadequate because it solves problems *for* managers and does not equip them to solve their own. What will be needed is a service that will educate managers to identify, solve, and implement the solutions to their own management problems. The services that will be in demand will range from conducting public and in-house seminars and providing prepared programs for in-house use to offering problem-solving consulting services. Calculating that each trained professional can generate three to five times his or her salary within 1 year and that you will have working capital available to support three professionals, you estimate first-year revenue of from $120,000 to $200,000, with $150,000 as the most probable. From these figures, you can develop your financial plan. You anticipate that this need will apply to business, government, and other types of undertakings and will extend throughout the world, although, because of limited resources, you anticipate that your best opportunities will be successively in the eastern, central, western, and southern United States and then in English-speaking countries throughout the world.

THE POSITION CHARTER

Your forecast sets limits in the form of the assumptions you make about the future. Within these limits you now develop the key and critical objectives and standards for your position. Some managers, especially at top levels, will also include key strategies. Your first step in developing your position charter is Commitment Analysis.

Commitment Analysis

Since resources are always limited, we need to commit ourselves as to how we will use those available to us. Again, we want to concern ourselves with the critical few resources that will give rise to the largest part of our results. Thus, we develop the Purpose, Product/Service, Customer/Client, and Scope Commitments and other critical commitments.

Continuing with our consulting example, in light of our forecast we determine that we can best use the limited resources available to build a profitable consulting firm. We do not intend to buy and operate businesses or go into executive search. We commit our resources to high-quality education and consultation services and decide to buy what research we need on the outside. Our marketing resources are limited, so we decide to concentrate on business and governmental clients. We will appeal not to individual managers but to enterprise clients. To conserve our capital and maximize our resources, we will expand only as fast as we can generate working capital to pay the costs. We will operate only in English-speaking countries until we have the funds and people to build multilingual capability.

The Focal Point: The Key Objective

Within the environment we forecast, on the basis of the commitments we have made, we can now state our overall, primary, continuing objective. This will serve as the focal point for our planning because it will define our purpose and set our overall direction. Since the key objective is the primary result we will use our resources to accomplish, it will enable us to determine the primary categories of work necessary to achieve it. We use the term key objective because it is the key to our plans, organization, and controls.

The key objective is equivalent to the mission statement or business definition. However, since it concentrates on the critical few success factors, it tends to be more concise and logical. The key objective defines a result to be achieved, so it is clearly an objective and should be classified as such.

An abbreviated statement of our key objective in our consulting example might be: To develop a growing, profitable, stable, and professionally managed consulting firm. This will be accomplished by providing high-quality educational and consulting services that will help managers to improve their practice of professional management. Clients will be sought primarily in business and government, successively in the eastern, central, western, and southern United States and then in English-speaking countries throughout the world.

The overall key objective is cascaded to all positions in the organization; hence, each is traceable and compatible. The key objective represents definite commitments of resources, ensuring consistency and support for the ongoing work of the organization. The key objective also provides a bridge to the organization structure, so that the work done can be balanced with the results desired and the resources available.

Key Standards: The Basis for Controls

We must know how effective we are in achieving our overall objective. This calls for controls. The foundation for control is "standards," which are the criteria by which we measure work and results. Since standards are directly related to results, we can develop them most logically to accompany our key objectives. The positioning of key standards in the position plan is shown in Figure 8-1. Key standards are also cascaded to all levels of the organization and thus provide the basis for an integrated set of controls.

Going back to our consulting example, our key standards might be:

1. *Profit.* 20% before taxes.
2. *Growth.* Revenues increase 12% per year in real terms averaged over 3-year periods.
3. *Stability.* Backlog at the end of each quarter exceeds actual revenues for the quarter.
4. *Client Evaluation.* Services are rated "extremely good" and "superior to competition" on annual surveys.
5. *Employee Evaluation.* Firm members evaluate management and technical work "extremely good" on annual surveys.

Key Strategies: The Direction Finders

After we know what primary results we want, we still must decide how best to go about achieving them. Usually this direction is set at top levels, most commonly by the chief executive officer. It provides guidance to all managers. In some cases the heads of the operating divisions, strategic business units, or line functions directly reporting to the chief executive will refine or interpret the overall strategy and apply it to their own areas of accountability.

Again in keeping with the principle of the critical few, we will develop strategies to implement our purpose, product/service, customer/client, scope, and other vital commitments.

In our consulting example our purpose strategy is to concentrate on our main business and not to diversify our efforts and resources into other tempting opportunities, such as executive recruiting. Our strategy for stability and growth is to maintain a lean, efficient headquarters staff and to concentrate our resources in marketing and professional services. Our quality strategy is to conduct annual surveys of our clients and employees and to implement the findings vigorously. Our product/service strategy is to help our clients tailor our services to their own needs and to train client personnel to do the internal consulting required. We decide to concentrate first on manufacturing and financial businesses and state government agencies. Our scope strategy is to decentralize to four regional offices but only as fast as we can generate funds internally to pay the costs.

Work Analysis Determines the Structure

From the key objectives we can devise the primary categories of work that must be performed on a continuing basis to provide the product or service and satisfy the needs of the customers or clients we have identified. These critical work categories are the equivalent of the Key Result Areas that are often used to identify the most important concentration points. However, through work analysis we have the opportunity of making a logical analysis of the continuing work that leads to continuing results instead of deciding arbitrarily what work seems most important.

In our consulting example, we decide we need a marketing function, so our primary work categories are program development, marketing, and client services.

The Critical Objectives

Our classification logic established that work leads to results. From the Work Analysis we derive the critical objectives that, if accomplished, will yield the key objective.

Since critical objectives cover the most important work and results necessary to achieve the key objective, they set the level of excellence we commit ourselves to achieve. For example, there is a world of difference between an objective "to deliver services of a recognized quality at least equal to that of competitors" and one "to deliver services of recognized quality clearly superior to that of competitors."

Because they establish the level of excellence for the enterprise as a whole, critical objectives are especially vital in the top executive's position. These objectives are cascaded all the way to the bottom, so the level of performance they specify becomes a requirement of every position.

In our consulting example, there will be seven critical objectives derived from the primary categories of managment and technical work. These will be for planning, organizing, leading, controlling, program development, marketing, and client services. The critical standards will be in the same areas.

Critical Standards

We also require standards to measure our secondary objectives. If we meet these critical few standards, there is a high probability we will attain our key objective. The critical standards for our consulting example will be developed to measure performance in the vital factors for each critical objective.

Update Your Position Charter

Your Position Charter is ongoing, but it should be reviewed and revised as often as changes are made in your superior's position charter or as you prepare new forecasts.

Here again it is most helpful if you can base these revisions on changes in the objectives, standards, and strategies of your superior, but you will find it valuable to develop these for your own position, even in the absence of organizational support, and to cascade your own updated position charter to members of your own team. You will want to secure understanding and acceptance from your subordinates, your peers, and, finally, your superior.

ACTION PLANS

The work done day by day is guided by precedent, habit, and procedures. Most tasks are already familiar or have been studied and procedurized so that the work can be delegated completely to the accountable individuals. However, there are always problem areas or opportunities which are not routine. Often these have a disproportionate impact on overall results and warrant special effort. This is the logical place for action plans. The analytical steps and planning activities included in action plans are shown in Figure 8-1. Needs analysis comes first.

Needs Analysis

We have set our overall, long-term direction. We know the level of excellence we expect to achieve, and we have developed a means of measuring our progress and results. Our control system provides us with records and reports. From these and other sources of data, we can identify problems and shortcomings in meeting our standards and achieving our objectives and can pinpoint our needs for specific action. We do this through an analysis of deviations from key and critical objectives and standards and an examination of new opportunities that have arisen. This is the process of needs analysis. It directs our attention to the vitally important areas that warrant the major share of our improvement effort.

Here are steps to follow in preparing the needs analysis:

1. Review your key objective and key standards in light of your forecast and assumptions. Determine the overall needs that will have to be met, giving particular consideration to the needs of your component.

2. Review each technical critical objective and its standards and your superior's objectives. Determine the needs you must satisfy to take advantage of opportunities, to overcome deficiencies in performance, and to maintain the levels set by your standards.

3. Determine needs that are created by the specific objectives and assumptions from your superior. List these needs.

4. Identify opportunities that have arisen or will arise. State them as needs to be met.

5. Review your management critical objectives and standards in the same fashion as your technical critical objectives. List your management needs.

Develop Specific Objectives and Standards

Your needs analysis enables you to focus on the areas which require action in order to overcome deficiencies and to maintain the other requirements of your position charter. It also opens up new opportunities important to your success. You are now ready to develop your specific objectives.

Each specific objective states a result that will satisfy a need you have already identified. You will usually find that each need leads to one specific objective. However, it is also possible for one need to generate several specific objectives or for one specific objective to meet several identified needs.

The work you do must support your superior's long-range objectives. Therefore, you will want to review your specific objectives and specific standards with your superior to be sure you have understanding and acceptance prior to developing the rest of your plan. This will help you to be certain that the completed plan does not overlap or duplicate work done elsewhere.

Complete Action Plans

After your specific objectives and standards have received your superior's approval, you flesh out your action plan by listing the program steps, scheduling completion dates, assigning accountability, and estimating the specific budget required.

1. *Program Steps.* Now you are ready to block out the action steps that will enable you to achieve your specific objective and satisfy your specific standards. Programming is the work of determining the sequence and priority of action steps necessary to reach an objective.

   To develop your program steps, you review the specific objective together with the specific standards to determine the logical action steps that must be followed to achieve the results you want.

2. *Schedules.* Since action plans are to be accomplished within a definite time period, you establish a time sequence for the program steps and for the plan as a whole. This is your schedule. For each step, you show the completion date or time; for each year that will elapse, you specify the beginning of the new year.

3. *Accountability and Authority.* For each program step and schedule time, you identify the accountable individuals by initials. You can also indicate the degree of authority delegated to those individuals.

4. *Specific Budgets.* Here we are concerned with the cost of resources necessary to carry out the program within scheduled limits and to meet the specific objective. The specific budget inputs to the business, financial, or control budget.

    For your specific budget, show the costs incurred in performing each program step. Consider the human, physical, and financial resources involved and convert them into monetary values.

    To simplify the collection of fixed and overhead expenses, charge to the program steps only direct costs, that is, money actually spent to carry out the step. You can collect the appropriate overhead costs on summary forms.

    If there are amounts that accrue to the whole action plan but cannot be assigned to individual steps, list these below the last step.

5. *Value.* You will find it very helpful to determine the *measurable* benefit that results from completion of the action plan. When you justify the costs and the benefits to be derived, you will find that this facilitates balanced decision making and valuation of the results.

    Values gained may be stated directly in monetary terms, such as revenue, reduced expenses, and costs or penalties avoided. You may also estimate the value of factors such as improved efficiency and improved morale or productivity. Financial benefits may accrue to the company as a whole or to components. Identify these.

You will want to secure understanding and acceptance of your action plans. Reconciliation and agreement is secured from the top down for the needs analysis and specific objectives and standards. Since the most detailed knowledge of methods, time, and cost is found at the operating level, the programs, schedules, and budgets are negotiated and reconciled from the bottom up.

THE POSITION-PLANNING CASCADE

Position planning is based on the logic that all levels of management must maintain both continuing and time-limited plans. We ordinarily think of missions and strategies as the exclusive province of top management, but if the operating levels do not understand the enterprise mission and strategy and do not implement their part, execution will be uncertain and imperfect. Corporate budgets are invaluable financial tools, but since most of the money is actually spent at the line of operations, it follows that we should be equally concerned with developing budgets at that level.

The vital question is: How can we integrate the plans of top and lower levels so that each fills its special role? The cascading process is a simple and logical way to do the job. Cascading means that a plan is delegated so that its essential requirements are translated into implementing plans at successively lower levels. As an everyday example, if a company has 20 sales regions and 5 divisions and commits itself to sell 100,000 units of product, the total is cascaded so that each of the 5 divisions commits to 20,000 units, more or less. And these quotas in turn are cascaded to the sales offices and individual salespersons.

While this is familiar in sales and cost reduction, it can be extended to virtually every important activity. To improve planning, for example, the president can begin by developing a position charter and then delegating the same task to all managers down to the first-line supervisor.

The pattern of the position-planning cascade is shown in Figure 8-2. Each planning component is cascaded. The position-charter cascade integrates continuing objectives, standards, and strategies at all levels. Cascading of the needs analysis and long- and short-range action plans ensures that strategic programs will be developed that will provide for orderly, consistent attainment of overall goals.

In the figure, you will see that position charters and action plans both are cascaded from the top down and reconciled from the bottom up. This ensures that plans are understood and accepted and that they have the realism and commitment necessary for effective implementation.

Cascade of the Chief Executive's Position Charter

The chief executive's position charter is a set of positive directions that will guide the overall use of resources. It is a living document because it is intended to be changed and updated on an ongoing basis.

A vital feature of the chief executive's position charter is that it is cascaded from top to bottom and reconciled and adjusted from bottom to top. The cascade ensures integration of key objectives and key standards. Key strategies spell out the general method that will be followed to meet the key objectives and standards. For example, it is critically important for every manager to know that the enterprise will use its profits to build working capital and to maintain cash flow rather than to invest in new growth. If the strategy is to move out ahead and capture

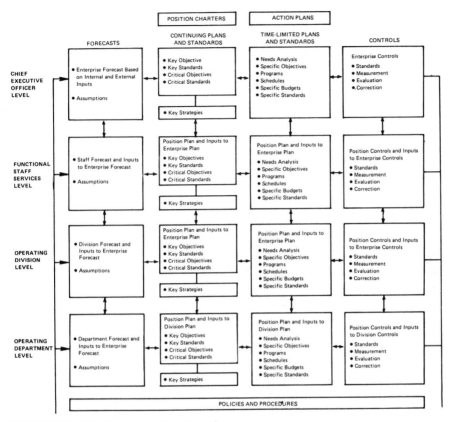

FIGURE 8-2 **The Cascade of Position Plans**

market position by innovation and quality, this directly influences operations as diverse as personnel selection and market research.

Systematic cascade of critical objectives and critical standards ensures that the desired level of excellence in performance is clearly defined for each organization component and that each function coordinates its future movements with those of the others directly involved.

Cascade of the Needs Analysis

Certain basic threats and opportunites (for example, the perils of illiquidity or the promise of a new technological breakthrough) confront every organization. These require coordinated analysis and action on the part of a wide variety of functions. At the same time, certain deficiences in performance may be common throughout the organization and can be corrected only if concerted action is taken. For example, if controls are weak, if productivity is low, or if there is a high degree of employee dissatisfaction, no one manager or group of managers is able to correct the situation. What is necessary is a broad and coordinated approach stemming from the top and implemented in every part of the organization.

Needs analysis is a mechanism for identifying and defining the critical few problems and opportunities that warrant this kind of action and setting the stage for the long- or short-range action plans that will correct the situation.

In one way, needs analysis is similar to what is commonly known as Gap Analysis, for it identifies the gap between long-range expectations and current actuality. However, needs analysis has the advantage of systematically analyzing each objective and standard that has been identified as critical to overall success and defining precisely the problems and opportunites that merit priority attention.

Cascade of Long-Range Action Plans

One of the most difficult moves in any organization is to get everybody to march in unison toward the desired end results. This is achieved by developing corporate strategies and then preparing medium- and short-range tactical programs, functional programs, or operational plans, which, in turn, are supported by budgets. All of these are concerned with detailing what steps to take to achieve the overall strategies and objectives. Their purpose is to bond the various components of the organization together in their planning and to encompass the diverse resources and efforts that must be blended if the enterprise is to move in the strategic directions its management has decided upon.

Long-range action plans serve this purpose in a concise and logical manner. They provide specific objectives accompanied by specific standards, programs, schedules, and specific budgets in the functional areas that have been identified as critical to success. By definition they warrant highest priority and preferential allocation of resources.

The long-range action plans are initiated at all levels in response to identified needs. However, they are cascaded from the highest-level manager to lower levels to ensure that there is vertical and lateral coordination.

Cascade of Short-Range Action Plans

Specific time-limited actions that are necessary to achieve the long-range action plans are documented in short-range plans. These usually extend for a year or less and detail the work for which resources will be used. Like the long-range action plans, the short-range ones are the clear accountability of individuals.

Short-range plans are reviewed periodically to check progress. Since the standards, program steps, and budgeted funds are directly measurable, short-range action plans are a most useful control device. In many cases, superior/subordinate reviews of progress and results are held monthly or even more frequently. This ensures participation, facilitates communication, and helps generate interest and enthusiasm for the work.

The cascade of plans from the chief executive to lower levels ensures that the planning structure will remain consistent and rational. It provides automatically for the coordination necessary to secure effective use of resources at each level.

The cascade can be effective only if managers use the same planning vocabulary and methods, so the cascade process itself encourages the training and education necessary for accurate, perceptive work. Since cascaded plans are based on the critical few problems and opportunities that are vital to success, they are a valuable means of focusing the resources of the entire organization on the work that will have the best payoff.

The Place of Policies

Policies are not part of the position plan because they apply to the organization as a whole. However, they are shown on the logic diagram (Figure 7-2) to indicate their relationship to the position plan. We consider policies to be continuing plans because they are standing decisions which are made to apply to recurring problems of concern to the organization as a whole. For example, suppose we are continually faced with the question of what level salaries we should pay. Should we try to get people to work as cheaply as possible? Do we want to pay a premium for superior skills? Would we prefer to pay at the same level as other enterprises? A policy might state that we would pay at least as much as similar enterprises in the same geographic areas. If we are convinced that superior people bring superior results, we might establish a policy that we would pay more than other enterprises to secure outstanding skills and competence.

Procedures

Procedures are also shown in Figure 7-2. A "procedure" is a standardized method of performing work that must be done in a uniform manner wherever it is performed. A procedure in effect is a continuing program. As we will see when we later discuss action plans, a "program" is an action step taken to accomplish a specific objective. If the program becomes routinized and is repeated over and over, we standardize it as a procedure. For example, suppose you develop a program to handle the acquisition, installation, and operation of word processing equipment. After it is installed and debugged, the work called for in the operations portion of your program is repeated endlessly by the machine operators. Instead of preparing new programs, you can have a careful study made of the best way to do the work whenever it is performed and capture the essence of this experience by preparing a procedure to cover it.

The Control Cycle

From Figure 7-2, it is clear that action plans lead to implementation; that is, the work is performed and the resources are used. Controls then come into operation to ensure that the plans are accomplished. Performance standards have already been developed to accompany objectives. Measuring and evaluating performance and results lead to required correction and improvement.

Management and Technical Action. A key characteristic of integrated planning and control is the feedback mechanism that provides both corrective and improvement action at appropriate points in the system. If your people do not meet standards, this prompts investigation of the causative factors and renewed action to satisfy the standards. At the same time, these same deficiencies should encourage you to review carefully the plans themselves to ensure that they are accurate and timely and that they are understood.

The action you and your people take directly to correct variances and exceptions is "technical action"; that is, it is applied directly to resources by the people accountable for the work. When you concentrate on correcting or improving the underlying plans, this is "management action," for it applies primarily to work that is intended to secure results through others.

The most important implication of this distinction between management and technical action is that you can largely delegate technical action, if, that is, you have people who are available and properly placed organizationally and who are trained and motivated to do the work as the standards require. Management work, on the other hand, is something you must do yourself, except to the extent you can delegate routine and repetitive aspects to others.

With a clear picture of position planning in mind, in the next chapter we will examine in detail the purpose commitment of the key objective.

KEY POINTS

1. *Position Plans.* These are made up of the continuing plans for a position and the position charter, consisting of key and critical objectives, key strategies as appropriate, and critical objectives and standards. Position plans also contain the time-limited action plans, composed of specific objectives, programs, schedules, and specific budgets.

2. *Position Forecasts.* These are developed to estimate and predict the future environment in which you will be operating. To secure emphasis on the critical few, data are grouped in the categories of purpose, product/service, customer/client, scope, and others that apply.

3. *The Key Objective and Standards.* An analysis of the primary commitment of resources is made, also under the critical-few category headings. The key objective is accompanied by overall standards that enable us to measure accomplishment of the key objective. Key standards become the basis for controls.

4. *Key Strategies.* A new definition and classification of strategy interprets it as the general approach to be followed in achieving an objective. Strategy is thus related directly to objectives. This narrow usage gives the term more precise meaning.

5. *Needs Analysis.* Continuing plans and standards define the level of excellence we commit ourselves to achieve. Through needs analysis, we determine deficiencies in accomplishing the plans and meeting the standards. This technique also enables us to spot opportunities that we might otherwise overlook.

6. *Action Plans.* These detail the specific actions we will take to overcome deficiencies, take advantage of opportunities, and continue to meet our continuing objectives and standards. Action plans are made up of specific objectives, specific standards, programs, schedules, and specific budgets.

7. *Cascade of Position Plans.* To secure integration both laterally and horizontally, position plans are cascaded from the chief executive to the lowest organizational level. The cascade includes both position charters and action plans.

8. *Policies and Procedures.* While not part of the position plan, policies are developed to provide continuing decisions that can be applied to repetitive needs and problems. Procedures establish the best way to perform work that must be done uniformly and consistently.

9. *Controls.* No plan is any better than the controls used to ensure that it is implemented. The control system is derived from the key, critical, and specific standards developed to accompany the objectives of the position plan.

QUOTES FROM CHAPTER 8

Significant quotations from this chapter that you will want to consider and discuss in greater detail:

- The position plan delineates responsibility, provides a basis for measuring performance, and minimizes overlap and duplication of effort.

- Needs analysis directs our attention to the vitally important areas that warrant the major share of our improvement effort.

- The chief executive's position charter is a set of positive directions that will guide the overall use of resources.

- A procedure is a continuing program.

THE KEY OBJECTIVE:
THE PURPOSE COMMITMENT

If you wish to live a life free from sorrow, think of what is going to happen as if it already happened.
EPICTETUS

THE CHAPTER IN BRIEF   We have seen that the position charter is probably the most important single document managers develop for their positions. Your charter will be framed by the limits and assumptions you establish in your forecasts. It will contain your commitment analysis: a clear statement of your major commitments of resources. These will include your purpose, product/service, customer/client, and your geographic, or scope, commitments. Based on these commitments, you will develop your key objective, key standards, and, if applicable, key strategies. You will also prepare your critical objectives and standards. This chapter will deal with the first commitment, which answers the seemingly simple but vital question: "What is our purpose?"

PLANNING BEGINS WITH PURPOSE

The Universal Electrical Services Company, a large electrical-engineering service company, grew rapidly and profitably in its specialty of providing technical services to electrical utilities. It seized upon an opportunity to acquire an electrical supply house with international operations. Then it set itself up to provide management consulting services to industry in general. Within 3 years, its profits had disappeared, the entire top management team had been turned over, and it was fighting off a takeover bid from its largest competitor.

Facing up to its problem, the company made a careful analysis of its growth pattern. It decided that the greatest probability of regaining lost ground rested in concentrating its resources and skills in the specialty it knew best—professional engineering services. But the chief operating officer and several key officers were yet to be won over. After almost a month of heated debate, the chief executive officer issued a statement that began: "The key objective of the Universal Electrical Services Company is to build a growing, profitable electrical-engineering service company."

Prompted by this commitment approved by the board, the company sold off its acquisitions and within another 3 years had forged to the front again.

This was the first position charter developed by the chief executive officer. As is often the case, the simple opening statement of the purpose commitment portion of the key objective carried a wealth of meaning and had a lasting impact on the business and characteristics of the company.

In developing your own position charter, whether you are at top or middle-management level, you will find that it will also provide guidance to you and all those with whom you work.

THE PARTS OF THE POSITION CHARTER

Your position charter is designed to respond to a set of questions you have about the future. Here are the questions and the answers provided by your position charter:

- What resources will be available in the environment in which you expect to operate, and how can you best commit those resources? You get these answers through commitment analysis.

- What kind of undertaking will you build, and what will you attempt to accomplish with the human and material resources available? This is your key objective.

- What alternative approaches are there to accomplishing your key objective? Which are best? These are your key strategies.

- What criteria will you use to determine how effectively you are accomplishing your key objective? These are your key standards.

- What are the primary categories of continuing work that must be performed to achieve your key objective? This is determined through work analysis.

- What continuing results must you accomplish for each primary work category in order to realize the key objective? These are your critical objectives.

- What criteria will you use to determine how effectively you are accomplishing your critical objectives? These are your critical standards.

We have already seen in Figure 7-2 how the position charter fits in the planning process. The parts of the position charter are shown in Figure 8-1. All of these parts are continuing in nature.

As we have noted, commitment analysis yields the key objective, from which key standards are derived. Key strategies are generally developed at top levels. Work analysis leads directly to critical objectives, on which critical standards are based.

Although we have discussed this before, it may be well to review the classification of standards. Because objectives and standards often have a symbiotic relationship and are closely linked in practice, we may be tempted to categorize standards as part of planning. However, this is no more the case than it is that a fungus is an algae because they are found in a symbiotic relationship in a lichen: objectives are *plans* and standards are *controls*. The term "position charter" is a convenient means of categorizing their joint use, just as the term "lichen" categorizes the symbiotic relationship of fungus and algae.

CASCADING YOUR POSITION CHARTER

Your position charter is valuable as a means of defining and orienting your own position and locating it within the organization as a whole. To be of real value, your charter should give you a brief, clear statement of what you must do to carry out your share of the overall objective. This means it must be derived from and reconciled with the position charter of your own superior. In turn, appropriate portions should be delegated and reconciled with those who report to you. Meshing and relating the different charters so they constitute an integrated whole is accomplished by cascading.

"Cascading" is *the process of conveying position charters in succession from top to bottom organization levels and reconciling them from bottom to top and with peer positions so that each charter states a balanced and proportionate part of the total results to be achieved and the standards by which they are to be measured.*

The cascading process follows the organization hierarchy, as do other parts of planning. This was shown in Figure 8-2, which outlines the cascade of plans and controls, including position charters, and the resulting information flows, from corporate management down through functional staff departments, operating divisions, and operating departments. The Feedback Loop is indicated.

The Key Objective Cascade

Each commitment is cascaded, narrowing in scope to fit the delegation made to successively lower positions. Thus, while the customer/client commitment of the chief executive officer of a food company is to "provide an integrated line of prepared foods to meet the identified needs of direct consumers," the Fido foods division narrows this to "provide processed, packaged foods for domestic pets to meet the identified needs of urban consumers." The Fido foods division marketing department repeats this commitment, for it is the group that directly accomplishes the division marketing commitment.

The Critical Objectives Cascade

Objectives for both management and technical functions are cascaded. Management objectives state the results to be achieved in planning, organizing, leading, and controlling work. Management objectives are much the same for all managers; however, they narrow successively from top to lower organizational levels, for example, from corporate to division to region to plant.

Technical critical objectives state the results to be achieved from technical work, such as engineering, accounting, marketing. These objectives will tend to differ from one enterprise to the next and even among components of the same organization. Therefore, the technical objective cascade will show the greatest variation. For example, the research critical objective in one drug company might be largely concerned with developing new drugs, while the research critical objective in a proprietary drug company might concentrate on establishing exclusive ownership of special modifications of new drugs discovered elsewhere.

When position charters are cascaded, you secure from your superior the basic information from which you develop your own charter and you pass this on in turn to the people who report to you. The cascading process enables you to achieve the vertical traceability and horizontal compatibility which we discussed earlier.

With this cascade in mind, we can now look to the process of developing the key objective. This begins with analysis of the commitments that are made to guide the use of resources.

PREPARING THE COMMITMENT ANALYSIS

"Commitment analysis" is *the process of identifying and defining the overall categories to which continuing allocation of resources will be made.* Your forecasts provide a reasonably clear idea of the important features of the future environment in which you expect to be working. Your task now is to provide a basis for allocating the resources of materials, tools, and people that will be available to you.

We will assume that this is not a start-up effort; although if you are starting a new business, professional office, or government agency, the method will apply with little modification. As part of an established enterprise, your need now is to review what is already in effect and to determine what changes are advisable.

The Critical Commitments

In accord with the principle of the critical few, you want to identify the relatively few areas that have greatest potential for payoff and concentrate your muscle and money there. Four basic commitments which answer the questions why, what, who, and where are generally recognized; however, you will probably want to consider others, such as commitments for human resources, social and environmental needs.

Purpose Commitment. You know that if your enterprise—or your component of the enterprise, however small—exists, it must do so for some purpose. Purpose, then, is the critical factor that will provide overall guidance in committing your available resources. The purpose commitment answers the question: *Why* does this enterprise, and its components, exist?

Product/Service Commitment. Every organized undertaking accomplishes its purpose by providing something of value to users—either internal or external. This is the product or service to which you will commit resources. Your product/service commitment answers the question: *What* will you provide to internal or external customers?

Customer/Client Commitment. You may provide this product or service to anybody and everybody who can possibly use it, or you can concentrate on the critical few who will give greatest promise of enabling you to achieve your purpose. Your customer/client commitment answers the question: *To whom* will you provide the product or service?

Scope Commitment. You may provide your products and services to customers and clients anywhere you can find them, but, as the principle of the critical few suggests, if you want to maximize your chances of success, you will concentrate your resources within the most promising geographic or other limits. Your scope commitment answers the question: *Where* will you provide the product or service to customers or clients?

Other Commitments. Depending on the type of enterprise, you may wish to make other commitments that will guide you in your overall use of resources. A human resources commitment might establish the obligations you undertake with respect to the people of the enterprise. A social commitment might relate to the community or the country or society as a whole. An ecological commitment might establish an obligation to use resources to help preserve and improve the environment.

For example, Hewlett-Packard Company, a leader in electronics, commits itself to "being an economic, intellectual and social asset to each nation and each community in which we operate."

In my discussions with Japanese managers, I have been impressed with a general attitude that business and government are working together. There is a joint commitment to improving the position of the country as a whole, so that productivity, quality, and social commitments are clearly stated and universally endorsed. What is most important is that these commitments are not platitudes: government agencies and individual firms develop coordinated plans and work purposefully to achieve them.

A typical cascade of the key objective commitments is shown schematically in Figure 9-1. Although additional narrative might be added, the core commitment is successively focused until it reaches the implementation level.

Every Person Has a Commitment

Ordinarily we think of commitments to use resources as the exclusive province of top management. However, these commitments are no better than our ability to carry them out and must be implemented at the operating levels by supervisors and nonmanagerial employees. It follows, then, that we can get better and faster results if we make sure that all people develop their own key commitments, which are derived from and reconciled with those of the company as a whole.

Often there is objection that employees who are not managers will resist the thinking and writing involved. In fact, however, if properly prepared, employees take great pride in charters which clearly relate their jobs to those of the chief executive officer and to the overall success of the enterprise. And when meaningful key and critical standards are incorporated so people can evaluate their own work, the charters become a valuable aid to communication and performance appraisal.

One caution: position charters should be developed in phases. The first time charters are attempted, they will tend to be clumsily stated, imprecise, and wordy. You will want to work on these until concise, understandable statements evolve. Anticipate that it will require two, or even three generations of position charters until you can use them with confidence.

	COMMITMENTS (Abbreviated)			
POSITION	PURPOSE	PRODUCT/SERVICE	CUSTOMER/CLIENT	SCOPE
President and CEO, Xxex Corp.	Build a growing, profitable diversified electric products company	Provide products, systems, and supplies that use electricity as a primary activating force	Satisfy the identified needs of direct consumers and distributors and franchised shops	In the United States, Pacific, Europe, and Africa
Human Resources Manager	Contribute to growth and profitability by building a corporate specialized staff department	Provide advice and service in making most effective use of human resources	Satisfy the identified needs of the President, Division, and Department Managers	In the United States
Finance Manager	Contribute to growth and profitability by building a corporate specialized staff department	Provide advice and service in planning, controlling, and conserving the assets of the company	Satisfy the identified needs of the President, Division, and Department Managers	In the United States, Pacific, Europe, and Africa
General Manager Electronics Division	Contribute to growth and profitability by building a profit center division	Provide TV, radio, and tape-recording units and parts	Satisfy the identified needs of direct consumers, and distributors	In the United States, Australia, and Africa
Manufacturing Manager Electronics Division	Contribute to growth and profitability of the Electronics Division	Provide TV and radio units and parts	Satisfy the identified needs of the Marketing and Engineering Departments	In Xxex Corp. facilities in the United States
Manager, TV Plant	Contribute to growth and profitability of the Electronics Division	Provide TV components, chassis, and parts	Satisfy the identified needs of the Manufacturing Manager	At the plant locations in Columbus
Supervisor, Fabrication, TV plant	Contribute to growth and profitability of the Electronics Division	Provide TV chassis and cabinets	Satisfy the identified needs of the Manager, TV plant	Columbus plant
Marketing Manager	Contribute to growth and profitability of the Electronics Division	Provide TV, radio, tape-recording units and parts	Satisfy the identified needs of direct consumers and distributors	In the United States
Sales Manager Central Region	Contribute to growth and profitability of the Electronics Division	Provide TV, radio, and tape-recording units	Satisfy the identified needs of direct consumers, distributors, and wholesalers	Illinois, Indiana, Michigan, Wisconsin
District Manager, Retail Sales	Contribute to growth and profitability of the Electronics Division	Provide TV and radio units	Satisfy the identified needs of direct consumers	Chicago, Illinois

FIGURE 9-1 Typical Commitment Cascade

133

Whatever your position, you will want to understand how you fit into the overall cascade. Therefore, we will look first at the process of developing commitments for the enterprise as a whole, then at the individual positions that go to make it up, in both line and staff relationships.

The Commitment Cascade

To ensure vertical traceability and horizontal compatibility, each commitment should have its source in the overall purpose. The commitments at successively lower organization levels come to focus on specific actions that are finally carried out by the operating components of the enterprise. We saw a typical cascade of commitments in Figure 9-1. While it may seem repetitious to provide similar purpose statements to a number of the organization units shown, keep in mind that individuals see only the commitments that apply to their organization components.

DEVELOPING THE PURPOSE COMMITMENT FOR THE ENTERPRISE

The "purpose commitment" of an enterprise or of its parts is *a statement of the overall, continuing ends to be accomplished for which all available resources will be used*. The purpose commitment establishes the reason the enterprise and its parts exist. Notice we specify that this commitment is both *overall* and *continuing*. It is overall because it states the results toward which everything will be directed. It is *continuing* because there is no time limit: everybody will continue to work toward the results until they are changed—whether that be in 5 years or in 50.

The statement of purpose for the components of an enterprise is vitally important. Accountants who act as bookkeepers instead of controllers or personnel managers who see themselves as hiring and firing and trying to beat the union instead of building human resources will be less effective than they might be because their efforts are not directed to a clear and unequivocal purpose.

The Two Parts of the Purpose Commitment

We have defined purpose as the overall, continuing ends to be accomplished for which all available resources will be used. If we want to state the purpose for something and also to have other people understand what we're talking about, logically we first state what that something is, that is, what type of enterprise or what type of component this will be. We then state what overall results it will use its resources to achieve.

Managers who do a good job of preparing a statement of purpose include these kinds of information:

1. A determination of what kind of enterprise or component this has been in the past
2. A commitment as to what kind of enterprise or component this intends to become in the future
3. A statement of the reason why the enterprise exists
4. Derived from this, a statement of why the department, division, or other component exists

Part 1 of the Purpose Commitment: What Kind of Enterprise?

Like the people who make them up, companies tend to become what their past has made of them. Even the largest enterprises bear the stamp of the strong personalities who molded them in early years.

The Case of Chrysler. The Chrysler Corporation, for example, was founded in 1925 by Walter P. Chrysler, the son of a railroad engineer. While working for General Motors, Willys-Overland and the Maxwell Motor Company, Chrysler evolved his own dream of an "engineered car" which would be safe, attractive, and comfortable and which could be sold at a moderate price. He gathered around him several outstanding engineers who took pride in their ability to design, engineer, and market durable, efficient automobiles. With this orientation, as we would expect, they emphasized design and engineering. During the 1930s, for example, Chrysler introduced the Air Flow, which was the most innovative car of its day, years ahead of its time.

Because its engineering and manufacturing departments dominated, Chrysler was slow to change to meet the new needs of customers. Although it was first to build small front-wheel-drive automobiles in the United States, Chrysler found its real problem was to define a new purpose to make a new kind of company of itself. The task was difficult, for it meant becoming totally competitive with other U.S. manufacturers and the burgeoning host of overseas competitors.

Establishing the Pattern. Before we can change anything, it is helpful to know exactly what we are attempting to change. A necessary preliminary to deciding what we want to make of our enterprise or component is to determine what it now is and how it got that way. This process may be called establishing the growth profile, identifying structural norms, or planning formative strategies. Planners often accumulate sales, cost, and other data and from it attempt to establish trends and reach the necessary conclusions; however, this may be no better than trying to identify what kind of person an individual has been by tracking statistics on weight, respiration, chlorophyll count, and basic metabolism. Most companies can track their own past accurately enough; their chief need is to exercise enough objectivity to sort out the trivial from the important and to arrive at conclusions that are supported by facts rather than pride and nostalgia. Often the task of self-assessment can be accomplished from within; sometimes an outside viewpoint is required. General Electric provides a good example.

The General Electric Company. General Electric evolved from the Edison General Electric Company, which was organized in 1878 by Thomas A. Edison. His purpose was to finance his laboratory work on a product that did not yet exist, the incandescent light bulb. At first the company bore the mark of the researcher and inventor. Although none of its chief executives after Edison was an engineer, the company used its resources for research and engineering and concentrated its training on engineers. It built its business on technological innovation. By 1953, 1 out of every 31 American engineers was a General Electric engineer and 1 out of every 92 American scientists worked in a General Electric laboratory. Each year since patents have been granted, General Electric has produced more patentable inventions than any other company in the world.

Paradoxically enough, however, General Electric does not see itself as an engineering company. From the earliest days, when Thomas Edison sealed a tiny carbonized piece of sewing thread into a glass globe and launched a new electrical era, the company has seen its purpose as that of creating markets by turning technology to serve the needs of society. Initially, it concentrated on electrical manufacturing, but decade after decade since, it has moved purposefully into such fields as aircraft engines, consumer products and services, transportation systems, medical systems, synthetic materials, information services, and natural resources.

These planned moves have been based on self-assessment as well as evaluation of the external world and its opportunities. In the mid-70s, General Electric found itself committing a heavy share of its resources to technological invention. But was it getting the results it should? The company undertook a deep and utterly candid corporate technology study that highlighted strengths and weaknesses, needs and opportunities in every part of the organization. The result has been a technological renaissance in General Electric, in which existing commitments have been screened and revitalized at the same time that new and challenging ones have been undertaken. Because of this eclectic orientation, for the 1980s and beyond the company sees itself strongly positioned to take advantage of profitable growth opportunities as they emerge.

Passing the Baton. As General Electric discovered, increasing size, diversification, and maturation call for evolutionary changes in management. And General Electric has responded with insight and great effectiveness.

The first and most critical crisis of growth occurs when increasing size dictates that an organization must be built. Then the person who created the still vivid picture of the future must pass it on, or it rapidly dims and becomes lost—and the sense of purpose with it. If circumstances change and the image of purpose is inflexible, the enterprise soon goes the way of all obsolescent organisms. Many railroads discovered, for example, that it doesn't help much if your purpose is to be a company that will run an efficient rail transportation system to move freight and people when, in fact, the times dictate you should be a transportation system that will move freight and people in the most economical and effective manner—whether by rail, road, air, or water.

Survival and success lie in the founder's ability to pass the baton—to get others to see this clear mental image and act upon it as their own. And since events change and visions must be altered with them, continued success depends upon developing the skills necessary to keep this changing picture clear and to communicate it vividly and convincingly to all who work to realize it.

Here, again, I have found that Japanese companies place great stress upon stating clearly the overall purposes of the enterprise and communicating them to every employee so the message permeates the entire organization. For example, if quality is a corporate commitment, it also becomes an obligation all employees take upon themselves. The story of the Honda worker who stopped on his way to work to adjust misaligned windshield wipers of Honda automobiles parked by the curb is probably quite true.

Whatever the mechanism that brings it about, for long-term success the enterprise must present a clear identity, both to its internal and external customers. As we have seen, the founders of the enterprise succeed because they have a sharp and vivid image of what they are trying to do. Almost invariably this begins to fade as the enterprise grows. New people have different ideas; the founder rarely communicates effectively; sooner or later the purpose that was once clear and compelling becomes an assortment of unrelated ideas.

Sea-Land Industries, Inc.: A Worldwide Fleet. In some cases the first vision of what the company is to become is strong enough and has sufficient potential over time to provide continuing guidance. Little more than 20 years ago, for example, Sea-Land introduced the concept of containerization to the transportation industry, and today it is the world's largest containerized freight carrier. Malcolm McLean, founder of Sea-Land Service, visualized a great fleet of container ships regularly circling the globe, carrying cargo to the ports of the earth. He conveyed that picture vividly to Charles Hiltzheimer, one of his managers, and to Paul Sticht, chairman of the parent company, R. J. Reynolds Industries. Working together, Hiltzheimer, as chief executive of Sea-Land Industries, Inc., and Sticht have made the picture a reality.

W. R. Grace & Co.: A Double Transformation. While many companies have extended their corporate image or have diversified successfully, I encountered only one that had the ability and resources to twice alter the nature of its business to meet the needs of a fast-changing environment. W. R. Grace & Co. has this remarkable record. Its experience has many valuable lessons. Grace was founded as a Latin American trading company. It soon went into shipping to transport goods from Central and South America to the United States. Today it is almost entirely out of both Latin America and the shipping business.

There were good reasons, most of which go back to the outstanding capabilities of Peter Grace. After World War II he saw clearly that the world was changing and that the central business of W. R. Grace would not support the growth and profitability he wanted. Grace Line, Panagra, and the trading enterprise had a dim future in the face of competition and change. Instead of looking around for a likely company to buy, as so many others did, Peter Grace purposely planned his way out of one business and into another.

Here's how he did it. In the late 1940s he put together a group of staff people to study a number of industries. The team made a careful analysis of available opportunities. They concluded that chemicals offered the best field. Peter Grace listened carefully and decided this was what he wanted.

He set about convincing his board of directors and his management team that the changes were imperative and the sooner they started the better. The board was uncertain. Some executives laughed at the idea as a personal whim. The financial community was surprised and carefully pessimistic about the probabilities of successfully steering a more than $300 million company onto a new course.

The strategy worked. Grace became a primary factor in chemicals. But the chemical industry also changed. Major competitors dominated vital markets. Foreign competition became a major threat. Profit margins leveled and then slipped as the industry matured. Grace again planned carefully, seeking opportunities afield from chemicals. The next move was into consumer products. Here competition was already intense, and establishing a beachhead was a grim battle. Grace chose the acquisition route, and in one year bought some 50 companies. Absorbing and integrating these was a crucial struggle. Some turned out to be bad choices. In keeping with a basic Grace philosophy that everything had to be the best—people, quality, products, service, and profitability—the losers were dropped as soon as their deficiencies became clear.

Grace also expanded into services as a complement to consumer products and natural resources. It is now a major international firm with balanced worldwide interests in specialty chemicals, natural resources, and consumer businesses. In retaining its leadership, it has demonstrated that the purpose of even a large enterprise can be changed but that it requires patience, courage, and strong management.

Armco Inc.: A Concept of People. Some of today's most successful enterprises did not begin with an image based on a type of industry or a new and powerful system but rather on a special concept of people.

George M. Verity, for example, the founder of Armco Inc. (formerly Armco Steel Corporation), had an idea that enabled him to compete successfully with the giant steelmakers of his day. He had no experience in steelmaking. He was not an engineer. He didn't even know what kind of machinery was required to fabricate the steel he intended to make. The product he visualized was people. He was a pioneer in recognizing that all people in business, not just a few at the top, have certain inalienable and equal rights.

At a time when workers in steel mills labored 11 to 13 hours a day, 6 days a week in unremitting heat and grime, Verity introduced a set of policies that committed the company to a new set of values. Armco policies promised all employees a square deal; they would be treated right for right's sake. The company pledged itself to pay its people well and to provide every possible and practical sound incentive. At a time when employee training and management development were virtually unknown in industry, Armco undertook to provide training opportunities so people could advance to the limit of their abilities.

Long before environmental matters became a matter of public concern, Armco declared its intention to maintain clean and safe living and working conditions and to encourage and support community efforts to all citizens. Armco took active measures to build effective teamwork before "team building" became a favorite subject on management podia, and it made "personnel policies" a meaningful term when employees were more often thought of as tools of production rather than as unique and significant human beings.

A. W. Robertson, board chairman of Westinghouse Electric Corp. said of George Verity, "His ideas lived after him and became alive through the men he had trained." These men included C. William Verity, grandson of the founder, who strengthened even further Armco's concept that its purpose was to serve the needs of people. Today, new managers, imbued with the same mental image to serve, lead Armco in its successful growth.

Part II of the Purpose Commitment: Why Does the Enterprise Exist?

Important steps for any enterprise are to define what kind of undertaking it is and to determine what it intends to become. An equally important step is to decide why it exists in the first place. Most companies that have formal plans set this forth in their mission statement or statement of purpose. However, it is helpful to go beyond such typical expressions as "We exist to serve our customers" or "Our primary purpose is profit" and to establish a clear logic as to the reason why the enterprise should survive and prosper. People believe and support the purpose commitment much more readily if they understand the logic behind it than if they are simply asked to accept it as a declaration from top management.

What logic undergirds purpose? We tend to think of business enterprises as economic agencies and to declare that they exist primarily to turn out goods and services for sale to customers at a profit. This is certainly part of the story. However, to get at the true purpose of a business, just as have Armco Inc., IBM, and many other businesses, we must look not at balance sheets and profit and loss statements but rather at the people who make up the business. Human enterprises must have human purposes if they are to continue and succeed.

Behavioral-science research establishes that the mainspring which drives us is needs satisfaction. We have adapted to changing environments over millions of years because we have been able to satisfy such basic needs as those for food, shelter, sex, and safety. Our genes drive us to secure this satisfaction. We develop needs also in relation to other poeple: we want to be considered important, we seek power, we enjoy companionship. These cultural needs are varied, but they also are powerful motivators.

The Duality of Purpose. Enterprises are organized because people have discovered that they can satisfy many of their needs better by working together in groups than they can by working alone. But when we work with others, we can satisfy our own needs only to the extent we help others to satisfy *their* needs. Primitive people who refused to share the venison they killed had as much chance of survival as the marketer who refuses to pass on lower costs to customers or to share increased profits with employees and shareholders.

Because all humans exist to satisfy needs, enterprises made up of people exist to satisfy needs. The special point here is that enterprises are organized because groups of people can satisfy their needs better by working together in groups than they can by working alone.

Internal and External Needs. We often overlook the fact that the first purpose of any group is to satisfy the *internal* needs of its own members. But a complex relationship prevails. No group is self-sufficient; its members must look to other groups for many of the things they want. Group members are able to satisfy their *internal* needs largely by becoming adept at satisfying *external* needs: the needs of external groups. This relationship is reciprocal. We accomplish our personal objectives by helping to satisfy the needs of others.

Enterprises are legion that rise and fall with the genius of one or a very few people at the top. We can learn far more from those enterprises that survive. If we study E. I. DuPont, General Electric, Sears Roebuck, we find in each case a clear identification of the internal and external needs that must be satisfied and an unyielding commitment to that end.

George Verity clearly identified the mutuality of business purpose: "Armco," he declared, "could secure results in largest measure by understanding and satisfying the needs of the working organization, its customers, its stockholders, and the citizens of the communities in which its plants would be located."

J. C. Penney: Serving the Customer. Another example is the J. C. Penney Company, one of the oldest and most successful enterprises in what is probably the most highly competitive industry in the United States, retail merchandising. James Cash Penney, the founder and entrepreneurial genius who built the company, started his career by developing a chain of "Golden Rule Stores." Son of a Baptist minister, he believed that he could succeed best by making both employees and customers partners in his undertaking. "There could be no lasting prosperity for us unless the people of our communities were better off and happier for our being among them" he said. Managers were sold stock in the stores. In this way they became part owners and worked hard to make the company succeed.

In 1913, Penney expressed the purpose of his fledgling company in "The Penney Idea." Its primary tenets were:

1. To serve the public as nearly as we can to its complete satisfaction

2. To expect for the service we render a fair remuneration, and not all the profit the traffic will bear

3. To do all in our power to pack the customer's dollar full of value, quality, and satisfaction

4. To continue to train ourselves and our associates so that the service we give will be more and more intelligently performed

5. To improve constantly the human factor in our business

6. To reward the men and women in our organization through participation in what the business produces

7. To test our every policy, method, and art in this wise: "Does it square with what is right and just"

The Place of Profit. Profit is not a purpose. It is a means of providing the resources necessary to achieve the purpose of an enterprise. The Hewlett-Packard Company explains this well. It states seven basic objectives, which together provide the reason for its existence and the basis for its success. The first of these is profit, as stated below:

1. PROFIT

OBJECTIVE: To achieve sufficient profit to finance our company growth and to provide the resources we need to achieve our other corporate objectives.

In our economic system, the profit we generate from our operations is the ultimate source of the funds we need to prosper and grow. It is the one absolutely essential measure of our corporate performance over the long term. Only if we continue to meet our profit objective can we achieve our other corporate objectives.

Our long-standing policy has been to reinvest most of our profits and to depend on this reinvestment, plus funds from employee stock purchases and other cash flow items, to finance our growth. This can be achieved if our return on net worth is roughly equal to our sales growth rate. We must strive to reach this goal every year without limiting our efforts to attain our other objectives.

Profits vary from year to year, reflecting changing economic conditions and varying demands for our products. Our needs for capital also vary, and we depend on short-term bank loans to meet those needs when profits or other cash sources are inadequate. However, loans are costly and must be repaid; thus, our objective is to rely on reinvested profits as our main source of capital.

Meeting our profit objective requires that we design and develop each and every product so that it is considered a good value by our customers, yet is priced to include an adequate profit. Maintaining this competitiveness in the market place also requires that we perform our manufacturing, marketing, and administrative functions as economically as possible.

Profit is not something that can be put off until tomorrow; it must be achieved today. It means that myriad jobs must be done correctly and efficiently. The day-to-day performance of each individual adds to— or subtracts from—our profit. Profit is the responsibility of all.

While profit is important, we must look to people to achieve our real purpose, that of satisfying internal and external customers. If the enterprise is not committed to discovering the needs of employees as well as customers, if it is not able to satisfy one as well as the other, it will not survive.

This is vastly more complicated than simply making a profit. Many enterprises overlook this mutuality of purpose. While single-minded concentration upon profit may lead to short-term success, it cannot be sustained unless the mechanism that creates profit is kept alive and healthy. This mechanism is the development of highly motivated employees who are committed to discovering and satisfying the needs of their customers, for each has customers.

Does this really work in practice, or is it an impractical idea? As we have seen, George Verity first hammered out this philosophy based on his own experience and his deep faith in people. After 80 years, C. William Verity confirmed that Armco has been profitable in its tough, competitive business directly in proportion to its ability to satisfy the needs of its customers, employees and stockholders and of the society in which it operates. As he summarized it, "Our real business is people."

How to State the Enterprise Purpose Commitment

We know that the purpose commitment will answer two questions: "What kind of enterprise is this?" and "Why does it exist?" The statement is intended to create understanding on the part of people at all levels of the enterprise and on the part of such external audiences as customers, stockholders, government agencies, and the public at large. Therefore, the purpose commitment should be stated clearly and simply and in terms everybody will understand.

Here is a typical statement:

> The Xxex Corporation commits itself to use its resources to build a growing, diversified, and professionally managed electric products company that will earn enough money to cover its costs, including equitable wages, salaries, and benefits that will help ensure the security and well-being of all personnel.
>
> It will use funds available for profit to pay for ownership shares for employees under the employee stock-ownership plan, to invest in growth and improvement of the company and its operations, to provide a reserve for emergencies, and to pay a fair return to stockholders for the money they invest in the corporation.

This statement makes clear what kind of company this is: it commits itself to manage professionally, that is, in a logical, orderly, and predictable fashion. It will diversify in electric products, which is a field that it knows and one that has satisfactory growth potential and the potential to fully utilize the company's technological resources.

Part of the money that would otherwise be declared as profit is used to pay for company stock, which is given to employees so they will have an ownership interest in the firm they are helping to build. Profit has an important place in the company's growth and future, and the statement attempts to bring this out.

Company Statements of Purpose

Each enterprise expresses its purpose in a different way, but the central tendency is to express what it is and why it exists. For example, The Prudential Insurance Company of America sees its purpose as helping to "provide security against an ever-increasing range of risks and hazards that threaten the financial welfare of individuals, families, groups and businesses at every economic level that can be served by the private sector."

To show the wide range of expression of similar purposes, here is the purpose commitment of Northwestern Mutual Life Insurance Company: "To provide the best value in individual life insurance and disability income contracts—highest quality products at lowest net cost."

Sea-Land Industries, Inc., states a brief, succinct purpose, "To continue to build a profitable, competitively strong, financially sound containerized sea and land transportation system."

DEVELOPING THE PURPOSE COMMITMENT FOR COMPONENTS

Usually we state the purpose of the enterprise and assume that all of our people will easily relate their component—division, department, or unit—to this. But often the corporate purpose seems vague and remote and has little or no impact on the people it is intended to influence.

Each component has its own unique role within the overall enterprise. This role may be established by happenstance and may not provide the clear, logical portrayal it should. For example, the sales department that considers its purpose that of selling goods and services has already declared its own eventual ineffectiveness. The personnel department that sees its purpose as merely that of hiring and developing people will never contribute its true potential.

Why Does My Job Exist?

Each part of the enterprise contributes to the overall purpose; however, the results the various units achieve are only part of the overall accomplishment and not all of it. For good understanding, desired results should be spelled out separately.

In defining your purpose commitment, you are answering the question, "Why does my job exist?" Usually a unit exists to contribute to the purpose of the larger component of which it is part and, in turn, to that of the overall enterprise.

You will want to consider several factors. First is the need to separate yourself as a person from your job as a position. Similarly, the purpose of your position should be determined without tailoring it to you as a person. If it is properly framed, you or a succession of people with different personalities should be able to fill the position, each following his or her own leadership style.

When the Position Doesn't Fit. It is important to keep the difference between the employee and the position clearly in mind; otherwise you will soon find that the commitments of the position are being changed to fit the special characteristics of the individual who happens to fill it. Some current theories prognosticate that this is desirable, but practical experience shows that two things happen. First, the person holding the position shapes it to fit his or her strengths and weaknesses. This may be acceptable until the incumbent is promoted or leaves; the next person then has to reorganize to bring things back to normal. A second concern when positions are customized too much is that overlap and duplication inevitably creep in and become a source of friction and inefficiency. For example, the public safety department in one large city maintained a fleet of medical emergency vans because the head of the department had early training in hospital administration and was vitally interested in rescue and life saving services. At the same time, the large municipal hospital from which the public safety head had been promoted continued to maintain an equally large fleet of inhalation and rescue vans. The duplication was eliminated only when several citizens complained because the competing vans took to racing one another with sirens screaming to reach the scene of an accident.

Is Your Job to Manage or to Operate?

When defining your purpose, you will also want to determine whether the position is primarily a management or a technical position. If your purpose is managerial, you contribute to the profitability and success of the organization by planning, leading, organizing, and controlling the efforts of other people. If your position is technical, you do not supervise others and you contribute to success or profitability by specializing in some kind of technical work, such as selling, designing products, or operating a machine.

It may be that your commitment is not just to manage, but, as in the case of Xxex Corporation, to manage in a logical, orderly, and systematic manner, in other words, to function as a professional manager. If this is so, you may want to specify your commitment, just as engineers may specify themselves as "professional engineers" or as physicians may be "thoracic surgeons" or "internists."

How to State the Component Purpose Commitment

The statement you develop to apply to the team of people you manage should make it clear that the component for which you are accountable, whether it be a division, department, or unit, exists to help the enterprise as a whole to achieve its purpose. Your purpose commitment should also specify what you contribute to. Here you will want to refer to the larger component of which your own is part. It is not particularly helpful to say that you contribute to the key objective. However, if your component contributes directly to growth and profitability, this is a useful identification.

Suppose you manage the television division of the Xxex Corporation. You might state your purpose commitment as follows:

> The television division of the Xxex Corporation commits itself to build a professionally managed television and radio business that will earn

enough money to cover its costs, including equitable wages and salaries and insurance, pensions, and other benefits that will help ensure the security and well-being of all its personnel. It will make adequate contribution to the profit of Xxex so that funds will be available to pay for ownership shares of division employees under the employee stock-ownership plan, to invest in growth and improvement of the division and the company, to provide a reserve that will be available to the division in emergencies, and to pay a fair return to stockholders for the money they invest in the corporation and the division.

Whatever your position, you will want to define your purpose as part of the commitment cascade. Assume you now have a clear idea of your purpose and the kind of enterprise or component you will build to accomplish it. Next you look to the products and/or services you will provide to accomplish that purpose. In the next chapter, we will examine the product/service commitment in some detail.

KEY POINTS

1. *Concentrating on the Critical Few.* A position charter helps you to establish priorities, to identify problem areas, and to shift your time commitment from the minor many to the critical few. Since the objectives and standards within position charters are vertically integrated, these guidelines are consistent throughout the enterprise. Your position charter responds to a set of questions which managers must answer if they expect to act with confidence and success in the future. From these we derive the commitment analysis, key objective, key standards, key strategies, work analysis, critical objectives, and critical standards.
2. *Parts of the Position Charter.* The position charter contains two planning segments—key objectives and critical objectives—and two accompanying control segments—key standards and critical standards. The objectives are developed through commitment analysis and work analysis.
3. *Cascading Your Position Charter.* Your charter should provide a concise, clear statement of what you must do to carry out your share of the overall objective. Cascading integrates and coordinates position charters from top to bottom and from bottom to top. Key objectives are cascaded, with each commitment narrowing in scope to fit successively lower positions. Both management and technical critical objectives are cascaded. Cascading encourages vertical traceability and horizontal compatibility.
4. *Commitment Analysis.* Four basic commitments common to all enterprises are purpose, product/service, customer/client, and scope. All managers develop their own key commitments which derive from those of the enterprise as a whole.
5. *The Purpose Commitment.* The two major parts of the purpose commitment are a clear determination of what kind of enterprise or component this has been in the past and an equally clear commitment as to what it intends to

become in the future. Needs satisfaction is the mainspring of purpose. *Internal* and *external* need satisfactions are reciprocal. Profit is not a purpose but rather a means of providing resources necessary to achieve the purpose of an enterprise.

6. *Stating the Purpose Commitment.* The purpose commitment should be stated clearly and simply. Each part of the enterprise should have a clear understanding of how it contributes to the overall purpose.

7. *Stating the Component Purpose Commitment.* The statement of purpose for your component should indicate that it exists to help the enterprise as a whole; the statement should elucidate exactly what your contribution is and to what larger component it contributes.

QUOTES FROM CHAPTER 9

Significant quotations from this chapter that you will want to consider and discuss in greater detail:

- Personnel managers who see themselves as hiring and firing and trying to beat the union instead of building human resources will be less effective than they might be.

- Like the people who make them up, companies tend to become what their past has made of them.

- Japanese companies place great stress upon stating clearly the overall purposes of the enterprise and communicating them to every employee so the message permeates the entire organization.

- Human enterprises must have human purposes if they are to continue and succeed.

- Profit is a means of providing the resources necessary to achieve the purpose of an enterprise.

THE KEY OBJECTIVE:
WHAT PRODUCTS?

Do not depend on one thing or trust to only one resource.
BALTASAR GRACIAN

THE CHAPTER IN BRIEF While it is true that customers make products, it is equally true that products make customers. And knowing what products to plan to satisfy the wants and needs of its customers is one of the primary concerns of every enterprise and of each of its managers. In this chapter, we will examine the product/service commitment, which becomes part of the key objective. As we will see, the thought and planning that lie behind the words of this commitment can have a significant impact on the success of managers at all levels. It will be clear that internal services and products provided for internal clients and customers can be as important as those provided for external ones. We will begin with the overall product/service commitment for the enterprise as a whole.

THE PRODUCT/SERVICE COMMITMENT

The Universal Electrical Services Company we met in Chapter 9 found that its commitment to remain an electrical-engineering service company still left many loopholes. Assignments were booked that ranged into the domain of construction and maintenance and that severely curtailed the availability of professional personnel. To define the objective even more clearly, the chief executive and his key officers developed their product/service commitment, which now expanded the key objective to read "The key objective of the Universal Electrical Services Company is to build a growing, profitable electrical-engineering service company *that will provide professional design, analysis, engineering, and management services. New services will be compatible with existing resources, skills, and customer requirements.*"

The addition accomplished several things. It alerted everybody to the concentration on professional services and promised a cold reception to renewed attempts to diversify. As the new planning cycle began, strategies were developed for divestment of the incompatible acquisitions and strengthening of the core services. Personnel and training staff built into their plans provision for selection and development of

149

professional skills. The marketing group realigned its marketing plan to stress the sales theme, to develop advertising and promotional materials, and to train marketing representatives to support the theme.

The product/service commitment is an effective means of concentrating resources on the areas with greatest potential. When cascaded from top to bottom, it helps ensure that the same parameters are observed throughout the organization. The product/service commitment is shown in its place in the key objective in Figure 8-1.

Importance of the Product/Service Commitment

As we develop our key objective, accurate and realistic determination of the product/service commitment is vital, for it will have a large bearing on our survival and success. In every field of endeavor, a relatively small number of enterprises will be the most successful. As the principle of the critical few establishes, some 20% or so of competing enterprises will command about 80% of the revenue and profits, while the remaining 80% will squabble over the 20% of revenue and profits. While the proportions tend to remain constant, the identity of the critical few enterprises changes. If we examine any 25-year period, however, we will find a number of companies that continue to stand out above the pack. Because they have found a successful combination, most of the durable ones have also become large. Companies, such as Bank of America, Armco Inc., J. C. Penney Company, Rockwell International, Union Carbide, Shell Oil, General Electric, are successful by plan, not by accident.

Setting the Stage. As we study companies that have been successful for many generations, several facts stand out. Their planning concentrates on building leadership in some critical aspect of the products and services they offer. Many are specialists, but each has developed unusual competence in certain significant aspects of its operations. Each offers something unique to its customers. This is what the customer buys and what the company is known for. Planning of the product commitment is a critical matter for every company and for every component of the company.

If we plan to manufacture mopeds, for example, we must, as a preliminary, assess the resources available to conduct the required research and engineering, to construct new or to modify existing plants, and to provide manufacturing facilities and warehousing. Money must be found for the capital improvements required to cover the cost of receivables and inventory until adequate income is generated.

When we plan our product/service commitment, we are at the same time setting the stage for our planning for research and new product development, acquisition and divestment. Clearly stated, the commitment provides guidelines for all who are concerned with preparing plans for creating or developing products or services. These may include research personnel, who develop plans to create new products and uses; design engineers, who need to know what uses and applications to consider in their planning; marketers, who are constantly engaged in designing plans that will mesh company capabilities and customer needs; finance specialists, who seek out sources of funds; and personnel managers, who must plan ahead to find or develop the specialized skills required.

Clarifying Roles. As you develop and cascade your product/service commitment, you will find that it is particularly valuable for clarifying the roles of different groups with whom you work. In fact, your attempts to define your commitment will almost certainly flush out troublesome gaps and misunderstandings. Typical of the questions you will generate is whether the research department should plan to use its resources to create new and different products, to improve existing products, or to modify products to satisfy customer requirements. Is the quality control department to control quality and the production control department to control production? Does the credit manager manage credit? As you work out relationships such as these, you will find that you are also eliminating a great deal of confusion and friction.

The Initial Product/Service Commitment

There is an evolutionary development both in an enterprise's ability to create and produce products and services and in the demand of customers for them. By the time top management becomes concerned about formalized planning, the initial product line is usually already established.

Products Precede Markets. Most enterprises do not plan their initial selection of products. They are pushed into it by force of circumstances, rather than by rational choice. The bright idea that vitalizes most entrepreneurs is a product or service, not a new or better way to discover and satisfy customer needs. Whether it is Henry Ford with his automobile, Chester F. Carlson with xerography, or Helena Rubenstein with her facial creams, in its entrepreneurial or natural-leadership stage, the enterprise tends to generate a product or service, then to look for ways to attract and satisfy customers.

If the idea is novel or a distinct improvement, the product or service creates its own following and sales fall into the role of keeping up with the demand rather than creating it. For example, Syntex Corporation was started by a small group of biomedical research scientists who were working on steroids—the artificial manufacture of synthetic human hormones. This led to breakthroughs from which the birth control pill evolved. For the first 15 years the company grew around its patent for steroid production. When the patent expired, Syntex planned a diversification that led it into a number of related fields which capitalized on its abilities in research.

Product obsolescence usually accompanies the demise of the founding natural leader, because there is a failure to plan product succession as well as management succession. One of the first tasks of successor management is to develop plans for revitalizing the product line. If formalized planning is introduced during the early, natural-leadership stage of growth, the product/service commitment simply confirms the existing product line; what is needed is careful determination of the improved or new products that will be necessary to satisfy the changing market.

Functional departments show this influence as well as the enterprise as a whole. A major textile company, for example, first established a personnel department in an attempt to resolve a long and bitter series of labor disputes with its unions. It selected a lawyer who specialized in labor law to head the new department. Twelve years later, the personnel department had become the human resources department, but the manager still spent most of his time in labor negotiations and in dealings with the union.

Markets Create Products. In developing your product/service commitment, you will want to study your existing products and to determine what share of success is the result of the product creating a market and what share is the result of aggressive marketing creating customer demand, which the product is tailored to fit. The perennial question must always be answered: does marketing create our products or do our products create markets? For many companies, the better part of wisdom is to plan to search carefully for new customers who will buy existing products with minor changes in format or packaging rather than investing in major modifications or completely new products. Like farmers, good planners figure out how to get the best out of the acreage they are cultivating before going on to turn over new soil.

This is also true for components. Many a marketing department has invested large sums in its advertising product/service commitment, overlooking the much smaller investment that would yield even greater returns if used to train and motivate the existing sales force to greater effectiveness.

The Established Product/Service Commitment

Soon enough the momentum of the inital product success begins to fade. At this time, development of a key objective with a logical product commitment may become an urgent priority. Choice of products or services is a concern of marketing as well as of the production, operations, or manufacturing department, and in fact, market factors will become the final determinants in most cases. Here are some of the factors that must be considered in planning the product commitment.

Competitiveness. Since the measure of success always depends upon competition, a primary factor is the vulnerability of the product to competition. The edge should always go to the products that can be patented or copyrighted or that have secret or proprietary features that are not easily matched. A brand new product that offers features not duplicated elsewhere has real advantages, but the appeal of the innovation must be matched against the cost of creating and sustaining enough demand to make it successful. Specialized production capabilities, an unusually alert and aggressive sales force, and professional management are factors that multiply basic product advantages.

Other competitive aspects of the product are also vital. A favorable price or a quality higher than that of competition are telling advantages. A quality product may carry a high price, or an unusually low price may compensate if quality, style, or other expense-adding requirements are not great. For example, Nikon cameras sell at a relatively high price to a quality-conscious group of customers who buy a status symbol as well as a camera; however, the simple utilitarian Kodak appeals to a far larger group of buyers.

The words that appear in your product/service commitment may appear simple, but if you have thought through your choices, they can have great significance. Palm Beach, Inc., for example, started its career with a single product—men's white summer suits. It has carefully planned its product commitment so that it has been able to diversify into both men's and women's clothing. From a high concentration of spring-season sales, it has been able to equalize sales volume throughout the year, with the attendant advantages in staffing, inventory, and financing.

Synergism. Two plus two can equal five if a new product has features that complement other products presently available. Advertising synergism is highly desirable. If the new product can be handled effectively by the existing and external advertising and promotion force, it will get off to a quicker and better start than if a new set of personnel must be broken in.

Products may enhance the value of the existing line if they fill gaps or add a new dimension which is sought by clients. For example, the early food-mill has given rise to a host of attachments that chop, blend, liquefy, and homogenize. Plain nylon stockings for women have been supplemented by adding patterns and tints so they can be bought to match wardrobes and accessories. Levi Strauss & Co. early concentrated so completely on men's blue denim work pants that "Levi's" became a synonymn for the habitual attire of cowboys and foresters. Today the company has expanded to clothe the lower extremities of men, women, and children with a variety of style and materials, and it has done this from the top to the bottom of society and in every country of the world.

Distribution channels should also be synergistic. If you plan so that the new product can be loaded onto the existing distribution setup at little additional cost, it will do better than if a new distribution system must be developed. Digital Equipment Corp., for example, has become a leader in minicomputers by developing the broadest product line in the industry. However, instead of using commissioned salespeople, it sells through a salaried sales force—thus avoiding the dangers of having salespeople push the high volume items at the expense of slower-moving products with greater long-term potential. This also encourages salespeople to service the customer's needs instead of chasing commissions.

Productive synergism is a distinct asset. If present facilities and equipment will be adequate or if only limited additions are necessary, the chances for success are greatest. This is particularly true if the new product can be produced on idle equipment or in empty facilities.

Human synergism is a key factor. While new or additional first-line operators skilled in the technical work will probably be required, it is advantageous if the new product can use existing staff and support facilities. This not only provides a broader base for allocating overhead expenses, it also avoids the cost of adding and training new staff personnel.

Synergistic integration can be especially helpful to a small company which is faced with the problem of growth at minimum cost. A small Massachusetts manufacturer of snow plows wanted to grow but lacked the capital. The firm found another company making power lawn mowers with a mulcher built into the design. After negotiation, the two companies merged, with no cash changing hands. By slightly modifying its consolidated equipment and facilities, the resulting corporation was able to produce the original lines of snow plow and blower plus the lawn mower, useful both summer and winter. This consisted of the basic power unit plus attachments which converted it, as desired, to lawn mower and mulcher or snow plow and blower.

How to State the Enterprise Product/Service Commitment

Through the statement of the product/service commitment, the chief executive officer has opportunity to express the collective judgment of the top management team and the board of directors as to what the enterprise will commit itself to provide for external customers. As we have seen, this is a key statement, for it provides limits for the expenditure of funds, for research and product development, for marketing, and for many other aspects of the business. Since it more specifically defines the type of business, it should be derived from and be consistent with the purpose commitment.

How can the most meaningful statement be made? It should not be too broad and general, or it will not provide guidelines for the key decisions that should stem from it. If it is too definitive, it will discourage the broad and innovative thinking that is vital to continued growth and success. Examples of useful statements follow.

Insurance Company of North America. "The Corporation brings together, in logical assortment, divisions of companies offering a broad range of financial services, real estate and property protection products. These services, with heavy accent on insurance and special products, are designed to enhance, conserve and protect the assets of individuals and business concerns."

INA brings out clearly the underlying logic of its business and the types of services it will provide within this framework. The company uses this statement as a general guide for managers in considering expansions of its services, the development of new businesses, and the acquisition of companies.

The General Electric Company. During its early history, General Electric's products were concentrated in three industrial fields—power, lighting, and electric railways. However, electricity was a significant new force. New applications multiplied, and General Electric's product lines with it. Today the company's product/service commitment centers on a core of consistently profitable product lines, including lighting, major appliances and components, aircraft engines, turbines, and contractor equipment. It sees its greatest future growth in products such as medical systems, transportation systems, energy systems, human-made materials, natural resources, and consumer information services.

Product/Service Commitment for the Xxex Corporation. The hypothetical Xxex Corporation continues its development of its key objective by adding the following product/service commitment: "The Xxex Corporation commits itself to use its resources to build a growing, diversified, and professionally managed electrical products company that will earn enough money to cover its costs, including equitable wages and salaries and benefits that will help ensure the security and well-being of all personnel.

"It will use funds available from profit to pay for ownership shares for employees under the employee stock-ownership plan, to invest in growth and improvement, to provide a reserve for emergencies, and to pay a fair return to stockholders for the money they invest in the corporation.

"This will be accomplished by providing products, systems, and supplies which use electricity as the primary actuating force."

DEVELOPING THE COMPONENT PRODUCT/SERVICE COMMITMENT

As we have seen, the corporate product/service commitment provides the logical framework within which all other product/service commitments will fit. Carefully developed, the corporate commitment ensures consistency, integration, and balance with the commitments of the organization components which are derived from it. Each component of the company exists to provide something of value to internal or external customers. The cascading commitment chain integrates the total effort so that resources can be focused on this end result and, at the same time, can provide for the needs of each component in the chain.

Line and Staff Differences

There are significant differences in the commitments made by components that are organized to satisfy the needs of either internal or external customers, for these usually call for differing line and staff roles.

The Line Role. Components in the line relationship to the overall objective are accountable for delivering the product or service to the customer; there is a direct line of accountability from the customer all the way back to the chief executive officer. The contribution of each line component is traceable directly from the client. This chain of commitments has significance in planning the product/service commitment, for it provides a logical succession from the customer to the chief executive officer. We show this in Figure 10-1.

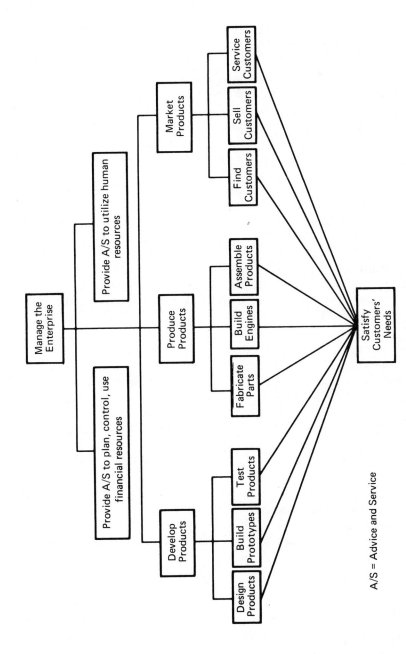

A/S = Advice and Service

FIGURE 10-1   The Chain of Commitments Begins with the Customer

157

Here the product/service commitment of each organization component is derived from its role in the chain. It becomes clear that the commitments of engineering (to develop products), manufacturing (to produce products), and sales (to market products) are all to satisfy customer needs. While this may be evident to most marketing departments, it may be a new orientation for many planners in other line departments, such as operations and sales.

The logic for the staff component product/service commitment chain is usually derived from its specialized role, which will be to provide advice and service in such technical work as accounts receivable and accounts payable and to provide advice and service in such management work as planning, organizing, leading, and controlling. We see this relationship in the role of finance and personnel in Figure 10-1.

Testing the Product/Service Commitment

The commitment chain should be traceable directly. The best way to do this is by input/output analysis. Simply stated, this requires that the input to one component becomes the output to the next. If there are gaps or overlaps, the need for corrective action is indicated.

An Aluminum Example. In Alcan Aluminum Company, we find the chain shown in Figure 10-2.

Other aluminum companies buy ingot and concentrate on manufacturing. Some fabricate their own ingot from purchased bauxite or alumina. The commitment chain is usually based on careful assessment of each step in terms of the factors discussed in the foregoing.

The Chain-Store Pattern. A typical commitment chain in chain-store merchandising follows the pattern shown in Figure 10-3.

Sears Roebuck gained a competitive edge and assumed leadership by adding three steps, as shown in Figure 10-4.

Maintaining testing laboratories adds to the expense, but it also enhances customer satisfaction and reduces returns. Product/service com-

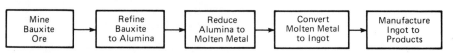

FIGURE 10-2   Alcan Aluminum Company Commitment Cascade

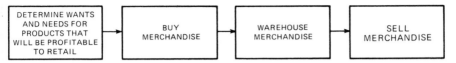

| DETERMINE WANTS AND NEEDS FOR PRODUCTS THAT WILL BE PROFITABLE TO RETAIL | → | BUY MERCHANDISE | → | WAREHOUSE MERCHANDISE | → | SELL MERCHANDISE |

FIGURE 10-3   A Chain-Store Commitment Cascade

mitment is common to other types of business, but Sears has made it into a powerful message that addresses itself directly to customer needs as: "We service what we sell."

The product/service commitment is a useful planning tool. If we are planning the product line for external customers, it forces us to examine our previous experience, to study competitors, and to make a rational choice that will best contribute to achieving our purpose. If we are planning for staff activities, our service commitment requires us to think through the logic of what we provide and to ensure that it fully satisfies the needs of internal customers.

In the next chapter, we will look at the product/service commitment's companion commitment, which will help us to plan so that we satisfy the final arbiters of our success—our clients and customers. We will also examine the scope commitment, which determines *where* we will operate.

KEY POINTS

1. *Developing the Enterprise Product/Service Commitment.* After deciding the purpose commitment of our key objective, we look logically to planning the products and services we will provide to customers to accomplish that purpose. The product/service commitment is an obligation to provide designated categories of products or services to external or internal customers.

2. *Importance of the Product/Service Commitment.* The most successful companies achieve and maintain unusual competence in certain significant aspects of their operations. When we plan the product/service commitment, we provide this emphasis. The product/service commitment sets the stage for research, new product development, acquisition, and divestment. It also clarifies the roles of various groups within the enterprise, eliminating friction and confusion.

3. *The Initial Product/Service Commitment.* For most enterprises, the initial product or service just happens. Often the demise of the founding natural leader also marks the obsolescence of the initial product line. At this point, a formalized planning system enables successor management to reassess and revitalize the products or services offered through careful planning of the product/service commitment.

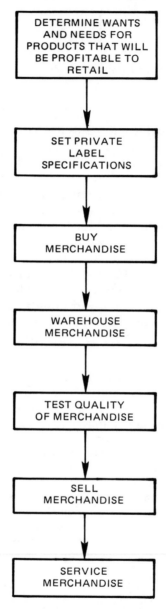

FIGURE 10-4 Sears, Roebuck, and Company Commitment Cascade

4. *The Established Product/Service Commitment.* Competitiveness is a major consideration in developing your product/service commitment. If you plan for patented or copyrighted materials (or features that cannot be duplicated), specialized production capabilities, an aggressive sales force, and professional management, you stand to gain a decided edge. A difficult choice in planning is to figure out either how to surpass competition in terms of quality or how to maintain lower prices. In developing their product/service commitments, staff services must similarly strive to make their services worth more than they cost.

5. *Stating the Product/Service Commitment.* The enterprise product/service commitment states what the company will commit itself to provide for external customers. It limits the expenditure of funds and more specifically defines the type of business. It is logically derived from the purpose commitment.

6. *Developing the Component Product/Service Commitment.* Cascading the product/service commitment ensures integrated effort. Line and staff play different roles in the commitment. Contributions from line components are directly traceable to the external customer or client. Staff components serve internal clients by supplying specialized advice and service to the organization as a whole.

7. *Testing the Product/Service Commitment.* An input/output analysis is the best way to trace the chain of product/service commitments—one component's output is input to the next. Component commitments should be reviewed regularly to avoid duplication and inefficiency.

QUOTES FROM CHAPTER 10

Significant quotations from this chapter that you will want to consider and discuss in greater detail:

- Internal services and products provided for internal clients and customers can be as important as those provided for external ones.

- There is an evolutionary development both in an enterprise's ability to create and produce products and services and in the demand of customers for them.

- Many a marketing department would secure greater returns if it invested in training and motivating the existing sales force rather than in advertising.

11

THE KEY OBJECTIVE: CHOOSING CUSTOMERS

As long as I have a want, I have a reason for living.
GEORGE BERNARD SHAW

THE CHAPTER IN BRIEF   Customers with wants and needs are the reason for the existence of most enterprises. However, no product, of itself, however good, can find its own clientele. A product must be identified, popularized, and invested with value and appeal. It must be serviced so it continues to satisfy the need for which it was created. In this chapter we will examine the notions that the success of every manager, as well as every enterprise, depends upon satisfying the needs of clients or customers and that we can consciously plan to do this. A first step is to develop the customer/client commitment of our key objective.

DEVELOPING THE CUSTOMER/CLIENT COMMITMENT

In the Universal Electric Services Company case which we left in our last chapter, we find that selling was done primarily by engineering specialists who were called "service consultants." A substantial part of their compensation was commissions; accordingly, they tended to develop prospect lists and to search out assignments wherever the opportunity arose. This led to several problems.

An increasing number of proposals were being developed for governmental agencies. While the projects were large and the potential commissions substantial, the regulatory morass and endless delays piled up huge costs which often could not be recaptured. A great deal of effort was also being devoted to securing management consulting assignments that dealt with problems with which the Universal Electric Services Company professionals were only marginally familiar.

In developing the key objective, the chief executive and his officers decided to clarify the situation and to focus all available resources on the most profitable market segments. They accomplished this by adding the following customer/client commitment: "The key objective of the Universal Electric Services Company is to build a growing, profitable electrical-engineering service company that will provide professional design, analysis, engineering, and management services. New services will be compatible with existing resources, skills, and customer re-

163

quirements. *These services will be offered to satisfy the identified needs of utilities, equipment suppliers, constructors, architects, engineers, and consultants concerned with the planning, design, construction, or operation of electric power facilities. Services will be offered to government agencies only if they are essentially nonregulatory."*

A series of interrelated decisions must be made in developing the customer/client commitment. We cannot consider our customers and their needs without also looking at the products or services we can most effectively provide. And these choices, in turn, will be influenced by the strategies we adopt. The decisions cannot all be made at once. In practice, we undertake each commitment individually, but we also review and revise our conclusions in light of the new insights we develop.

THE MARKETING-MANAGEMENT CONCEPT

Companies often are intimately familiar with the characteristics and features of their own products but have little real knowledge of how customers can best use them. When they recognize this, the results can be significant. The Carborundum Company, for instance, once saw itself primarily as a specialist in abrasives; it manufactured and sold several thousand different types. In recent years, however, it has studied its customers and realized that their real need was to remove stock or to provide a specific finish—and abrasives were just one way to do this. Recognition of this basic fact led Carborundum to change its organization, its planning, and the very nature of the company to become a supplier of stock-removal and finishing systems rather than merely of abrasives. This was an application of the marketing concept.

Definition of the Marketing-Management Concept

The following definition helps to consolidate the best current thinking: The "marketing-management concept" is the fundamental idea that the best way for an enterprise to accomplish overall objectives is by committing the enterprise and each of its components to manage their activities so as to satisfy the identified needs of internal and external customers or clients.

Planning the companywide effort so that each component satisfies the needs of its customers or clients leads to a reorientation of effort. Since few enterprises have the resources to satisfy all customers, once more this calls into use the principle of the critical few. Here managers select the critical few customer groups—say 20%—they can best serve in order to accomplish their key objective and to meet their key standards. As we have seen, from the critical few customers will flow 80% or more of sales and profits. This is a process of conscious selection: it may involve finding the best customers for an existing product, developing new products, or modifying existing ones to meet the needs of specific customers.

The marketing-management concept often fails because managers, from the top down, think in functional or product terms rather than in terms of customer needs. The objectives and other plans they develop inevitably reflect this orientation and preclude fully effective operation.

At the top management level, this is especially true if executives have come up through finance, engineering, manufacturing, research, or some other technical function. Emphasis then may be on developing new and better products, on increasing manufacturing efficiency, on improving the balance sheet, or on some other facet, without relating this to satisfying customer needs.

EVERYBODY HAS CUSTOMERS

The work of marketing is not unique to business. Every organized enterprise has customers. That is why it exists. And the enterprise continues to survive and succeed only to the extent it satisfies its customers. A church has customers. Its parishioners have needs, which must be identified. They must be persuaded of the rightness of the creed or dogma. They must be sold on the idea that the benefits of belonging are worth the costs in time, energy, and money they invest.

Every school and university and every club and institution has its customers. And these enterprises continue and prosper only so long as they identify their customers, determine their needs and wants, persuade the customers that their needs are being satisfied, and deliver the goods. Sometimes there are several customer groups. A school must satisfy students, parents, and the governmental entity that provides funds. A national government must satisfy both the constituency that empowers it and the newspapers, radio, television, and other media that mold the opinions of the voters.

One of the greatest benefits of developing the customer/client commitment for every position in the organization is that it brings home the fact that each job exists primarily to help satisfy the needs of people. In other words, everybody has customers. The more clearly people understand the needs of their customers, the more effectively they will work to satisfy them and the greater the rewards both to the organization and the people themselves will be.

The following, from a state manager of Ansett Airlines of Australia, traces the customer commitment explicitly: "The position of the Queensland Manager exists to contribute to the growth and profitability of Ansett Pioneer and to the achievement of the Ansett Transport Industries' Key Objective by marketing intercapital express services, extended tours, day and half-day local tours, and charter services directly to the travelling, holidaying or touring public and indirectly through travel agents."

INTERNAL CUSTOMERS

It is equally significant that every internal component has its customers. In a manufacturing company, the research function must satisfy the needs of the engineering and manufacturing departments as well as the needs of external customers. In a bank, the investment department must concern itself with the requirements of lending. A hospital nursing staff has as its customers the surgeons and anesthetists as well as the patients. The human resources department must service the needs of all other groups, so its customers include all personnel.

Satisfying the needs of internal customers is a vital aspect of planning, for the plans we develop are the means of ensuring that this satisfaction takes place. People will understand our plans and will be motivated to make them succeed to the extent our plans take their needs into consideration and provide for the action that will result in satisfaction.

Satisfying Internal Customers

While positions in a continuing line relationship generally have their commitments to external customers, those in a staff relationship commit themselves to serve internal customers. We often fail to recognize that one of the strengths of the marketing concept is that it applies to internal customers as well as to external ones.

Every component of the organization must have users of what it produces—in other words, customers—or it will have no reason for survival. For example, the engineering department does not exist to satisfy its own needs and wants; rather, it designs and develops products to meet the needs of the manufacturing and marketing departments who, in turn, are interpreting customers' needs. While we may have little or no choice in deciding what groups we will work with in a staff relationship, we do have many options in determining how best to work with them.

The personnel department exists to help select, train, develop, and compensate people for all other positions and components. The controller must satisfy the organization's requirements for accounting, financial planning, and asset-conservation services. The measure of success for both the personnel head and the controller is not only the technical excellence of the work they do, but also how well they satisfy the needs of their customers.

Understanding of the marketing concept can be revealing. For example, an accounts-receivable supervisor in a textile company had worked in her position for 12 years in the belief that her job was "to keep accurate and timely record of the money owing from customers." She participated in developing her customer/client commitment, which read "to keep record of the money owing from customers so as to satisfy the identified needs of the credit and budget departments and the division manager."

Her immediate question was "What are the needs of the credit and budget departments and the division manager?" After a series of discussions with people from the two departments and an interview with the division manager, she and her collaborators recommended to the controller that the timing of several reports should be changed and that one series of reports should be dropped because it was of no value to the credit or budget departments or the division manager.

Customers Can Be Created, As Well As Discovered

When we seek to determine who are our customers, we can start either with the product or the customer, and we do not want to overlook the potential of either. This applies to internal as well as external customers. We usually interpret the marketing concept as requiring that we go to those who are currently buying our product or could be persuaded to buy it and then that we modify the product to fit their needs. If we are concerned with new product development, we may use customer panels, surveys, or interviews to determine what customers will buy and then develop a product to satisfy that need.

However, the customer commitment can be satisfied by finding the right customer for existing products as well as by developing new products for existing customers. We find it as effective to find customers whose needs are satisfied by what the product offers as it is to revamp our products to fit customer needs.

For example, McDonald's hamburgers is one of the success stories in modern merchandising. One of the strengths of McDonald's is that the product and the way it is delivered vary little for different types of customers. Instead of developing new types of foods or diversifying widely, McDonald's Corp. has become highly successful by finding customers whose needs are satisfied by its fast service, prices, and standardization of a limited menu. That segment of the population which counts these high finds its needs satisfied at McDonald's. Others will go elsewhere.

The product makes the customer as much as the customer determines what the product is to be. This is particularly true of innovations. While a predetermined pattern of desirable characteristics may serve as a guide to research and development efforts, new discoveries and significant innovations often occur as a seeming by-product of the creative process. The problem then becomes one of finding the customer segment to which the new product can be sold.

While the relationship of marketing to the customer is vital, we may overlook the importance of internal groups satisfying the identified needs of their customers.

Staff Department Clients

The advice and service offered to other components by staff departments tend to be tailored to the interests and abilities of the staff managers rather than to the identified needs of the internal customers. Advertising departments, for example, frequently are prone to strive for technical excellence and dramatic impact, rather than sales revenue. Data processing and management information specialists frequently pride themselves on the sophistication and complexity of the analytical tools they provide, rather than on the ability of the internal clients to use them. Most line managers have only a smattering of accounting expertise, yet accountants ordinarily feed them data reports designed by and for accountants.

We can see how the product/service and customer/client commitments of a staff human resources department is cascaded in Figure 11-1.

The customer/client commitment of the key objective identifies the customer groups and market segments that offer greatest returns for the resources expended. Internally, the commitment specifies the clients

POSITION	PRODUCT/SERVICE COMMITMENT	CUSTOMER/CLIENT COMMITMENT
Manager, Human Resources	Provide advice and service in selecting, developing, compensating employees	To satisfy the identified needs of all corporate personnel and Division Managers
Manager, Selection and Placement	Provide advice and service in hiring and orienting employees	To satisfy the identified needs of all corporate personnel and Division Managers
Supervisor, Executive Selection	Provide advice and service in locating, testing, interviewing managers	To satisfy the identified needs of the President and Division Managers

FIGURE 11-1   Cascade of Staff Product/Service; Customer/Client Commitments

who must be served. Next. we will look at the related commitment: that which determines *where* we will operate. This is the scope commitment.

DEVELOPING THE SCOPE COMMITMENT

As is true of other aspects of conducting a business, we have the choice of reacting spontaneously to customer demand wherever it arises and diffusing our capabilities over a large area or of rationally selecting those areas that promise greatest returns. Enterprises that apply the principle of the critical few to concentrate their greatest resources upon the most promising areas come out ahead in the long run. The scope commitment is a conscious choice of the preferred area of operations.

We define the "scope commitment"as *an undertaking to remain within given organizational, geographic, or other limits in working toward objectives.*

Factors in Determining the Scope Commitment

The Universal Electric Services Company, whose key objective and commitments we discussed earlier, found its professional services so much in demand it was sending teams all over the world. Some of these were unprofitable and did not perform well because the members were limited to English, the cost of bringing the necessary skills together was too high, or the political climate was unfavorable. The chief executive decided that it was the better part of wisdom to determine where the company could best operate rather than to let circumstances dictate. The scope commitment shown below set up the guidelines.

"The key objective of the Universal Electric Services Company is to build a growing, profitable, electrical-engineering service company that will provide professional design, analysis, engineering, and management services. New services will be compatible with existing resources, skills, and customer requirements. These services will be offered to satisfy the identified needs of utilities, engineers, and consultants concerned with the planning, design, construction, or operation of electric power facilities. Services will be offered to government agencies only if they are essentially nonregulatory. Operations will be limited to clients who can conduct business in English, primarily in the United States and Canada, Australia and South Africa."

Geographic Scope

Geography is usually an early concern in determining the scope commitment. At some point, growing companies find it desirable to disperse their operations beyond the original geographical limits. A single-state operation looks to a national scope; the national enterprise surveys the prospects in other countries.

Many factors influence selection of the areas that have greatest potential for expansion. The availability of lower cost, more available, or better quality raw materials or components often is decisive. Countries like the United States and Japan and most European nations buy over half of their natural resources and semimanufactured goods from other nations. Reasons for the decision of U.S. steel manufacturers to buy chromite in South Africa or of Japanese aluminum fabricators to go to Australia for bauxite, the aluminum ore, are readily obvious. However, we often overlook other opportunities. Investment in operations in other countries can be more profitable than in the home country. Costs are often lower, quality may be higher, technology may be more available.

Expanding Mental Scope

Mental exports can be even more valuable than physical, but the determination to search for new ideas and the willingness to adopt them call for as much of a commitment as the acceptance of new technical inventions or better operating methods does. H. J. Heinz Company, for example, has strong autonomous affiliates in many countries. One of the chief articles of trade among these national enterprises is ideas. In the United States, Heinz learned how to cut waste in growing tomatoes by 20% and in the process was able to get twice the bushels per acre at double the gross value. The new methods were quickly exported to other Heinz operations.

The Brain Pickers

Another approach to enlarging the scope of mental trade is the use of facilities in other countries either by contract or purchase. American and Japanese companies such as DuPont, IBM, Union Carbide, Toshiba, and Mitsubishi find much to be gained by picking the brains of productive research centers in Europe, the United States, and elsewhere. Differing backgrounds and orientations encourage different approaches and enhance the probability of new research discoveries. They also encourage creative solutions to operating problems.

Smith Kline and French Laboratories, a leading U.S.-based drug company, operates a large research laboratory near London. This provides a cross-fertilization of research philosophies and approaches that complements the work done in each country. For instance, SK&F Laboratories in the United Kingdom are concerned with altering well-defined pharmacological mechanisms in the belief that these effects will translate into therapeutically useful drugs in humans, while the U.S. research program emphasizes the biochemical and pharmacological aspects of human disease models in experimental animals.

Scope of Internal Staff

The scope of components in a staff relationship should also be defined carefully. The advice and service provided by one organization component to others can be made generally available on demand, or it can be limited to preselected internal clients. For example, in one international oil company, members of the corporate staff organization development group were in demand from refineries, depots, and sales offices in the United States, Europe, Africa, and the Far East to conduct team-building programs. In an attempt to respond, the human resources director, to whom the organization development manager reported, spread the skilled specialists available so thinly that they did an incomplete and unsatisfactory job at every location. The effort faded away because, as one refinery reported, "It died of malnutrition. We just didn't get enough help to find out what it really could do."

STATING THE SCOPE COMMITMENT

The scope commitment relates to both the product/service and customer/client commitments. For line components, it delineates both the location of the physical facilities where the product or service will be developed and produced and the geography within which customers will be served.

Setting Guidelines and Limits

The scope commitment can be of value in clarifying territorial limits. If no clear separation is made, operations in plants or offices tend to spread where opportunity affords—always operating on the general rule that a vacuum, such as an empty office or an unused portion of a building, gets filled first. Since those with squatters' rights are hard to dislodge, the better way is to delineate clearly the scope for each position and group.

The scope commitment can be very useful in setting guidelines. Anchor-Hocking Corporation, for example, has committed itself to maintain production facilities and to market products through its own organization in the United States and Canada and to sell throughout the world through its international division, using brokers and independent agents.

The scope commitment can also provide criteria for operating in some countries and staying out of others. A midwestern chemical corporation, for example, commits itself to market its products and technology in all countries of the world in which it has a reasonable opportunity both to earn and remit profits. However, it will maintain facilities and investments only in those countries that offer reasonable security of investment. It further commits that this is to be done only to the extent consistent with existing governmental policy.

Stating the Staff Scope Commitment

For components in a staff relationship, the scope commitment sets limits, both physical and organizational. The maintenance department, for example, may provide emergency repair service only in the north

POSITION	SCOPE COMMITMENT
Division Manager, Electronics Division	Market in North and South America, the Pacific except Japan. Manufacture in the U.S., Singapore.
Manufacturing Manager, TV Operations	Conduct operations in the Illinois, South Carolina, and Singapore plants
Plant Manager, Container Plant	Conduct operations in the South Carolina plant
Production Manager, TV Cabinet Department	Conduct operations in Buildings #1 and #3, with common use of receiving area
General Foreman, TV Cabinet Department	Conduct operations in north end of Building #3, as assigned
Supervisor, Assembly Department	Conduct operations in the south bay of Building #1, with exclusive use of Storage Area G

FIGURE 11-2   Cascade of Line Scope Commitments

plant. The employment office may provide services only for corporate personnel at headquarters, exclusive of the operating divisions.

The Chain of Scope Commitments

A typical cascade for the line scope commitments is shown in Figure 11-2. Here the chain of accountability runs from the chief executive officer to the division manager and down through the manufacturing function. Other functions, of course, would show similar cascades.

The delineation of a "territory" for each manager clearly establishes this part of his or her accountability and avoids the overlap and duplication that often result when the demarcation is not clear.

The cascade of staff scope commitments is shown in Figure 11-3.

With the key objective completed, in the next chapter we look to the development of key standards. These will provide us with criteria which we can use to measure how well we are achieving the key objective.

KEY POINTS

1. *Developing the Customer/Client Commitment.* No product finds its own clientele: profitable products are planned. The enterprise must commit itself to studying potential customers and planning to satisfy them. The customer/client commitment is an obligation to satisfy the identified needs of internal and external customers.

POSITION	SCOPE COMMITMENT
Manager, Human Resources	Provide service in North America, with advice to components in South America and Singapore
Manager, Selection and Placement	Provide staff services in the United States, arrange for retention of Positions International for management positions in Mexico, Brazil, Singapore, and Toronto
Supervisor, Executive Selection	Provide staff services through Salary Grade 9 in the United States and Canada, use Positions International for all positions above Salary Grade 9

FIGURE 11-3   **Cascade of Staff Scope Commitments**

2. *The Marketing-Management Concept.* This is a formalized approach which requires that, in its planning, the enterprise commit itself and its components to satisfying the identified needs of internal and external customers.

3. *Everybody Has Customers.* Churches, schools, clubs, institutions all have customers. One great benefit of the customer/client commitment is that it reminds all managers that the more they understand customer needs, the greater will be their effectiveness in achieving objectives.

4. *Internal Customers.* It is equally significant that every *internal* component has clients. Satisfying the needs of these internal customers is an important part of planning. Staff commits itself to serve internal customers. If staff departments focus their efforts on their own interests and abilities rather than on those of internal clients, they will lose effectiveness.

5. *Developing the Scope Commitment.* As with other aspects of planning, with the scope commitment it pays to rationally select the critical few areas on which to concentrate our resources. Externally, there are a critical few geographic areas; and internally, there are a critical few components and a critical few parts of each person's job.

6. *Expanding Scope.* Mental exports—the sharing of ideas and technology—is one way of expanding scope. Another means is to plan the use of facilities of other countries through contract or purchase. Exchanges between research centers are common.

7. *Stating the Scope Commitment.* The scope commitment relates to both the product/service and customer/client commitment. For line functions, it clarifies territorial limits, preventing confusion and friction; sets guidelines; and provides criteria for geographical dispersion. For components in a staff relationship, the scope commitment sets physical and organizational limits.

QUOTES FROM CHAPTER 11

Significant quotations from this chapter that you will want to consider and discuss in greater detail:

- The Carborundum Company once was a specialist in abrasives: it has now made itself a supplier of stock removal and finishing systems.

- Every organized enterprise has customers.

- One of the strengths of the marketing concept is that it applies to internal customers as well as to external ones.

- Mental exports can be even more valuable than physical ones.

- If staff departments focus their efforts on their own interests and abilities rather than on those of internal clients, they will lose effectiveness.

12

KEY STANDARDS: MEASURES OF PERFORMANCE

Everyone complains of his memory but no one complains of his judgment.
FRANCOIS DE LA ROCHEFOUCAULD

THE CHAPTER IN BRIEF We know that judgment is even more fallible than memory, and we devise standards to make judgment as correct as it should be. Standards are part of the controlling function. Key standards, which provide overall, continuing criteria by which to measure progress and results, are best addressed to the critical few areas that control the largest measure of results. Key standards are cascaded to provide an integrated set of controls for the entire organization.

CONTROLS MAKE PLANS HAPPEN

The real professionals in management are not those who develop plans but those who make plans happen. While it is important to know *what* to do, this knowledge comes to nothing unless it can be realized. Controls ensure that plans succeed; and if our plans do not get us what we want, controls ensure that we revise the plans or change our actions until we are successful. Sound controls are based on sound plans; at the same time, the best plans may fail if they are not supported by equally good controls.

The place of controls in the planning and controlling process is shown in Figure 7-2. Although sequentially we place controls after planning, we do not complete our plans and then concern ourselves with control; rather, as is true of other parts of management, we do the work of controlling at that point where it is most appropriate. Often this is in concert with planning activities.

DEFINITION AND CHARACTERISTICS OF KEY STANDARDS

Key standards are the keystone in the control process. We define "key standards" as *the overall, continuing criteria used to measure and evaluate progress and results in achieving the key objective.* Key standards are control segments as shown in Figure 7-2. Since they are derived from key objectives, they are most conveniently discussed with the plans they accompany.

177

Key standards are used to summarize the total effectiveness of all the work done. Since the key objective is *ongoing* in nature, we continually move it ahead; therefore, the key standards are measures of progress as much as of results.

If properly developed, key standards are impersonal and unbiased. They represent our best consensus of what represents the level of performance we want. Once set, they can be used to indicate shortcomings, diagnose problems, and reveal opportunities. The great value of a key standard is that it stands as a recognizably fair and objective measure that can be interpreted in a similar fashion by any knowledgeable person.

Key Standards Encourage Creativity

We may think of key standards as impediments to free and imaginative action, as a means of forcing people to conform to the criteria set by the organization. In fact, however, sound standards facilitate innovative thinking and give a wider range of freedom than is possible without them. Standards mark limits and boundaries within which an individual can be given wide authority. Outside these limits other people are also pursuing their objectives, within limiting standards. If all plow their own fields. they can be creative and express their own individuality as much as they like. It is only when people begin to encroach on the territory of others that friction and confusion arise. Key standards are positive guides to accomplishment. They help to raise the level of performance by encouraging people to work harder and better so that they can reach levels they have set for themselves.

Key Standards Are a Basis for Performance Appraisal

Many approaches have been developed for determining how well or poorly people are performing their jobs. Enterprises use methods ranging from personal opinion to elaborate schemes for quantifying each nuance of activity. Many of these methods fail because they are too elaborate. Some are so unrealistic or inflexible that they get short shrift from the people who are expected to use them.

You can measure performance accurately only if you have an answer to the question: What is good and what is poor performance? How to determine this accurately, so those being measured will agree to it, has always been the problem. I have found that part of the answer is to separate out key standards and use them as continuing criteria against which to measure overall performance. Used in this way, key standards can serve as the basis for a hierarchy of standards that will help measure vital aspects of performance.

Key Standards Are Measurable

Because they apply overall and on a continuing basis, there often is a tendency to skip over key standards and concentrate on the more definitive specific standards that measure short-term progress and results. But there is little point in measuring the success of individual projects if the overall department or division is sliding unnoticed to disaster. Measurability is a primary feature of useful key standards; a standard that does not measure is about as useful as a compass without markings. You can expect to invest time and work in quantifying key standards. However, this is the only way you can get an accurate fix on where you are and where you are going. You will find the effort worthwhile, for sound key standards will remain in effect for months and sometimes years.

Do the Measures Measure? The perennial question in measurability is the basis selected for comparison. Will we compare this year's costs with last year's? Our own quality level with that of competitors? Our productivity with the national average?

Problems arise in selecting almost any criterion because it is rare that any two things are precisely comparable. One hundred thousand dollars this year is not the same as last year because of a spell of prolonged cold and the general onslaught of influenza, because machinery was under repair, or because of a dozen other reasons. Unless these mitigating circumstances are given appropriate weight, the comparison will suffer.

Budgets give rise to particular difficulty when used as standards because they are stated in precise terms and appear to be unequivocal measures when actual expenditures are compared with those planned. Most knowledgeable managers are expert in stating budgets so that they will have enough elasticity to cover changing circumstances. As one division manager put it: "The law of the budget is that you ask for more money than you need and forecast less than you expect to take in."

Key Standards Concentrate on the Critical Few

Your key standards measure your overall, continuing results, which is to say they continually measure progress toward an end point rather than the end point itself. Since many affairs of considerable importance are underway even in small enterprises, an early question is "How many key standards do we need?" Managers often find themselves confronted with lengthy computer printouts detailing results for a host of standards. Usually these are derived from the accounting system and are detailed and precise as well as comprehensive. However, the ease with which these documents can be compiled is often their undoing, for the net result usually is a proliferation of standards, most of which receive a cursory glance but little real understanding and even less corrective action. Standards and controls that do *not* prompt corrective action are useless exercises.

The president of a multibillion dollar department-store chain is a case in point. He had begun his career as a controller in a large metropolitan store. With a prodigious memory and a high number aptitude, he absorbed detailed financial reports with ease. After the chain grew to nationwide scope, he continued to take home a stack of reports, which he read with the avidity of a detective-story fan. Each morning he placed in his "out" basket a sheaf of blue slips bearing his personal logo. Each slip carried instructions on what he wanted done about items he had noted. Some of these commands reached into the lowest reaches of the organization.

During this period, five of the chain's newest and largest flagship stores ran into trouble. They had been built in outlying suburban locations to capitalize on expected growth patterns, but energy shortages and rising prices changed the demographic pattern. The president was so involved in noting inventory shortages and merchandise returns that he failed to give appropriate attention to these ominous new trends. Three of the five stores were in danger before an alert board member forced the retention of an outside consultant, who identified the problem and helped institute corrective measures. The president was encouraged to take early retirement.

MEASURING TOTAL PERFORMANCE

Key standards provide a summary statement of overall performance. They serve as an index to accomplishment for each level of the organization. Supported by critical and specific standards, they help you to analyze and evaluate performance, whether it be company or unit, function or division.

Identifying the Critical Few

We know that a small number of standards, if properly identified, can enable us to measure the largest part of our results. How to identify the few standards on which to concentrate our control efforts is the question.

When achievement comes easily there is little concern with these critical few; however, adversity tends to force attention on the really important things that make the difference between success and failure. For example, the British Steel Corporation, plagued by a succession of bad years, identified the critical factors in its success as profits, return on capital, productivity, labor-relations harmony, exports, management strength, and industrial stability.

Faced with a changing market, tightening competition, and falling demand, Philip Caldwell, chairman of the Ford Motor Company, summarized basic factors of success that apply to many other enterprises. As he put it, "Suitable products for the market at the right time, low production costs, good quality and good backup service. When any one element gets out of phase, it causes a telescoping effect all through the organization. When they all work right, it goes like a charm."

The terminology used and the methods followed to identify the critical few areas in which outstanding performance is required vary widely; however, as is true in most other aspects of management, we can distill from the hodgepodge of current practice a clear rationale.

Our concern is to identify those areas of the business that have a critical influence on our overall success. If we do a good job in those areas, we will have a high probability of meeting our key objective; if we fail in any of them for a significant period, our success will be jeopardized. As is true in many other aspects of professional management, we can look to General Electric for a pioneering example.

General Electric's Key Result Areas. Some 25 years ago, Ralph J. Cordiner, president of General Electric, saw the need for accurately measuring increasingly complex technological operations. In General Electric, this need was heightened by the company's move toward decentralization of authority to over 100 divisionalized management teams.

General Electric was probably the first to attempt to set formalized standards for the work of managing as such. In developing its overall standards, the company identified eight key result areas which were used to measure the performance of General Electric as a whole. The criterion that General Electric used for the selection was:

"Will continued failure in this area prevent attainment of managerial responsibility for advancing General Electric as a leader in a strong, competitive economy, even though results in all other Key Result Areas are good?" The key result areas selected were:

1. Profitability
2. Market position

3. Productivity, or the effective utilization of human capital, and material resources
4. Product leadership
5. Personnel development
6. Employee attitudes
7. Public responsibility
8. Balance between short-range and long-range goals

Can You Use the Key Result Areas? Operating under the assumption that business enterprises are much the same, a great many companies have adopted the General Electric key result areas intact and continue to use them even though General Electric feels other measurement approaches are more useful.

The chief obstacle that arises in the attempt to use universal measures is that the work done and the results achieved in enterprises differ enough that the same criteria do not apply. For example, a bank or life insurance company might cite investment safety and return as measures, while a textile company whose profit depends as much on the price it pays for fibers as on the selling price might specify purchasing effectiveness.

After their initial experience in using a standard list of key result areas, many companies have found that, while every component from top to bottom is expected to achieve its own overall results, these will vary from one function to another and at different levels. It quickly becomes clear that key measures that are sound for the president might not apply to the treasurer or a research department. As specific examples, marketing position does not apply to the accounting department but accuracy of reporting does. The first-line supervisor is concerned with personnel development but has little or nothing to say about product leadership.

There are many similarities among companies, of course, but rather than blindly adopting factors developed by another enterprise, you will probably do better if you identify those that apply specifically to your own business.

If we began the development of our key objective with a sound logic, we can expect it to apply also to identifying the critical few areas vital to overall success. This is the case. We established that every enterprise exists to satisfy internal and external needs and that these can be expressed in the form of the basic commitments. We suggested a basic four—the purpose, product/service, customer/client, and scope commitments—to be augmented by others that apply in specific cases. Logically, then, we can expect these to be the critical few areas in which outstanding performance is required.

The Hierarchy of Standards

Since planning, organization, and controls are logically related, we want the overall standards based on the key commitments to fall into the pattern we have already established. We can accomplish this by having the hierarchy of standards follow that for the planning structure. Each objective and the work category that leads to it thus become the indicators for standards which measure the progress of the work and the results attained. Taken together, the objectives in the hierarchy identify and provide controls for each position and for the enterprise as a whole. They measure each significant aspect of operations in relation to every other one.

Usually the standards for each position and level of the organization are established without developing their logical relationship. This forecloses the opportunity to integrate standards so that changes in one will lead to the necessary adjustment in others. Just as every person depends on others, so sound standards always must be supported. Solitary, unrelated standards have little value.

The hierarchy of standards is shown in Figure 12-1. As it logically should, this closely follows the hierarchy of plans, thus establishing the organic relationship between planning and controlling. Cascading both objectives and standards ensures that this relationship is maintained and that it extends to all the derivative plans and controls.

In this figure, the key, critical, and specific standards all derive from those of the chief executive officer. The standards for the line components, here shown as manufacturing and sales, cascade down the hierarchy from those of the chief executive officer. The staff department standards are for financial services and human resources services. The key standards for these staff components are stated in terms of the advice and service provided to satisfy the needs of the line components.

WHAT KEY STANDARDS SHOULD YOU USE?

While we can establish a clear rationale for key standards, the difficult question is how to develop them in practice. While each situation is different, there are enough similar considerations in dealing with each category of key standards to provide some useful guidelines.

Developing Purpose Key Standards

The overall factors that enable an enterprise to achieve its purpose will vary. As we have seen, a primary consideration in selecting those that

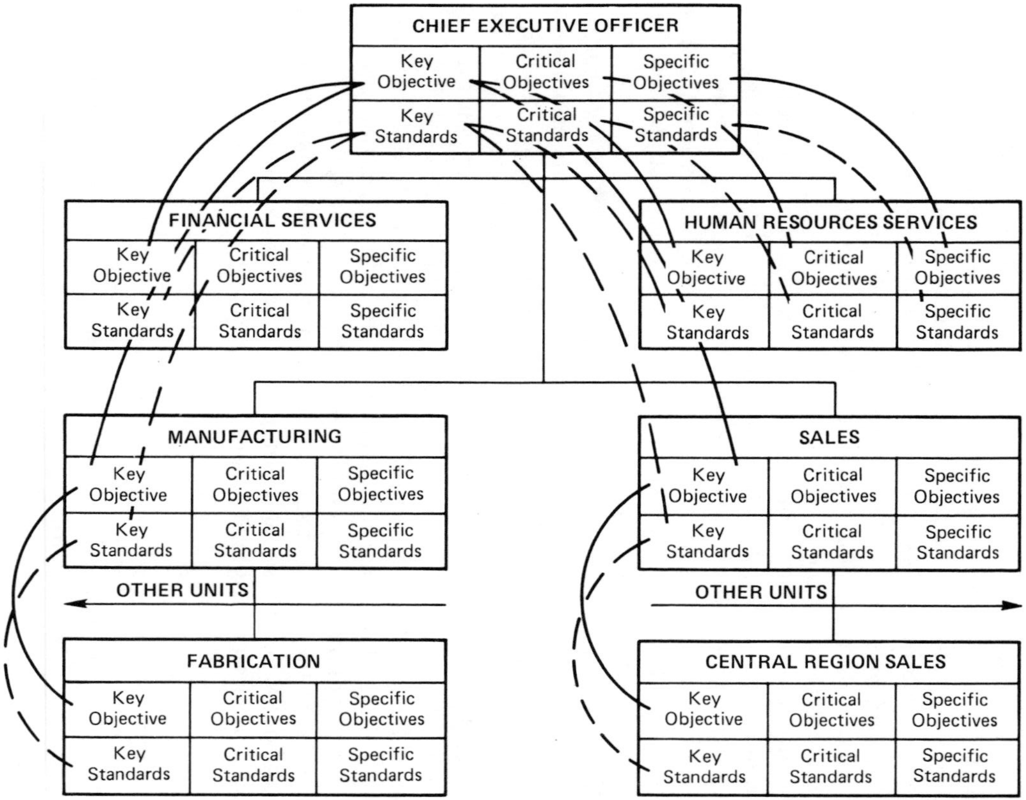

FIGURE 12-1 The Hierarchy of Standards

will be used to measure the performance of the enterprise as a whole is that they should be translatable so that they can be used in a derivative form to apply to each component that contributes to overall success.

Profit, Revenue, and Sales as Key Standards. For business enterprises, as we have seen, a common purpose is to provide products or services that have a value greater than the cost of producing them. The value to customers is represented by the price they are willing to pay. When we translate this into financial terms, we can show it as the relative degree of profitability.

We can hold an organization accountable for profit only if it has command over the elements that go to make up profit. In most cases this means both the revenue that is received from the customer and the costs involved. The company as a whole falls into this category, as do divisional components. Functional groupings, both staff and line, generally have control of costs and, in the case of sales or marketing, the growth in revenue or sales volume. Thus the level of profit, the level of revenue, and the level of costs are vital and interrelated factors. These we can cascade from top to bottom, and they are measurable.

Profitability, which is highly measurable for most businesses, is most meaningful if it is further broken down into standards such as return on investment, return on assets, or return on equity. Since profit depends directly upon cost, many companies state profit standards so that they reflect the cost of providing superior quality or service. Consistency of profit can be as vital as the amount. Standards can help to stabilize the profit flow by encouraging profit planning over a sufficient number of years to even out the ups and downs.

Return on Investment as a Key Standard. Many executives believe that the most informative criterion is the ability to secure optimum returns from the money invested in the business and its components. Return on investment is readily calculated as a key standard by dividing the total amount invested into the amount realized from that investment or by dividing net income by net worth. ROI (return on investment) as a standard encourages managers to think in terms of the costs and growth potential as well as in terms of the maximum use of their present productive sales capabilities.

Since return on investment is a direct measure of what the owners of the business—the stockholders—receive for their money, it is most significant in a publicly held enterprise, for knowledgeable stockholders expect the management of the company to use their funds in a way that will enhance their investment.

Return on Assets as a Key Standard. This measure is developed by dividing assets into net income. Thus it shows how effectively the company is using its assets. Variations include using net assets and fixed assets as the denominator. Large investments in assets that have a prolonged payout period will tend to distort the return-on-assets figure, as will failure to make the investments necessary for growth. Because of this, both ROI and ROA (return on assets) are most useful when they measure trends over several years.

Level of Costs as Key Standards. Organization components that cannot be held accountable for profit or revenues can always be held for costs. These may be budgeted costs or standard costs.

Costs may be those established in the agreed-upon budget. Usually this includes direct costs, that is, money spent that is under the control of the accountable manager. Allocated or indirect costs represent the manager's share of general expenses, such as the cost of computer services, office facilities, and the finance and human resources departments.

Standard costs are usually developed for repetitive operations, such as manufacturing, order processing, or printing. Here the cost of each unit of output is calculated based on the normal or standard amount of direct labor and direct materials and, sometimes, of overhead or burden charges. The manager, usually at the first or second level of management, is held accountable for the actual compared to the standard costs.

Level of Revenue as a Key Standard. The two most common line technical components are sales and manufacturing or their equivalents. In attempting to cascade profit down the hierarchy to the manager accountable for selling the product or service, we find that sales has virtually no control over the cost of the product. However, sales can control selling costs as represented by the budget. While sales managers have a voice in pricing, they may not have control over it. As a key standard for sales, level of revenue represents the ability to use all the resources represented by the sales budget to secure the desired level of sales revenue.

USING RATIOS AS STANDARDS

Almost everything of consequence that occurs in a business results from and impacts upon a great many related other factors. This is especially true of profit, which is directly affected by everything from the productivity of people to the costs of inventory.

Ratios are used by many companies to show these relationships. Typical are those developed by determining what level of sales, operating expense, and profitability represents the desired level of performance and by comparing current performance to this.

One company calculates the average monthly sales, operating expense, and profit for 2 or more selected years and then uses the percentage ratios as the standards. Another company uses ratios as standards. Three examples follow:

1. Net profit after taxes on net worth is 14 to 16%.
2. Current assets to current liabilities are 2 to 1.
3. Average collection is 20 to 30 days.

Many texts are available which cover the use of ratios and ratio analysis. Properly used, selected ratios can provide much useful information about the inner workings of the enterprise and its components.

There is nothing new in the use of financial and other measures as indicators of overall performance. However, we are beginning to recognize that while the numbers in themselves are useful, they can be of greatest value when they are related directly to key objectives and when they are cascaded.

CASCADING KEY STANDARDS

Key standards apply throughout, so they can be translated into similar factors that apply at lower levels of the planning structure. Return on investment and return on assets for example, can be cascaded to divisions and even smaller profit centers to measure how effectively accountable managers are using the money invested in their operations.

The accounting system provides operating statements and balance sheets for each profit center. It will also break down operating-statement and balance-sheet items into their constituents. Inventory totals on the balance sheet, for example, will break down into subtotals for the costs of raw or component materials, work in process, and finished goods.

Cascading key ratios enables us to develop a direct relationship among the ratios for different levels of positions. This provides the basis for integrated controls. For example, we know that increasing sales will move finished goods faster and will reduce inventory. This information is most meaningful when we can track it from beginning to end and take purposeful action at the point where it will yield the results we want.

Development of meaningful ratios at each level of the cascade is not difficult. Since the data are already generated in the normal accounting process, effective standards can be maintained at small additional cost.

EXAMPLE OF KEY STANDARDS

To be useful, key standards must cover the vital factors critical to attainment of the key objective. They must be measurable, and they should be capable of being cascaded.

A Chemical Company Example

A typical set of key standards from a chemical company follows:

KEY STANDARDS   The key objective will be achieved successfully when the following standards are met:

1. Gross profit is 22% of sales.
2. Pretax profit is 7% of sales.
3. Return on investment is 16% per year.
4. Asset growth is 14% per year.
5. Net sales increase 6% per year, averaged over 3-year periods.
6. Capital turnover is 16% per year.
7. New ventures provide a 24% return on investment after 3 years.

A Hospital

Here, cost, not profit, is significant. Standards for patient care and other aspects of operation are formalized and made available through various hospital associations. Thus the following standards are supported by a comprehensive set of audit criteria.

KEY STANDARDS   The key objective will be met when:

1. *Growth.* Patient-care days increase at an annual rate of 4%.
2. *Costs.* Sufficient revenue is generated to meet all current obligations, including short- and long-term debt service.
3. *Professional Performance.* All departments meet or exceed approved operational standards as evidenced by an annual audit.

The overall objectives and standards we have developed mark the destination we will set out to reach and provide the direction signs that will ensure we get there. However, there may be different routes we can follow and different methods of travel. Before we get under way, we want to look at the different approaches that may be open to us and decide which is best to follow. This calls for a consideration of strategy, which we will discuss in the next chapter.

KEY POINTS

1. *The Place of Controls.* Controls ensure that plans succeed and that revision and correction take place if the desired results are not achieved. Controls do not come *after* planning, but in conjunction *with* planning.
2. *Key Standards.* These are central to the control process; we define them as the overall continuing criteria used to measure and evaluate progress and results in achieving the key objective. Properly developed, key standards are impersonal and unbiased so that they can be interpreted in a similar fashion by any knowledgeable person.
3. *Limits Encourage Creativity.* The boundaries set by key standards promote creativity in that they prevent people from encroaching on the territory of others; thus they reduce friction and confusion and encourage people to work harder and better to reach levels they have set for themselves.
4. *A Hierarchy of Measures.* Key standards serve as a basis for a hierarchy of standards that measures vital aspects of performance. Measurability is a primary factor of useful key standards.
5. *The Critical Few Standards.* Key standards concentrate on the critical few. This concentration on causative factors helps analyze and evaluate the total performance and prompts corrective action.
6. *Identifying the Critical Few.* Enterprises vary enough so that a standard set of key measures is inadequate. A logical beginning for all companies, however, is found in four basic commitments: purpose, product/service, customer/client, and scope.
7. *Integrating Standards.* The hierarchy of standards closely follows the hierarchies of objectives and work categories. This congruence gives standards a logical relationship, so that they are integrated into an effective supportive whole.
8. *Types of Key Standards.* A primary consideration in selecting key standards is that they can be cascaded. Profit, revenue, and sales are often used as key standards. Profitability is more meaningful if it is broken down into return on investment or assets employed. Return on investment can be effectively cascaded to lower levels; however, it is rendered less accurate by inflation and short-term variances of costs and availability of capital. Sales controls only its own costs, hence this component cannot be held accountable for profit; but sales revenue can be effectively used as a key standard. Components which can be held accountable for neither revenue nor profit can always be held accountable for costs.

QUOTES FROM CHAPTER 12

Significant quotations from this chapter that you will want to consider and discuss in greater detail:

- Sound controls are based on sound plans.

- Sound standards facilitate innovative thinking and give a wider range of freedom than is possible without them.

- A standard that does not measure is about as useful as a compass without markings.

- The law of the budget is that you ask for more money than you need and forecast less than you expect to take in, as one skeptic says.

- Standards and controls that do not prompt corrective action are useless exercises.

- Key standards serve as an index to accomplishment for each level of the organization.

- Many companies have adopted the General Electric key result areas even though General Electric feels other measurement approaches are more useful.

- We can hold an organization accountable for profit only if it has command over the elements that go to make up profit.

- Financial measures can be most useful when they are related directly to key objectives.

- Since the data are already generated in the normal accounting process, effective standards can be maintained at small additional cost.

- Controls ensure that plans succeed.

STRATEGY AND GROWTH

Where absolute superiority is not attainable you must produce a relative one at the decisive point by making skillful use of what you have.
KARL VON CLAUSEWITZ

THE CHAPTER IN BRIEF   The literature on strategy would stock a fair-sized library. Unfortunately, this intelligence is often confused and sometimes contradictory. Our concern is to fit strategy into the logic of managerial planning—to attempt to bring some order and consistency out of the welter of valuable information that is available. A necessary beginning is to differentiate strategy from objectives and other types of planning. A moot question is: Should strategy development be classified as a planning activity? Because it is helpful to encapsulate and generalize the experience of others, we state two concepts of strategy: the learning curve and product-life concepts. These directly influence the most important strategy for an organization—that which will guide its growth. We classify growth strategies into two *segments:* concentration and diversification, with their appropriate *elements.* Finally, the question of how to choose the best strategy arises. We suggest a logical approach which uses the objectives and standards already stated as the criteria of choice.

WHAT DOES STRATEGY MEAN?

One aid in determining what a word really means is to trace its origins. The idea of strategy has its roots in military usage. The term is derived from the greek *stratos* for "army" and *ago* for "lead." The military interpretation related to the leadership of armies, the direction of large military movements, especially by maneuvers or stratagems. In fact, the idea of using schemes or ruses to deceive an enemy is very much part of our general understanding of strategy.

A Logic for Strategy

To establish a logic for more precise definition of strategy, we begin with the basic idea that strategy has to do with determining the direction of things. Since going somewhere requires an objective, we can conclude that strategy is related to objectives but is different from them. An objective is a result you intend to accomplish. You perform work

191

and use resources to achieve an objective, but the objective is neither the work nor the resources. But knowing what result you want is not enough if you wish to predetermine your course of action. There are probably many different approaches you could follow. For example, if making a profit is your objective, you may have the options of raising prices; increasing volume; introducing new, high-margin products; or some combination of these. Whatever your choice, you want to state it explicitly so that it is understood and followed by all. You get this understanding and support by stating your strategy.

A Definition of Strategy

In terms of this logic, we can define "strategy" as *the general approach to be followed in achieving an objective.* By "general approach" we do not mean the action steps you take to achieve the objective. In other words, a strategy is not a program or a program step. For example, if your objective is to reduce costs, you begin with the assumption that most of the problem arises from only a few causative factors. You identify the cutting back of operations, the reduction of overhead, and the improvement of productivity as strategic options. Your strategy may be to follow one or all of these. Once the strategic decision is made, you can then develop the program, that is, the series of action steps you will take to achieve the objective and meet standards. The implementing program is also known by such names as the tactical program, strategic program, or operating plan.

Classification of Strategy

An immediate question arises as to whether strategy is an activity of the planning function. It would seem that we do not yet have enough data on and experience with the connotations of strategy to so classify it. It is clear that a strategy cannot exist by itself. It must always be related to an objective, for it is a way of attaining an objective. We can consider strategy as an adjunct to setting objectives or as one step to follow in developing objectives. In this sense, however, strategies are similar to programs, which also become meaningful only when related to objectives, or to schedules, which have a symbiotic tie with program steps.

Not all objectives require the support of strategies; in fact, the larger number of objectives do very well without strategies. Therefore, strategies may seem to lack the degree of differentiation and universality that characterize the other activities of work. For these reasons, it does not seem timely to classify strategy as the eighth planning activity.

We show strategy in Figure 7-2 to indicate this transitional status. However, since strategy is an important aspect of planning, it should receive appropriate consideration.

Strategy Can Be Accidental

Like other aspects of planning, strategies may not be thought through consciously but may arise from the situation and may be arrived at by trial and error. In a very real sense, strategy then becomes a matter of making explicit something we do intuitively.

Often when we set out to accomplish an objective, we take the first step that seems timely and opportune without attempting to think through a strategy. Just as often, we come to realize later that the first step inevitably leads to others. If the direction is right, our efforts are crowned in glory; however, if we're heading in the wrong direction, it requires time and effort to correct the heading or to go back and start all over.

As a case in point, before getting into the chewing gum business, William Wrigley, Jr. sold soap produced by his father's Philadelphia factory. Looking for a greater challenge, as a young man he moved to Chicago and established the Wm. Wrigley, Jr. Company to distribute his father's soap throughout the midwest. When competition in the soap business became fierce, young Wrigley took on baking powder as a second line, which soon became more profitable than soap.

To stimulate sales, he experimented with various premium items that could be sold along with a quantity of baking powder at a reasonable price. First there were silver-plated teaspoons, then a Wrigley cookbook, then umbrellas, and finally chewing gum.

Once again he recognized the potential of a new product, and decided to concentrate on chewing gum. He used baking powder for a while as part of a combination sale with gum but soon found that gum outsold baking powder. Thus after several tries, William Wrigley, Jr. hit upon the product that brought him fame and fortune.

Strategy and the Art of Warfare

Strategies still retain their military connotation, for they are developed primarily to outthink, outfox, and outmaneuver competition. Usually this means that your resources are less than those of your competitor but that you want to use them in such a manner as to take the advantage. There is not much point in a head-to-head confrontation, because the cost in resources is likely to be high even for the winner. Recognizing this, a basic rule in all strategy development is to seek out your competitor's weakness and bring your greatest strength to bear in that area. You do this in the expectation that the competition will either respond or will abandon its position to use its resources elsewhere—often against your own weakest point.

For example, K-Mart Corporation and Sears, Roebuck and Company compete strongly for the same customers. For years, Sears followed a strategy offering quality goods that it backed by customer service. K-Mart lacked a quality image and customers tended to go to Sears if they wanted high quality. Sears strengthened its reputation for low prices by adopting a strategy of offering low prices on a selected list of items that had high visibility, such as television sets and certain appliances. K-Mart countered strategically. It built its quality image by featuring nationally branded items that had achieved their own quality image, but at the same time, it kept prices down with simple, utilitarian surroundings and streamlined services. As a result of these strategies, customers began to see K-Mart as offering quality merchandise and Sears as offering low prices.

We have adopted many other military techniques in our effort to shape strategies to fit the needs of the marketplace. Our purpose here, however, is not to develop these techniques in detail but rather to find their rational place in the planning process. Here we find that strategies begin at top organization levels, but they are most useful if the guidance they provide is extended throughout the organization.

Strategy Is Necessary at All Levels

To be effective, any strategy must apply to all who work toward a common objective. Most strategies are developed at top levels where, too often, they become a corporate staff exercise, with little or no input from operating components. In a few of the cases I have encountered, the corporate strategies are kept secret—unknown even to the functional managers who are to carry them out. However, when many groups must work together, each with its own objectives and considerable authority to perform as it thinks best, the vertical integration and horizontal coordination of strategy becomes vital.

Each component of the organization will want to consider its own strategy as a means of helping to carry out the corporate strategy. Usually the marketing group carries the major responsibility for strategy, but production, research, engineering, finance, human resources, and other functions have a vital role in strategy development. In many enterprises, the contribution and value of such services as management information systems, organization development, accounting, and purchasing can be greatly enhanced if we think through the general approach, or strategy, we will follow in providing them.

For example, the organization development group of a large department-store chain had an objective of helping to improve management performance so that the survival and profitability of the stores would be enhanced. The organization development director was unable to get acceptance or support from the store managers, so she was encouraged to state her strategy. As she put it, she intended to improve management performance by "sharing new findings in behavioral science with store managers and personnel and helping them to adopt humanistic values and management styles." The strategy was discussed with the internal customers—the store managers. It quickly became obvious that they both resented and resisted the attempt to get them to adopt more humanistic values and management styles. A more productive direction was established when the strategy was changed to "Make every effort to understand the objectives and needs of store managers and personnel and help them to develop the knowledge, attitudes, and skills they feel are necessary to improve management performance."

Strategies Are Interdependent

Although strategy is set by top management, inevitably its success depends upon the ability and willingness of lower levels to carry it out. We expect every manager to have a key objective that contributes to the overall key objective; so with time and experience we can expect all managers to develop their own strategies for accomplishing their part of the total task.

Just as all the key commitments directly influence one another, each key strategy we adopt will open or close doors for other strategies. When General Mills decided to change its market strategy from milling and flour and to diversify into such things as toys, jewelry, and sporting goods, it also had to change its product and scope strategies.

Magic Chef was a leader in kitchen ranges, and its limited product commitment gave it the advantages of specialization. When it moved into dishwashers, it satisfied its product commitment by buying its products from a private label manufacturer, Design and Manufacturing Corporation. However, when Magic Chef decided to become a full-line manufacturer, adding refrigerators, freezers, and clothes washers and dryers, it also had to rethink its market and scope strategies to compete with industry leaders, Whirlpool and General Electric.

Because each strategy has both its own implications and an overall impact, the total strategy must be worked out with careful evaluation of each component. Since the whole is dependent upon its parts, individual managers need to think through their own strategies with clear understanding of the overall direction and to refit and reconcile as the total strategy unfolds.

WHAT KEY STRATEGIES DO WE NEED?

As in other aspects of planning, the principle of the critical few can be helpful in concentrating our efforts on the most productive strategies. We have already established the key factors in overall success: purpose, product/service, customer/client, and scope. Again, we recognize that people and money are vital parts of all of these.

The strategies we develop to facilitate our accomplishment of the key objective will be related to these and other commitments. Many marketing texts contain excellent and detailed analyses of market strategies, encompassing both the product and customer commitments. We will not cover this ground again; however, we will look at the application of the classification logic to growth strategies, as this area has been neglected.

THE STRATEGY OF GROWTH

As it grows, every enterprise has the choice of expanding fortuitously or of determining in a rational, orderly manner what it will make of itself. The Wrigley Company pattern is quite typical. The company grew fortuitously into chewing gum, but it adopted the strategy of concentration and soon became the world's leading purveyor of gum.

The early history of most outstanding companies follows a common pattern: they build their competence and reputation around their greatest strength so that they are difficult or impossible to dislodge in their chosen markets. So it is that "Kodak" and "Coke" have become popular synonyms for proprietary products.

However, this strategy also can carry the seeds of disaster. The Swiss watch industry led the world for a century or more. Swiss watchmakers honed one set of skills to the highest level. A Swiss watch was a quality watch. But this very success made change difficult, and Japanese competitors were able to capture the market with a new technology that made possible both low prices and accuracy. The Swiss strategy now is to stress high-priced, exclusive watches.

Growth Strategies for Components

Changes in strategies are necessary to facilitate the growth of individual functions as well as the enterprise as a whole. A leading commercial bank in New York developed an overall corporate growth strategy of stressing friendly, individualized service to attract and keep depositors. It provided a full range of complementary services. But the intuitive strategy of the savings and lending departments since the bank's founding, built on the first president's personality, had been one of caution and suspicion. This drove customers to more friendly competitors. The new bank strategy was meaningless until the heads of each functional department changed their own attitudes and instigated intensive training programs to implement new strategies for their departments.

Growth Strategies and Market Leadership

A number of factors influence our choice of market strategy. One of the most important is the experience curve or learning-curve concept. This establishes that the total cost, including production, marketing, and research, tends to go down as a company gains experience in a specific market segment. In part this is because of the economies of scale. There is also the impact of greater efficiency and increased ability to mechanize and automate and to use substitute materials.

One consequence is that the largest producer will tend to have the lowest costs. Since each company must compete on price, no matter what it costs, the ability to attain and hold market leadership is a vital factor in determining the growth strategy. Thus General Motors has a decided edge over Ford because it has been able to follow a strategy of maintaining leadership in the more profitable sector of the vehicle market and, as a result, has had the resources to develop a wider array of products to meet changing market demand. The Mead Corporation, for example, invested heavily in a furniture and home-furnishings business, but as soon as it determined it could not continue to make the investment necessary to dominate the market, it sold off the fledgling but promising undertaking and put its money where it could dominate.

The Logic of Classifying Growth Strategies

As is true of other aspects of planning, it will be helpful if we can identify, define, and classify the different types of growth strategies. While no accepted classification exists, I believe it will be helpful to develop a clear logic so the choices available can be identified, defined, and classified.

The logic on which the classification is based is that an enterprise satisfies the needs of customers by offering one or more combinations of products and services to one or more markets. This offering is on a continuum: it may be one to a thousand or more products offered to a like number of markets, or any combination of the two. The chief distinction lies in concentration or diversification. And this comes back to the basic question: Is it most to our advantage to invest our resources in one product or market, or in a number of related products and markets, or in unrelated products and markets?

CONCENTRATION AND DIVERSIFICATION GROWTH STRATEGIES

Using our classification logic, we can classify the different types of growth strategies into two primary categories: Concentration Strategies and Diversification Strategies. The classification logic diagram is shown in Figure 13-1. The work category is identified and defined, and the objective which is the outcome of the work is stated.

We can see how the work of developing growth strategies fits into the taxonomy in Figure 13-2. The function is Planning, the activity is Developing Strategy and the segment is Developing Growth Strategies.

We expand the definitions into more complete statements below.

1. *Developing Concentration Growth Strategies.* A means of achieving the growth commitment of the key objective is to concentrate resources to provide related products to related markets. This may range from one category of products to one or multiple categories of related markets or to multiple related categories of products to single markets.

   a. *Developing Unified Growth Strategy.* You can achieve growth by concentrating resources to provide one category of products to one market category.

   b. *Developing Product Growth Strategy.* You can achieve growth by concentrating resources to provide multiple categories of related products to one market category.

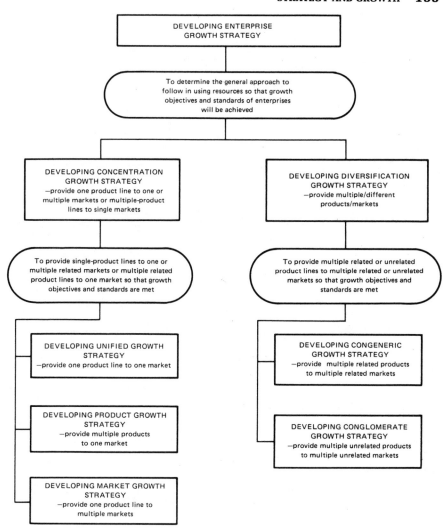

FIGURE 13-1   The Growth Strategy Classification Logic Diagram

  c. *Developing Market Growth Strategy.* You can achieve growth
     by concentrating resources to provide one category of prod-
     ucts to multiple, related market categories.

  2. *Developing Diversification Growth Strategy.* You can achieve
     growth by using resources to provide multiple, product cat-
     egories to multiple market categories.

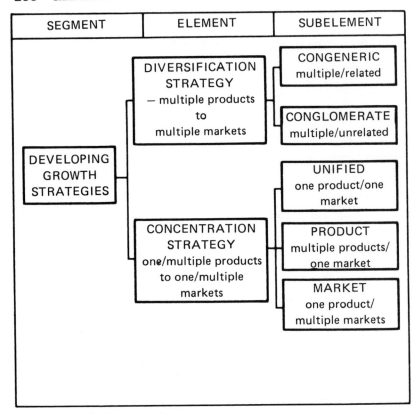

FIGURE 13-2 A Taxonomy of Growth Strategies

a. *Developing Congeneric Growth Strategy.* You can achieve growth by providing multiple, related product categories to multiple, related market categories.

b. *Developing Conglomerate Growth Strategy.* You can achieve growth by providing multiple, unrelated product categories to multiple, unrelated market categories.

Each of these strategies will impact the product and customer commitments of the key objective. Each has its own characteristics and merits consideration at various stages of growth. We will look at each in more detail.

Concentration Growth Strategies

Here resources are used to expand one set of products or markets. Concentration may be in one product line and one primary market. It may involve growth around a single product line with multiple, related markets, or it may involve growth around one primary market to which multiple, related products are offered.

This strategy may appear limiting, but it has advantages. Many companies grow and prosper by planning to continue to do what they know best. Expansion and improvement of existing products, markets, and skills is more efficient than using the same resources to move into areas that have distinctly different demands. However, this concentration can easily become a rut. If investment has been heavily concentrated, there may be inadequate resources to support the changeover to a new technology. In human terms, an innate preference for the known, familiar, and successful develops, and resistance to change may become a fatal handicap. Many a company that sells out at the close of the tenure of the founding entrepreneur does so because it cannot make the changes necessary for growth and survival. We can identify three types of concentration strategies: unified, product, and market.

Unified Concentration. Many enterprises leap to the front because of specialized expertise they develop in a single product line which is sold to one homogeneous market. This integration of effort has the advantage of building great competitive strength. However, as this concentration brings success, it inevitably draws competitors.

Ford Motor Company provides the historical example. Under Henry Ford, the company built the famous Model-T. Ford appealed to one category of customers: those who wanted an efficient, utilitarian automobile in the color black. This concentration was extremely successful and enabled Ford to head off competitors in the burgeoning automobile industry. But Ford rode his success story too long. General Motors, under Alfred P. Sloan, catered to the needs of different customer groups. It outsold Ford not because it made better automobiles, but because its strategy was superior.

Product Concentration. A strong product frequently has appeal to many different customer categories. General Motors, by use of styling and function differentiation, fitted the basic automobile to the needs of customer categories from rich to poor, from farmers to salespersons. In all its permutations, the primary characteristics of the gasoline-driven automobile in the hands of General Motors have remained remarkably consistent. One result is that GM has been able to blanket the market-place while greatly benefiting from the experience curve. Here again, however, the difficulties of changing course for a great corporation under full headway are evident. With energy shortages, increased costs and sharp competition, General Motors has had to summon the full capabilities of its management team to move out of a once-successful pattern and keep its primary product in a leading position.

Market Concentration. While companies with successful products naturally evolve to a strategy of seeking other market outlets, the reverse is not as common. Product features, patent protection, and complex technology help sustain product concentration. Mastering a market to the degree that a range of different products can be sold successfully calls for unusual skill and persistence. Procter and Gamble uses its superb marketing system to bring more products to the grocers' shelves at steadily reducing distribution costs. Republic Steel gives highest priority to new products that can be sold by its existing sales force.

A highly successful example of market concentration is Avon Products, Inc. A leader in home selling of personal products, primarily cosmetics, toiletries, and fashion jewelry, Avon began by providing cosmetics and toiletries to housewives who had limited access to retail stores.

A unique marketing strategy was developed, that of appointing sales representatives, usually women, who sold to their friends and neighbors on a part-time basis. Today, skill in recruiting, training, and motivating over 1,200,000 sales representatives in the United States and 29 other countries has given Avon its competitive edge. To this primary customer group Avon offers over 700 products. A strong field-operations function headquartered in New York provides centralized direction for the marketing effort.

It is far easier to set up production or manufacturing facilities and to operate them successfully than it is to develop and maintain a top-notch marketing capability. For this reason companies with strong marketing tend to do better by adding product lines rather than by creating new marketing forces. Organization of product- or market-manager positions can often expand the scope of a single sales force so it can handle a number of products.

Cascading Concentration Strategies. Concentration strategies apply at all levels of the enterprise. They may be cascaded from the top, or they may originate at lower levels. For example, the human resources department of a Massachusetts electronics company served its purpose extremely well by following a strategy of hiring technically skilled people trained by competitors. This brought technical competence quickly. However, as other electronics companies moved into the area, the price commanded by skilled people increased sharply and the supply of them dwindled. Company growth slowed until the human resources department was encouraged to follow a new strategy: one of identifying, training, and motivating technical specialists internally.

Frequently, concentration strategies are successful during the early growth stages but become outmoded. Concentration strategies give way to diversification for many reasons. Most common are uncertainties, limitations, or changes in the market. Pressed Steel Car Company moved out of its early specialization in freight cars to avoid the cyclical feast and famine typical of the industry and became U.S. Industries, Inc. Minnesota Mining and Manufacturing Company made an early hit with its sandpaper but found this an inadequate vehicle for sustained expansion. It diversified to find the growth space it needed.

Diversification Growth Strategies

Sooner or later most companies diversify into multiple products and multiple markets, either related or unrelated. Diversification has been the primary growth strategy for many leaders, ranging from General Electric to Rockwell International Corp.

The central problem in planning a diversification strategy is not the availability of capital or the availability of suitable acquisitions or even research and development capability. It is the suitability and adaptability of management. It is necessary to plan for the development of competent and flexible management skills at many levels of the organization to handle the complex demands of successful diversification.

Diversification strategies usually are either congeneric or conglomerate. Either may come about spontaneously, through the pressures of the operating situation, or rationally, through careful analysis and orderly, logical action.

Congeneric Diversification. Companies that have had experience in diversifying generally conclude that it is best to make additions only if they complement and expand what is already in place. Internal growth maximizes the probability that management and production and marketing capabilities will be synergistic.

Digital Equipment Corporation, for example, has forged to a front position in minicomputers against such competition as Hewlett-Packard, IBM, and Data General Corporation. It did so by diversifying within its primary business. Its products range from minicomputers to computer systems, from $50 in price to $2 million. Its customers vary from small business to aerospace. It sells through its own sales force and its own retail stores. Each part of the enterprise complements the others, maximizing the contribution of its highly effective management group.

As a company grows, it tends to build a pool of skills in its basic functions. Some companies have found that they can diversify most successfully by moving into new businesses which utilize these skills. Marketing is a most common example; however, research and engineering may have an even greater catalytic effect in high-technology industries. Emerson Electric Co., for example, specialized in electric motors and machines driven by electric motors. Expanding from this reservoir of know-how, it has built a strong position in businesses related by the technology—ranging from chain saws to electric fans.

Congeneric diversification is also called concentric diversification and other names. However, I believe the important distinction between this kind of diversification and others is the difference between the relatedness and unrelatedness of the components. For this reason I propose that "congeneric" is the preferred term.

The particulars of congeneric diversification fill a steadily expanding bookshelf, but the key factors remain constant. Once a company has paid the price for developing specialized research, engineering, manufacturing, and marketing skills, it stands to gain most by planning to increase the work and output of these groups. If it has selected its markets wisely, the greater its experience, the higher its volume will be. Increased volume, carefully controlled, brings lower costs and prices, improved market position, and enhanced profitability.

Conglomerate Strategies. While there is some consensus that congeneric diversification is generally best, there are strong arguments—and success stories—in favor of the conglomerate route. At first glance, the task of melding different products, markets, and especially managements would seem to be enormous. And many a conglomerate that has come apart at the seams can attest to the fact. However, it is also true that if an enterprise does not find the potential it seeks in congeneric growth, conglomeration may be an acceptable alternative.

The difference between a successful congeneric diversification and a conglomerate is that the congeneric can specialize in a related line of products or markets but a conglomerate can have only one primary specialization—management.

Conglomerate Portfolios. Top executives often view their accountability as managing a pool of assets to be invested in business operations that will yield a maximum return to stockholders. This portfolio approach may be espoused by chief executives of conglomerate diversifications, who recognize the impossibility of understanding and monitoring the operating problems and needs of the varied functions they attempt to govern. The usual consequence is that the chief executive and his or her staff treat the conglomerate businesses as relatively autonomous enterprises, holding them to account primarily for profit.

Unfortunately, the portfolio approach overlooks a key requirement in successful organization of a conglomerate. This is the need to decentralize authority so that the profit makers can make as many of their own decisions as possible but yet remain accountable for meeting standards and achieving their part of overall corporate strategies. Since decentralization rests upon effective controls and plans, which are mutually interdependent, a first need in any conglomerate diversification is a fully effective planning and control system. To be successful, this must go far beyond the financial planning and control which is at the heart of the portfolio approach.

The Management of Conglomerates. Effective conglomerates tend to flourish best under professional managers who do not have a strong predilection for any one of the dissimilar products or functions they manage.

John Snyder, Jr., who refabricated Pressed Steel Car and made it into U.S. Industries, Inc., was a specialist in finance, not in freight cars. W. R. Grace & Co. has been able to accommodate a wide diversification because Peter Grace stressed the vital role of professional management in building and nurturing—and divesting when necessary. R. J. Reynolds Industries was unable to diversify beyond its tobacco core until it brought in Paul J. Sticht, a professional manager, who carefully designed a highly successful conglomerate enterprise.

The failures have been conspicuous. National Distillers found that expertise in liquor does not translate easily into success in chemicals. International Harvester ventured into such unfamiliar fields as air conditioners, refrigerators, and household appliances but withdrew when it found the mix more than it could manage. Professionally managed companies such as General Motors and Ford identify their incompatible additions and plan orderly divestment. After trying for several years to compete, Ford backed out of air conditioners. General Motors marketed its refrigerators for several decades but finally beat a strategic retreat.

Where Conglomerate Strategies Fail. While good management is the most important single requirement in a conglomerate diversification, we often overlook the fact that seeds of failure are sown at the operating levels, not in the office of the chief executive officer and corporate staff. The strategy that is carefully enunciated at the command post may fall apart when an attempt is made to implement it in the field.

Marketing and sales strategies tend to be the weakest points in a conglomerate strategy. When unrelated products are added, they invariably bring with them separate sales forces, with accompanying office and warehouse facilities. Because these are costly, there usually is a move to consolidate. If a salesperson can sell beer, why not also magazines? If the representative calls on the hardware stores in his or her territory, why not travel a few more miles and include the furniture dealers? This may seem logical enough to the head office planner, but it overlooks the Principle of Technical Priority. This establishes that when salespeople are called upon to sell differing products or technologies to differing markets, they will tend to show preference to one over the others.

The reason is familiar. Salespeople develop expertise in one product or a related set of products and markets. They become easy and confident in their specialty and pride themselves upon their expertise, especially if technical knowledge is required.

We can see this in the case of a New Jersey company that attempted to diversify from furniture waxes, polishes, and sprays to small household appliances. Two small-appliance companies were acquired, and the headquarters staff attempted to consolidate the three existing sales forces. The benefits were obvious.

The wax and polish salespeople had developed expertise in their speciality. They considered their customers their friends and enjoyed easy and confident relationships. The new lines required technical knowledge. They had to be demonstrated and serviced as well as sold. And competitors were well established and highly competent. Consolidated sales fell off dismally from those the separate lines had enjoyed.

The decline was arrested only when the field sales manager was invited to review and revise the strategy. She opted to split the sales forces but to add related products so each sales force would carry a full line.

Growth strategy can be discussed separately, but in practice the choice of growth strategy and its success depends upon the corollary success of our customer/client and product/service strategies. We will look at these in the next chapter.

KEY POINTS

1. *Strategy Defined.* "Strategy," though it is vital, suffers from semantic ambiguity. Strategy is the work we do to assess our options and set a general

direction toward an objective. We define strategy as the general approach to be followed in achieving an objective.

2. *Strategy Is Necessary at All Levels.* Vertical and horizontal integration of strategies within a firm are necessary. Successful strategy depends as much upon the ability and willingness of lower levels to carry it out as of top management to develop it.

3. *The Key Strategies.* Strategies established at the top set the direction for the firm as a whole and strongly influence supporting strategies. While the number and type of strategies will vary with the enterprise, we usually find it necessary to develop strategies to implement the purpose, customer/client, and product/service commitments of the key objective. Since our intention is to set forth a logical framework for planning, we will concentrate on the classification of one type of key strategy: growth strategy.

4. *What Kind of Growth Strategy?* Growth strategies determine the nature of the business and the allocation of resources. The experience curve concept is an influential factor in deciding on a growth strategy. This concept states that total cost (production, marketing, and research) tends to go down as a company accumulates knowledge and experience in a specific market segment. Costs are lowest in the largest firms. Thus, growth strategies are most advantageous if they enable the company to be among the two or three leaders in each market segment it enters. With this in mind, we must decide between concentration or diversification.

5. *Concentration Growth Strategy.* We classify this into three types. Unified concentration strategy focuses on one category of products and one market segment. Product concentration strategy requires marshalling resources to support a single category of products and multiple, related markets. Market concentration strategy centers resources on multiple, related products and one market segment. Concentration strategies are generally more efficient; they have pitfalls because the greater the concentration is, the greater the resistance to change will be.

6. *Diversification Strategies.* We classify these into congeneric and conglomerate types. Congeneric diversification strategy involves expansion into products and markets which are logically related, while conglomerate diversification involves expansion into products and markets which are not logically related. The success of any diversification strategy depends upon the suitability and adaptability of management. In general, congeneric diversification is more favorable because skills and knowledge are more readily transferable. Managers of conglomerates are most successful if they have no predilection for any one of the dissimilar products or functions.

QUOTES FROM CHAPTER 13

Significant quotations from this chapter that you will want to consider and discuss in greater detail:

- A strategy cannot exist by itself. It must always be related to an objective, for it is a way of attaining an objective.

- Strategy is often a matter of making explicit something we do intuitively.

- When Magic Chef decided to become a full-line manufacturer, it had to rethink its market and scope strategies to compete with industry leaders.

- W. R. Wrigley Company grew fortuitously into chewing gum, but it adopted the strategy of concentration and soon became the world's leading purveyor of gum.

- General Motors outsold Ford not because it made better automobiles, but because its strategy was superior.

- R. J. Reynolds Industries was unable to diversify beyond its tobacco core until it brought in Paul J. Sticht, a professional manager, who carefully designed a highly successful conglomerate enterprise.

- National Distillers found that expertise in liquor does not translate easily into success in chemicals.

- The central problem in planning a diversification strategy is not the availability of capital, of suitable acquisitions, or of research and development capability; it is the suitability and adaptability of management.

- The strategy that is carefully enunciated at the command post may fall apart when an attempt is made to implement it in the field.

14

CRITICAL OBJECTIVES AND STANDARDS: THE CONTINUING LINK

I think what has chiefly struck me in human beings is their lack of consistency. I have never seen people all of a piece.
W. SOMERSET MAUGHAM

THE CHAPTER IN BRIEF   Critical objectives and standards provide a model of the level of desired performance. They state the most important, overall, continuing results and the criteria for measuring them. Using the classification logic again, we identify and define the most important results, or critical objectives, as outcomes of the most important work categories we classified in work analysis. The work categories necessary to achieve the product/service and customer/client commitments become the line technical functions, from which we develop the line technical critical objectives and standards. Staff technical critical objectives and standards are those necessary to provide advice and service to the organization at large. Cascading both critical objectives and standards is key to their use. Suggestions and examples are given for developing the objectives and standards.

BRIDGING THE PRESENT AND THE FUTURE

We need a bridge between the long-range future and the short-range present if we are to plan consistently. Conventional strategic and operational plans often fail to provide this, because they are "owned" by different groups and suffer from the periscope syndrome we noted earlier. One approach to closing the gap is to revise and update our short-range plans on a sliding or rolling basis so that the time gap never becomes uncomfortable. However, this fails to build the bridges we need between present and future and between the enterprise plan and those of individual managers.

To provide for the integration of future and present of different organization levels and to reconcile the needs of the individual and the organization, we develop continuing objectives.

DEFINITION AND CHARACTERISTICS

Critical objectives are statements of the most important, overall, continuing results that must be accomplished to achieve the key objective.

Critical objectives identify the critical few results that warrant use

209

of the largest share of our resources and effort; therefore, they enable us to define the criteria by which we can determine whether those results are being achieved satisfactorily. They provide the basis for a reasoned, orderly allocation of resources.

Critical objectives help to further strengthen our controls, for if we know the most important results we want, we can quickly determine what are the most important reports and other controls we need. And, finally, when we are ready to appraise the performance of those accountable for achieving the results, critical objectives enable us to focus on a few central issues rather than try to cover all the windrows and thickets of responsibility. Critical objectives can provide an exemplar of successful operation: to the degree we fail to meet those objectives, we will also fail to achieve our key objective.

WHAT ARE THE MOST IMPORTANT RESULTS?

Our critical objectives should represent the vital few results that will be instrumental in accomplishing our key objective. There are a number of approaches to determine what is most important. Some companies rely upon the judgment of individual managers. Others prefer collective determination arrived at by a panel of knowledgeable persons. A few use statistical techniques such as multiple-criterion ranking and paired comparisons. However, these methods tend to be subjective and unwieldy.

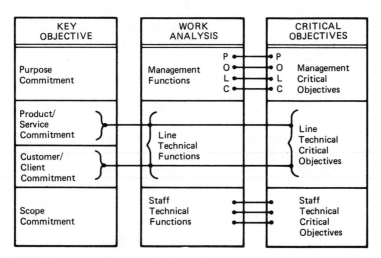

FIGURE 14-1   Derivation of Critical Objectives

We already have a means of getting a clear shot at what is most important in the logic of work classification. The task now becomes quite simple: we determine the most important categories of work necessary to accomplish our key objective. These categories, in turn, should lead us directly to the most important subobjectives necessary to achieve our key objective. These are our critical objectives. The derivation of critical objectives from the work analysis and the key objective is shown in Figure 14-1.

The Line Technical Critical Objectives

Here we see that the work categories necessary to satisfy the product/service and the customer/client commitments are the line technical functions, that is, the work categories accountable for direct accomplishment of the key objective.

Product/Service Work Categories. An enterprise must provide something of value, something for which customers, in order to secure the benefits provided, will be willing to pay more than it cost the enterprise to produce. What are the primary categories of work that must be performed on a continuing basis to provide this product or service?

In some enterprises, the conversion of a raw or semifinished material to a salable product is involved. This is the case, for example, in Procter and Gamble, Coca-Cola or Levi-Strauss. Here, typically, the product/service work category is manufacturing or production.

In a containerized sea- and land-transportation business, such as Sea-Land Service, Inc., the work categories necessary to satisfy the product/service commitment are land and sea operations. A bank, such as First City Bank of Dallas, might be concerned with investing and lending money and providing trust services; a department store, such as Macy's, might buy and sell merchandise. A company that is committed to developing new products might have engineering as well as manufacturing as the work categories necessary to satisfy the product/service commitment.

The line technical functions are the primary categories of technical work. We know from our classification logic that work gives rise to results; therefore, the line technical functions will give rise to the line technical critical objectives. We see this in Figure 14-1.

For example; if one of the line technical functions in Figure 14-1 is engineering, we know it will lead to a line technical critical objective. This might be, "to design and develop new and improved products so that marketing and manufacturing specifications are met."

Customer/Client Work Categories. Enterprises succeed only to the extent they find, persuade, and sell to customers. The total package of work performed to accomplish this is usually identified as marketing.

The customer/client commitment requires the performance of marketing work. This will contain some or all of the basic constituents, or subcategories, of marketing: finding the right customers, identifying their needs, persuading them of the benefits that will satisfy their needs, making the sale, delivering the goods, and following up to make sure the customers stay satisfied.

These subcategories of work have many labels. Finding customers and identifying their needs is generally called market research or market development. Persuasion most often goes under the name of advertising and promotion, selling may be called by such names as customer counseling or client development. Delivering goods may be called distribution, transportation, installation, or counseling. Ensuring satisfaction after the sale most often is known as customer service. In some cases this involves provision for physical servicing of breakdowns or malfunctions.

Giving Muscle to the Work. The subcategories of work determine the character and nature of the categories. We can call a function "marketing," but if our plan provides only for sending out salespeople to persuade people to buy, it is still only selling and not marketing. Our general tendency is to continue performing the subcategories of work that have always existed, no matter what the change in title. For example, companies that develop plans to integrate marketing often will organize a staff marketing group while leaving unchanged the work done by salespeople dealing with customers. But marketing cannot be merely a new department; it must expand beyond the range and capabilities of a staff function. Marketing is a way of life for the enterprise. The only way to make it so is to specify in our plans that the primary responsibility of salespeople and their ranks of managers is to find customers, to determine customer needs, to persuade customers that their needs will be satisfied, to make the sale, and to follow up to make sure their needs are satisfied.

The Staff Technical Critical Objectives

The ball carrier needs help to make gains on the football field, and the surgeon cannot operate successfully without an anesthetist, radiologist, and other skilled coworkers. So also in every business we must provide skilled specialists who will share in the task of accomplishing the overall objective.

As we have seen, for convenience we identify the categories of work directly accountable for achieving the overall objective as the line technical functions and subcategories of work. Those that we organize to provide skilled advice and service in achieving those same objectives we call staff technical functions and subcategories of work.

We can determine what staff technical functions we need only after we have organized our line technical functions. The staff technical functions exist to provide advice and service to the line organization and to other staff functions. Thus if our line technical functions are engineering, production, and sales, our staff technical functions might be financial services, personnel services, and administrative services.

The Critical Objectives Cascade

In a team effort, the objectives of each member of the team must contribute to achievement of the overall or key objective. If left to themselves, people will tend to set some objectives that vary from or even contradict those of the team as a whole; therefore, we must have some method for integrating objectives and standards. We can accomplish this by cascading objectives.

Objectives are cascaded from the top down. You will want to ensure that all have a clear picture of how the critical objectives cascade from the chief executive officer to the supervisory level. This will establish the accountability of each person in unmistakable terms and greatly simplify further position definition and delegation. The cascade is shown in Figure 14-2.

A clearly defined cascade of your critical objectives can help you in several ways.

Helps People to Write Their Own Objectives. Generally people wait to have their objectives handed to them. Or they are cut out of the whole cloth by the planning department or the MBO specialist and distributed. In the best of circumstances, people will have an opportunity to participate in this process and to develop a feeling that, at least in part, they own their objectives. People may fail to write their own objectives because they don't know how or, if they do, they are so uncertain of what their managers want that they are reluctant to take the first step. Developing a cascade chart clearly shows all where they fit into the picture and gives them guidelines so they can do a good job.

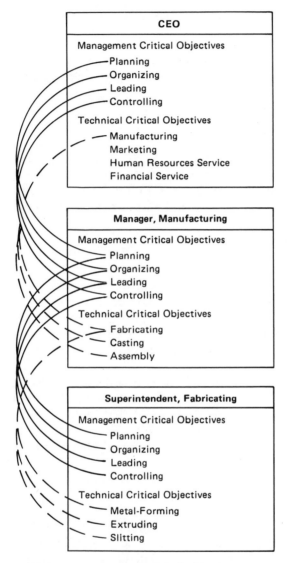

FIGURE 14-2   Cascade of Critical Objectives

Establishes Accountability for Each Position. By clearly defining the results expected and the standards by which both the work and the results will be judged, critical objectives and their accompanying critical standards make very clear what each person is to accomplish. This, in turn, provides an accurate and reasonable basis for performance appraisals both by individuals and their managers.

Eliminates Overlap and Duplication. Because it follows a logical classification of work, which defines each category and subcategory, the cascade almost automatically eliminates overlap and duplication in the most important functions and activities of work. Once accomplished, this also greatly minimizes the tendency for overlap in developing more specific and detailed plans and standards.

HOW TO STATE CRITICAL OBJECTIVES

Your critical objectives will define the results that must be accomplished as an outcome of each of the critical work categories you have already identified. Some helpful guides in stating your critical objectives are: (1) find your place in the cascade, (2) state continuing results to be achieved by your position, (3) use the work to guide you to results, (4) make sure the objective is continuing, (5) test for completeness.

Find Your Place in the Cascade

You are accountable for the work and results of your own position and also that of all the people in your component. To get a clear picture of the scope and depth of your continuing objectives, you will want to fit yourself in the objectives cascade. To do this you review the critical objectives of the person to whom you report and, if they are available, those of other positions with which you have working relationships.

Just as your key objective was derived directly from that of your manager and in turn was cascaded, so also are your critical objectives. If there is overlap or if inconsistencies exist, you will want to reconcile the differences.

Cascading your objectives will ensure that your contribution to overall company objectives is clearly delineated. No matter how far down the organizational hierarchy you are located, you will be able to relate what you do to what the organization as a whole is trying to accomplish.

State Continuing Results to Be Achieved

Just as being healthy, happy, and wise are conditions you never fully achieve but constantly strive toward, so the really important results an enterprise seeks to accomplish are continuing in nature rather than finite and terminal. To be profitable, to maintain high quality performance, and to satisfy customers are definable results which directly determine success or lack of it. Since these are ongoing and not intended to be achieved at any set time, we do not expect them to culminate in a quantifiable result. However, we can accurately measure our progress in moving toward them by developing, in parallel, criteria or standards.

The continuing results toward which managers work depend on the efforts both of their subordinates and peers. Therefore, stating the continuing results to be achieved can never be a personal exercise; it must always have the active participation of those who are directly involved. One of the best ways to accomplish this is to schedule 2 or 3 days of intensive meetings at a location away from business. Managers bring to the meeting the plans they have already worked out with their own teams. At the session, the objectives and other plans of the top-ranking manager are studied and discussed. This can be done by showing them on a screen, using an overhead projector. The plans of others are then reviewed and reconciled, so that an integrated, understood, and accepted plan results.

Use the Work to Guide You to Results

Following the logic we have already established, we know that each category of critical work will have as its outcome a critical objective. For example, we have defined marketing as the work of finding, persuading, selling, and servicing the needs of people. So we ask ourselves: "What ongoing, continuing results will be the outcome of this work?" The critical objective might then be stated: "to maintain leadership in volume, profit, and customer satisfaction." Another way to state it might be: "to maintain the largest market share for all segments but municipal hospitals, in which we will be among the first three."

These are brief statements, but they identify the outcomes we intend to use our resources to achieve on an ongoing basis. Subordinates and peers both can relate quickly to statements such as these. With this kind of guidance, instead of proposing projects that appear worthwhile, all concerned can justify requests by answering the question: "To what degree will this project help us maintain the market share we want?"

To develop your critical objectives, you review your management and technical work categories, then state the outcome you desire for each. At first your statements will tend to be vague and generalized. Use them in the best form you can generate. As you work with your objectives, keep asking such questions as: "Why should we continue to perform this work?" and "What tangible outcome must we get from this work?" Gradually you will find your statements becoming clearer, sharper, and more useful.

Test to Make Sure the Objective Is Continuing

If you have been accustomed to writing only quantified objectives, as most of us have, you will find yourself stating your critical objectives in specific numbers; for example, "to maintain a quality level of 0.017%" or "to keep vacancies below six per year." Unfortunately, this quantification encourages short-term perspective. The quantity specified probably reflects a level that will satisfy customers now. To get at the continuing result, you ask yourself "Why do I want to maintain a quality level of 0.017%?" What you may really want, on a continuing basis, may be a quality level that will encourage customers to select your product over that of competitors. Instead of specifying "vacancies below six per year," if you ask "Why do I want to keep vacancies below six per year?" you may conclude that your continuing objective is "to generate sufficient rental income to cover debt service."

You will have ample opportunity for developing measures when you write your critical standards, your specific objectives and standards, and your specific budgets. In stating your critical objectives, concentrate on what continuing outcomes you want from your critical work and why you want those outcomes.

Test for Completeness

Your critical objectives will establish a verbal picture of the level of excellence you will use your resources to attain. We know that mental images consciously developed directly influence our actions and those of others who participate. It is important that your critical objectives cover all of the vitally important aspects of your position so the action that follows will be comprehensive.

One good way to test for completeness is to perform a simple through-put analysis of the work categories necessary to achieve your key objective. If there are gaps or disparities in the work, inevitably the objectives will be incomplete.

Here is how one company used this analysis very effectively. The functions involved were human resources, which was defined as "the work of providing advice and service in making most effective utilization of human resources," and industrial relations, which was "the work of maintaining good relations with unionized employees and labor unions." The work categories of the two different components are shown in Figure 14-3.

It is clear that the objectives overlap to a large degree; to secure congruency, both sets of work categories should culminate in making

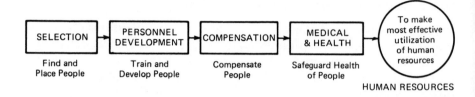

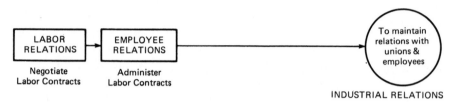

FIGURE 14-3   Using Work Analysis to Consolidate Functions

most effective utilization of human resources. The overlap, duplication, and cross purposes that ensued were clearly evident. The reason the split was maintained was an historical schism between the legally trained and oriented people who handled labor relations and the behavioral-science orientation of human resources personnel.

The situation was corrected by cross-training the younger head of industrial relations for 2 years and providing similar rotational experience for several other members of both groups. When the human resources head retired at the end of the 2 years, the two organizational entities were merged and their objectives were realigned and integrated.

DEVELOPING CRITICAL STANDARDS

Just as we need standards to measure our accomplishments of key objectives, we also need critical standards to establish the level of excellence we expect to attain in the critical areas of performance.

Critical standards are developed following a technique similar to that we used for key standards. Here the important requirement is that we provide measurable evidence that the desired result has been achieved. If all the standards are met, the objective will have been achieved.

Several considerations are worth reviewing as you develop your critical standards.

Use Vital Factors

The most important criteria are identified and stated as the critical standards for each critical objective. The vital factors are best known to the people who actually perform the work. Ask a knowledgeable person "How do you know when a person has done an outstanding job in performing this work?" or "What evidence would you accept that the work has been done in an outstanding manner?" and you will elicit the information you want.

Make Standards Measurable

Critical standards should be measurable. Often they cannot be quantified, but usually it is possible to specify some tangible evidence that the desired result has been achieved. For example, if the standard requires completion of position charters, their physical presence can be observed. If we want to measure the quality of the position charter, we will need criteria and some objective person or agency to evaluate the quality in terms of the criteria.

Secure Understanding and Acceptance

Since people will be judged on their ability to meet the standards, it is of first importance that they understand them and agree that they are fair and equitable. The best way to ensure this is to have your people recommend their own standards, rather than to have yourself or a staff group develop them. The more your people participate, the greater their emotional ownership of the standards.

USES OF CRITICAL OBJECTIVES AND STANDARDS

Taken together, your critical objectives and standards define your job. They provide a means of measuring performance and are indispensable in performance appraisal. Most importantly, they serve as a basis for needs analysis.

Defining Your Accountability

Because they cover the most important work and results you are expected to accomplish and define what constitutes acceptable performance, your critical objectives and standards provide a clear statement of your accountability. You can add the authority limits for each objective, if you wish, and thus have a set of job specifications you can get in no other way.

Use in Performance Appraisal

Determining how well—or poorly—people are performing is often a difficult and thankless task. However, if you ask your people to develop their own critical objectives and standards, which you approve, you will find that they can serve as a valid means of self-appraisal. Almost always the persons who complete their own appraisals using their critical objectives and standards as criteria will be quite realistic in identifying their own strengths and weaknesses. Your role in performance appraisal then becomes a matter of confirming the agreed-upon ratings and devoting most time to discussing the critical few exceptions.

A Basis for Needs Analysis

As we will see when we discuss needs analysis, your critical objectives and standards enable you to check each important area of your accountability and to determine where you are strong and where you are weak. You can then concentrate on identifying your real problems and developing specific plans to overcome them.

Examples of Management Critical Objectives and Standards

Management critical objectives usually follow the sequence of work classification. It is difficult to quantify management objectives or standards, but it is usually possible to specify tangible work products or to secure informed judgment.

You will find that when you standardize the format of critical objectives and standards, you will simplify preparation and communication. A system of numbering is advisable. The critical objectives may be given decimal numbers, which can be used to identify and track them. Decimal numbers for specific objectives dealing with the same areas can then be derived from these base numbers.

In the first example below, an introductory sentence is used which helps set the stage and which facilitates understanding of what is being done. In the second example, there is a briefer, more terse statement of the same information.

CRITICAL OBJECTIVES AND STANDARDS

In order to meet the key objective and standards, continuing satisfactory results must be met in achieving the critical objectives below, as measured by the critical standards.

C.O.1.0. Planning Performance

To maintain a logical, integrated planning system so that the desired growth in earnings and return on capital is achieved.

Standards

1. *Forecasts.* The significant external and internal factors determining the company's success are identified and projected annually and updated quarterly and are used to develop objectives and strategies.
2. *Position Charters.* These are maintained for all positions and provide measurable, understood, and accepted objectives and standards.
3. *Action Plans.* These are the basis for the annual financial accounting budgets, which schedule authorized capital and operating expenditures.
4. *Policies and Procedures.* Written policies and procedures are maintained and disseminated in regularly updated manuals to provide direction on matters of corporatewide significance and on recurrent work tasks.
5. *Evaluation.* The planning system and use of plans is evaluated "very good" (4/5) by managers in an annual management performance survey, on the basis of understood and accepted criteria.

The following statement of critical standards is used by a bank:

Standards

1. *Position Charter.* An ongoing position charter is revised and updated by each manager by September 1 each year.

2. *Action Plans.* These cover the critical few needs and are one basis for operating budgets.
3. *Policies and Procedures.* These are reviewed and revised as needed each year.

Examples of Technical Critical Objectives and Standards

These lend themselves more readily to quantification. To show the degree of measurability customarily achieved, an example from a chemical company appears first. The factors vital to attainment of the critical objective are identified; then a standard is stated for each vital factor. Taken together, the standards will yield the objective.

C.O.6.0. Operations Performance

To engineer, construct, operate, and maintain production facilities so that production and marketing requirements are met.

Standards

1. *Production Facilities.* State-of-the-art technology is incorporated to ensure that product performance and cost requirements are met.
2. *Costs.* Estimates of controllable costs for construction or rehabilitation of production facilities prove to be within 5% of actual for all projects over the calendar year and within plus 10% and minus 5% on individual projects.
3. *Completion Dates.* Estimates on date of completion for major construction or rehabilitation projects are accurate within 10 and 20% for projects involving rehabilitation or reconstruction of parts of existing production facilities.
4. *Quality and Delivery.* Products are produced and shipped to meet understood and accepted quality and delivery time requirements of the marketing department 95% of the time, and customers rate delivery service "satisfactory."
5. *Production Efficiency.* Efficiency, as measured by controllable units of consumption of labor, materials, supply, and energy per unit of production, meets established standards 95% of the time, and an ongoing cost reduction program is maintained, which results in regular and continuing im-

provements in annual cost reduction totals as measured by a 3-year moving average.

6. *Safety*. Lost time due to accidents and accident severity and frequency rates are continually improved down to a realistically practicable minimum, and an ongoing safety program results in specific improvements to the working environment.

A bank example is given below. The vital factors again are used as titles for the critical standards.

C.O.8.0. Investment Portfolio

To optimize investment portfolio yields to the bank while maintaining adequate liquidity, stressing quality without seriously affecting yields and remaining aware of pledging requirements and community responsibilities.

Standards

1. *Liquidity*. The bank's liquidity ratio remains at or near 20%.
2. *Investment Portfolio*. The investment portfolio primarily consists of bonds rated "A" and better, with "BAA" bonds considered on a selected basis.
3. *Maturities*. The maturities are staggered, with none being in excess of 20 years.
4. *Credit*. No concentration of credit exceeds 20% of the bank's capital, with adherence to regulatory limitations.

Action is the necessary end product of all useful objectives. Neither key nor critical objectives are designed to lead to action. They provide a basis for determining where resources should be directed to ensure that the action that does take place is productive and timely. This is accomplished by developing action plans, which we will discuss in the next chapter.

QUOTES FROM CHAPTER 14

Significant quotations from this chapter that you will want to consider and discuss in greater detail:

• Critical objectives provide the basis for a reasoned, orderly allocation of resources.

- Companies that develop integrated marketing often organize a staff marketing group while leaving unchanged the work done by salespeople dealing with customers.

- Cascading your objectives will ensure that your contribution to overall company objectives is clearly delineated.

- Your critical objectives will establish a verbal picture of the level of excellence you will use your resources to attain.

- The more your people participate, the greater their emotional ownership of the standards that are set.

15

ACTION PLANNING:
SPECIFIC OBJECTIVES AND STANDARDS

All action is involved in imperfection, like fire in smoke.
BHAGAVAD-GITA

THE CHAPTER IN BRIEF   Action plans serve as the bridge between the future and the present. Intended to be completed within a definite time period, they may range from a day to a decade or more. Action plans emerge logically from a needs analysis of our continuing plans and standards. In developing action plans, it is important to formalize and standardize their preparation, to ensure acceptance by contracting, and to make them measurable.

DEFICIENCIES IN SHORT-RANGE PLANS

The heart of the planning process is the work done by individual managers to plan the day-to-day actions of their own groups. This is as true at the chief executive level as at the first line of supervision. Stress is largely on operating plans; that is, those that refer to the technical work to be performed within a short time—usually a year or less. Production plans, sales plans, and project plans, including PERT and networking plans, all fall in this category.

Short-range plans *are* vitally important. But most operating or technical plans apply to repetitive projects and needs. They quickly become routine and often are stereotyped. They may be so detailed that they can only be controlled by the person directly accountable for carrying them out, in which case there are no checks and balances. Conversely, they may be so general that there is no opportunity to identify specific control points, so control by exception is ruled out.

The greatest limitation of much short-range planning, however, is that it is not integrated with the overall enterprise plan; that is, it does not have a logical position in the enterprise plan and fails to support and reinforce it. Plans are useful to the extent that their articulation binds them to other plans. If we want teamwork, our plans must ensure that the moves of each player are integrated with those of the team as a whole.

225

Most managers need help in developing short-range plans that will fit properly into an overall structure because this larger framework is beyond their own accountability. As we have seen, action plans provide this bridge. They ensure that the total effort can be properly coordinated and that each individual can have challenging tasks, the authority necessary to make most decisions, and a means of self-control.

DEFINITION AND CHARACTERISTICS

We define an "action plan" as *a plan that is intended to be completed within a definite time period*. Action plans translate overall, continuing plans into plans that will prompt specific action by individuals. Action plans do not cover everything you do: they concentrate on the critical few matters that warrant immediate, planned action. They are supported by repetitive plans, such as procedures, operating instructions, and rules and regulations.

The idea of action planning is hardly new to practicing managers. However, as is true with other aspects of planning, many interpretations and much contradictory terminology have sprung up. Action plans are also called Time Lines, Activity Programs, and Objective Plans. Some see the operational, or action, plan as the basis for functional plans. Most of these variations turn out to be either the business budget with line items supported by selected action plans or a combination of long- and short-range objectives, often with appended tasks, programs, or schedules.

Time Periods and Accountabilities

Action plans may cover any length of time from a day or less to several years. In this sense, they can be both short- and long-range. While each action plan is the accountability of one person, many different people will be accountable for carrying out different program steps in the plan.

People involved in action planning play two primary roles. The person who is accountable for the overall plan will make the decisions relating to accomplishment of the action plan, subject, of course, to approval of the supervisor concerned, when this control is reserved. This is as much as to say that if you are making a trip to Timbuktu, you are accountable for how and when you get there, no matter how much help you may have from travel agents, airline personnel, and your local purveyor of travel attire.

A variety of people may help by carrying out individual program steps. They are accountable for the content and quality of their own work, not for the overall result. If your travel agent issues you a ticket to Kinshasha instead of Timbuktu, you can hold the travel agent accountable for that mistake, but it's up to you to control, that is, to catch the mistake and have it corrected. Because they cover both roles, action plans guide and integrate both individual and group action.

Action Plans Are Part of the Management Process

While we discuss action plans as separate entities, they are most effective when we use them as part of our total approach to managing. Action plans provide the basis for effective controls. They help you to delegate and to develop good working relationships. Action plans can only be as good as the decision making that goes into them. They must be *communicated,* and people must be *motivated* to carry them out effectively.

You can couple your action plans with other management activities and make them even more versatile and valuable. Specific standards are most readily developed to accompany your specific objectives and to give you a convenient means of measuring both progress and results. As you work with programs, you will discover that many of them are repeated in much the same way. With a little additional effort, you can standardize these repetitive programs and convert them into procedures. And finally, when considered together with key and critical objectives and standards, you will find that your action plans can help you make well-rounded performance appraisals and to counsel and coach your people for improvement and career development.

Recent experience shows that action planning can be one of the most useful methods for encouraging people to take more interest in their jobs and to work harder and more productively. This follows, because to use action plans effectively, you must secure participation and get agreement on what is to be accomplished. The process calls for regular review of the work that is being done. It provides for evaluation and feedback so that people always know where they stand. And, finally, it gets you out of the role of critic and controller and into one of coach and helper.

THE LOGIC OF ACTION PLANNING

We have already seen how action planning fits into the overall planning process. Now we can examine the rationale for the action-planning format.'

In formalizing the logic flow for planning, earlier we developed the sequence of forecasting and then developing key and critical objectives and standards. We established that forecasts enable us to estimate and predict what the future will be like. Position charters provide the continuing objectives and standards that establish a clear picture of what the enterprise intends to become; they guide our long-term progress and enable us to determine how well we are accomplishing the overall results we want.

The Logic Bridge

Now we need a bridge between our continuing objectives and standards and our time-limited plans. There have been many approaches to this problem. Some rely largely on an extension of budgeting; this is the genesis of both responsibility budgeting and zero-based budgeting. Others develop a second echelon of plans—operational plans—for which the strategic or long-term plan serves primarily as background information. The most effective approach is to identify the deficiencies in action that are preventing us from satisfying our continuing objectives and standards, then to seek out the opportunities which have been lost or buried in the press of daily operations so that we can pursue the most promising of these. In doing so, we provide a basis for expanding and enriching our continuing objectives.

Needs Analysis Is the Key. A careful examination of the key and critical objectives and standards in terms of deficiencies and opportunities will provide a consistent, meaningful foundation for time-limited plans. Since continuing plans are already fully integrated with those of supervisors, subordinates, and peers, the time-limited plans that emerge will automatically relate in the same manner. This will ensure attainment of a long-desired end: congruency of individual and organization objectives. It will also coordinate long- and short-range planning so that an artificial distinction becomes unnecessary.

Completion of the Logic Flow

Putting this all together, we can see the completion of the logic flow, as indicated in Figure 15-1. The key and critical objectives and standards, which constitute the position charter, picture in needed detail what constitutes the desired level of performance on a continuing basis for every component as well as for the enterprise as a whole. The action plan, which begins with needs analysis, brings this overall picture to sharp focus on the problems and opportunities of day-to-day operations.

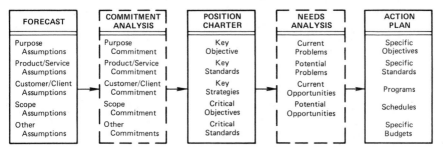

FIGURE 15-1   **The Logic Flow Extended to Action Planning**

It does this for each individual, but always in terms of the overall picture. From this process we derive a realistic, measurable statement of the results to be achieved, a means of measuring those results, the action steps to be taken, and the time and resources required. These are formalized in the specific objectives and standards, programs and schedules, and specific budgets.

LOGICAL DECISION MAKING AND ACTION PLANNING

We often confuse action planning with decision making. Since a decision is a conclusion or judgment, every plan has imbedded in it a multitude of decisions. The plan itself is really a process for putting all these subsidiary decisions together into one overall conclusion. If we accept this, we would expect that the same logic design would hold for both decision making and planning.

This is the case. Although there have been many variations dating from the inception of Aristotelian logic, we can show the essential steps in the logical thinking process as follows:

1. Define the problem.
2. Identify the alternative solutions.
3. Select the best solution.
4. Determine a course of action.

The Logical Basis for Action Planning

We can establish a useful framework for developing action plans by combining the logical thinking and planning sequences. Here is a suggestion:

1. Define the need.
2. Weigh the alternative results that will satisfy the need.
3. Select the best result.
4. Determine a course of action.

When we recognize that an objective is a predetermined result and that a course of action is a plan, we can further refine and simplify the process of needs analysis as follows:

1. Conduct a needs analysis.
2. Identify the possible objectives that will satisfy the need.
3. Select the best objective, and define it as a specific objective.
4. Determine the program, schedule, and specific budget necessary to achieve the specific objective.

This sequence is repeated for each action plan. It ensures that objectives are based solidly on identified needs. It requires us to develop the reasonable alternatives, to assess them, and to select for action the one that gives highest probability of success. This examination of the options crystallizes out of our generalized thinking the specifics of what is reasonable and possible in the light of the objective we've set.

The Place of Control

This chain of planning activities will help overcome some of the inherent weaknesses of the business plan. It provides a clear logic that ties together the activities of planning and control so that each can fulfill its proper role without overlap or duplication.

The controls necessary to monitor and realize the plans become an integral part of the process, not an unwelcome mechanism imposed from outside. The specific standards necessary to initiate the control function are developed to accompany the specific objectives. The activities of Performance Measurement, Performance Evaluation, and Performance Correction now complete the process.

We show the combined planning and control sequence in Figure 15-2. Here the connecting link provided by needs analysis is again indicated. The control activities provide continuing feedback, both to assess and regulate the work and results and to provide a basis for revising the different parts of the plan.

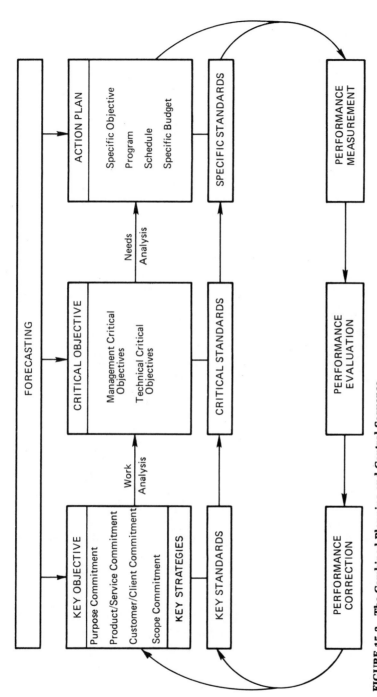

FIGURE 15-2 The Combined Planning and Control Sequence

231

HOW TO USE ACTION PLANS EFFECTIVELY

In spite of its common use in MBO programs, action planning often dies of neglect and malnutrition. One reason is that objectives are developed without reference to an overall system and hence cannot be coordinated or controlled. Another reason is failure to recognize that action planning demands constant effort and attention. You can anticipate that most problems will crop up during the early stages of your use of action planning. As you get these in hand, you will soon find that action planning becomes a way of life. Experience shows that several factors are particularly important in developing your approach. We will look at these before getting into the specifics.

Formalize the Action-Planning Process

Much good planning is done informally, but if you want to be sure of predictable results, all those involved should know what is happening, why it is happening, and what part they are to play. This calls for logical, clearly stated methods of planning that are as well known to people on your team as the plans are to members of a football team. To accomplish this, you will need to provide training and education, practice and coaching on the job and written guides for reference.

Contract Action Plans

A contract is an agreement between two or more people. This agreement is the heart of good action planning. If it is to work, your team members must agree on the need and feasibility of what is to be done, and you must also agree on the fairness and practicability of the means of measurement—the standards.

The process of contracting, or securing agreement, is directly opposite to the one-way edicts that often characterize planning. Contracting requires skill in establishing a climate of trust and confidence, in negotiating, and in securing feedback. Once a contract is agreed upon, however, you can expect people to feel a real commitment to what they—and you—want to accomplish.

Contracting action plans gives you an opportunity to get suggestions from the people who will be accountable for carrying out the plans. It enables you to contribute your own ideas as part of a joint effort, not as a set of commands.

Review Progress Regularly

Situations change, and plans must change with them. How can you stay on top of potential problems and make sure your people are taking preventive, rather than emergency, action? Your action plans will do the job if you review them with each person and carefully evaluate the progress that is made. Errors and deficiencies can be identified promptly, and good work can be recognized.

Anticipate changes when you review action plans. As the principle of the critical few suggests, most problems and changes will demand attention during the early steps of any program or project. Therefore, you will want to give new programs added attention by holding more frequent reviews or by giving them more detailed attention during regular reviews.

One indicator of effective progress reviews is how much change must be made in the plan. If at each progress review you do not modify or improve program steps, schedule times, or the standards and objectives, it is highly probable that the plan is too general, that you are not asking the searching questions you should during the review, or that you are holding the progress reviews so close together that significant changes are not evident. The conclusion: Expect to make some changes in almost every action plan at each progress review.

Make Action Plans Measurable

One of the greatest problems in action planning lies in developing quantified, measurable objectives. In an attempt to achieve this, the statement of the objective is often expanded to include time and cost requirements or other criteria by which to determine how well the objective is achieved. As an example, here is an objective submitted by the engineering manager of a large New Jersey factory: "To improve design performance by submitting subassembly proposals to manufacturing within 36 working days at a cost of less than $12,500 each."

This was accepted without question because it appeared to have all the necessary ingredients: it stated a clear result, and it was quantified. However, it soon became clear that the 36 days were unrealistic. The industrial engineer developed a PERT chart, and a more acceptable figure of 48 days was set. This at once brought into question the $12,500 cost. The plant accountant budgeted the activities listed in the PERT chart, and $16,800 was accepted.

When we look to the logic, we see the fallacy of attempting to use specific objectives as the primary measurement. Plans set the course of action we will follow; controls tell us how well we are accomplishing the plans.

Measurability is vital if we expect to use our plans as a basis for control; however, measurability does not always require quantification. Often, it is neither feasible nor necessary to pack our measurements into the objective. Properly developed, an action plan will furnish a complete array of measurable points in the form of the specific standards, the program, schedule, and specific budget.

Provide Both Long- and Short-Range Action Plans

Because action plans are time-limited, we tend to think of them as short-range. However, action plans can extend for whatever time period will be required to complete them. Since they will be reviewed periodically and updated during each planning period, they can bridge the time gap for you.

In most cases your own action plans will be longer-range than those of the individuals on your team because you are planning for the group as a whole. As an illustration, assume you are the metal products division manager of Xxex Corporation. You have engineering, manufacturing, and sales line technical functions and personnel and controller staff technical functions as shown in Figure 15-3. Your critical objective regarding engineering, is to design, operate, and maintain manufacturing facilities so that understood and accepted cost and efficiency stand-

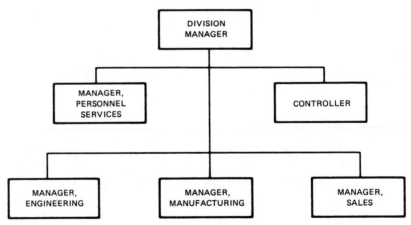

FIGURE 15-3   Organization of Division Manager, Xxex Corporation

ards are met. Energy costs have been a primary concern. The engineering manager is accountable to you for maintenance of plant facilities, including energy usage. One of his critical objectives with critical standards is as follows:

C.O.7.0. Electrical Systems Maintenance

To provide maintenance services so that electrical distribution systems in the plants are operated at lowest cost consistent with uninterrupted service.

Standards   (The objective will be met when):

1. *Maintenance Costs* are 0.004 per kilowatt.
2. *Unscheduled Downtime* is 0.001% or less.

With this example in mind, we can examine the steps involved in developing effective action plans. We will look at each part in turn, beginning with needs analysis.

CONDUCTING A NEEDS ANALYSIS

The first step in needs analysis is to determine whether current performance is satisfactory. If not, a need exists, for a need marks a lack. To identify the critical few needs that warrant action plans, you may want to find answers to questions such as these:

- What deficiencies have arisen in working toward my key and critical objectives and meeting my key and critical standards?
- What *current* problems have surfaced?
- Are there *potential* problems that might arise?
- What new opportunities have appeared that will contribute significantly to achieving my key and critical objectives or may even lead me to revise them?
- Are there any parts of the work that can be improved?

If current performance is satisfactory in all critical areas, there is still the possibility of improvement and of taking advantage of new opportunities. This also is part of the needs analysis.

Brainstorming the Possibilities

An excellent approach is to meet with the members of your group and encourage them to generate ideas. A brainstorming approach works well. As we have noted, this requires that every idea is listed, with no attempt to question or verify. When the list is complete, you can screen out the critical few by testing each idea against such decision criteria as the following:

1. Will satisfying this need contribute significantly to meeting the critical standards?
2. Can action be taken within a reasonable time?
3. Are resources available to secure the results desired?
4. Is the desired result within my area of accountability, or can I get approval if it is not?

Examples of Needs Statements

The deficiencies and opportunities you finally isolate should be written out clearly and concisely. If done well, these statements can be converted directly into specific objectives, thus saving time and ensuring that the result does truly satisfy its antecedent need.

We can return to the example of reducing energy costs in the Xxex Corporation division we cited previously. Here is the critical objective again:

C.O.7.0. Electrical System & Maintenance

To provide maintenance services so that electrical distribution systems in the plants are operated at lowest cost consistent with uninterrupted service.

Standards (The objective will be met when):

1. *Maintenance Costs* are .004 per kilowatt.
2. *Unscheduled Downtime* is .001% or less.

Needs Statement. Unscheduled downtime for minor repairs to the distribution system has increased 50% over the past 3 months—most of it concentrated in the assembly lines at the Pilkey plant. The reason is that we have installed electronic controls based on our new distributed data processing system. The crews are inexperienced, and it takes too long to find trouble spots in the system and to make the necessary repairs. There is still question whether personnel, including our professional staff, are sufficiently trained in the new electronic controls and whether we have the testing equipment we require.

One of our needs is to investigate and improve distribution system maintenance so that unscheduled downtime is reduced to meet standards. We also need to consider hiring an engineer with the specific skills we require.

The needs statement may be condensed into a few sentences. However, two points should be stressed. First, a careful analysis of the need should be made, determining where the problem occurred and why it happened. Second, the conclusions on which the needs statement are based should be included, so that others who work on the specific objective that will emerge will not have to retrace any steps.

Systematic review and analysis of the critical objectives and standards will generally result in a fairly comprehensive list of needs. Since it is probable that you cannot take action on all of them at once, you can single out the critical few and concentrate your efforts on those.

We can now proceed to develop specific objectives based on our identified needs.

HOW TO STATE SPECIFIC OBJECTIVES

Advice abounds on the writing of specific objectives. However, a few points may serve as useful reminders.

State Both the Work and the Result

Most guides to writing specific objectives emphasize the need to state results and to avoid the trap of specifying "activities." For example, "to increase sales" is held to be an activity and is to be avoided, while "$94,000 sales by June 30" is a desirable statement because it specifies a result.

In practice, this is confusing. It overlooks the logic that objectives or results are always the outcome of work. An "activity" such as "to increase sales" is really a statement of the work to be performed. Although "$94,000 sales by June 30" does state a desired result, it becomes much more meaningful if introduced by a statement of the work, so that we have "to increase sales to a level of $94,000 monthly." As we noted earlier, this calls into play a different type of thinking. Although closely related, the timing is probably best calculated separately from the objective and stated as a standard.

Below are examples of statements of both work and results. Combine them and see how they improve understanding:

Statement of Work or Activity: to hire a new electrical engineer.

Statement of Objective: to reduce electrical energy costs by 6%.

Combined Work and Results Statement: to hire a new electrical engineer so that electrical energy costs are reduced by 6%.

Statement of Work or Activity: to improve durability of plastic motor housing.

Statement of Objective: to maintain customer returns of cracked motor housings at 0.01% or lower.

Combined Statement: to improve durability of plastic motor housings so that customer returns are at 0.01% or lower.

Differentiating Between Work and Results. How can you tell what is work and what is a result? Work requires that you exert mental and physical effort. Work consumes time, materials, resources. Work is stated as a verb: "to build," " to design." Work states *what* is done; it does not tell *why.*

A result is the outcome of work. It is the condition brought about by the exertion of mental and physical effort. A result does not consume time, materials, or resources. It states why work is done and why resources are used. An objective is stated as an outcome of the work: "to design thermocouples so that contract specifications are met."

There is a simple way to ensure that you have developed a meaning-packed objective. Use an action verb such as "to increase," or "to test" to introduce the statement of the work, for example, "to increase the holding capacity of the ore bins," or "to test the space shuttle in preorbital flight." Follow whatever you have written with the phrase "so that," and add the ideas necessary to clarify the conditional clause.

Using this method, our examples now become much more meaningful. "To increase the holding capacity of the ore bins so that trucks can be fully loaded in one pass with no downtime," and "to test the space shuttle in preorbital flight so that all potential malfunctions are identified and backup systems are provided that pass all test categories."

How Measurable Should Specific Objectives Be?

The objective you prepare must be capable of measurement, or you cannot control the work effectively, and the statement will be of little value. By "measurable" we mean capable of being compared to a standard. Keep in mind that you will be developing standards after you state your objective: the objective will specify what result you want to achieve; the standard will provide evidence of progress and accomplishment. Your program, schedule, and budget will furnish further means of measurability.

While your specific objective should always be capable of measurement, it need not always be quantified. You may prefer to state in your objective the conditions you want to bring about and to quantify your standards.

For example, assume that you are a sales manager and many complaints are received from new customers about equipment breakdowns. A lawsuit is threatened. You and your team decide that the objective is "to follow up all equipment installations by timely personal calls so that complaints and returns will be held to a minimum."

You find out from the area sales supervisors within what time limits they can make the personal calls and what they are willing to accept as "minimum" complaints. You then write measurable standards as follows:

1. Personal calls are made within 2 days following each installation.
2. All complaints are answered within 90 minutes, and corrective action satisfactory to the customer is initiated within 1 working day.

To Quantify or Not to Quantify?

Your brain does not deal comfortably with developing ideas and making explicit their quantities at the same time because each function is located in a different side of your brain. Therefore, it is better first to concentrate on conceptualizing the result you want as the statement of the objective. Then, as a separate thought process, you can quantify the evidence of accomplishment as the standard. If numbers or other quantities come out easily as you state the objective, by all means use them, for you will measure results against *both* objectives and standards.

Verbs can be used to indicate the quantification that should follow in the accompanying standards. For example, the objectives "to train nurse trainees so that they will earn their certificates and qualify for nursing positions at Deaconess Hospital" leads easily to such standards as "at what cost," and "within what time limits?"

Make Specific Objectives Clear and Understandable

Since we intend them to guide people in the action they take, specific objectives should be stated in simple terms that will explain clearly what is intended to all the different people who use them.

Avoid technical terms as much as possible, or explain them briefly so they can be understood readily. Although technicalities may be unavoidable in certain situations, it is always better to use a common term a layperson would understand, in the confidence that the specialist will mentally substitute the technical term without effort. In any event, the addition of a few explanatory words will help. For example, instead of stating "steroids," something like "the steroid group of drugs" would be helpful. While an objective "to reduce the cost of flongs so that a price increase can be avoided" may be understandable to the printing superintendent, it would be much more clear to the accountant and the personnel manager who are also involved if the statement were worded: "to reduce the cost of flongs (papier-mâché molds) so that a price increase can be avoided."

Unnecessary verbiage can also cloud meaning. For example, a fund-raising professional set an objective "to develop sufficient funds to underwrite anticipated inflationary impacts." This sounded impressive to the specialist, but it became much more understandable and useful when it was changed to read: "To raise enough money so that an anticipated 11% cost-of-living increase can be covered."

Make Specific Objectives Reasonable But Challenging

There is often a tendency to set specific objectives too high, in the hope that this will lead to greater achievement. As we noted earlier, when it becomes apparent that the target is unrealistic, just the opposite occurs. There may be reasons other than the level or dimensions set. The objective may call for a 12% improvement, for example, which is perfectly reasonable. However, the people involved may not have the skills, or the time, or the ability to accomplish what has been set out. The costs may be greater than anticipated. As soon as it becomes clear that the objective is not reasonable, it is better to restudy the situation and modify it rather than to urge people to achieve what is obviously impossible.

As we also noted, the reverse of this is true. People may be more capable than the goals that are set. If rewards hinge on accomplishment, there will always be the few who will set their sights as low as you will permit so their personal payoff will be correspondingly higher. Generally, however, you will catch this the first time around and, thus alerted, will have little difficulty keeping the objectives at a more realistic level. If you do a good job of quantifying standards, this will become relatively easy.

You will have greater assurance that the objectives are both reasonable and challenging if you make it a point to schedule regular performance reviews. These are weekly, monthly, or quarterly face-to-face sessions in which you discuss current progress, identify problem areas, and probe for the reasons that deficiencies occur. This feedback not only helps you set the most meaningful levels for accomplishment, it also assures people that you are interested and concerned and that you really understand what is happening.

Specific objectives enable us to focus narrowly on the most important actions we need to take to keep our performance at the level of excellence we desire. As is true with all objectives, specific objectives should be supported by specific standards. We will discuss these next.

SPECIFIC STANDARDS

As with key and critical standards, specific standards are the starting point in the control process and, for convenience, are generally developed to accompany the specific objectives to which they relate.

Definitions and Characteristics

If you are driving through strange territory, you need a map to tell you where you are going; this is your plan. Signs posted along the highway inform you what speed limits are acceptable. The limits are your standards. Your speedometer, which monitors the miles and which points to your speed, is your means of measurement, your reporting system.

In addition to being posted, speed limits sometimes are printed on highway maps. In effect, the standard accompanies the plan. One consequence is that both you and the highway police officer will be currently informed of what constitutes acceptable speed. In the same way, specific standards accompany specific objectives so that all those working together will know what constitutes good and poor performance.

We define "specific standards" as *the criteria used to measure progress and results in achieving specific objectives.* We use the standards as a basis for comparing what we are doing with what we set out to accomplish.

We can provide two kinds of standards: those that measure the actions of people and those that measure the action of things, such as tools, machines, and systems. Measuring things is usually precise, quantifiable, and satisfying. Measuring people tends to be imprecise, elusive, and frustrating.

Skill in setting specific standards of either kind requires effort, application, and practice, just like the mastery of any other skill. As in learning bridge or golf, your first few tries will be awkward and imperfect. If you keep at it, learning from your mistakes, you will find that standards are an invaluable aid when you want to delegate. They are the backbone of performance appraisal. Used carefully, they are a potent means of motivating high effort. And controls without performance standards would be no better than a highway system without speed limits.

Uses of Specific Standards

People suspect specific standards because they are seen as means of coercion and discipline. In fact, however, they have many uses. Specific standards are most effective as measures of progress. They signal problems before they become crises. With sound standards, people know exactly where they stand at all times and do not need to devise strategies for protection.

Specific Standards Generate Information. Although we often do not realize it, the kind of information we get is determined by formal or informal standards. The more knowingly we can set the standards, the more appropriate and explicit the information will be. It is uneconomical and ineffective to attempt to keep people informed about all aspects of the work that is being done. However, it is equally futile simply to provide information about results, when we can identify the points where significant changes in work take place—and generate information at these control points.

Specific Standards Facilitate Control. You set zones of variance within which accountable individuals can control their own work. If people have understood and accepted standards, it is relatively easy for them to agree also on what constitutes acceptable limits of tolerance, above and below the standard. For example, if a standard calls for "2300 sales conversions per week," the zone of variance may be ± 10%, so you become concerned only when the records show over 2560 or under 2070. The important need, of course, is to observe the limits strictly, or soon the variance will become the standard.

Specific Standards Help Improve Performance. You can get the best from standards if you look upon them as a means of helping people to improve their own performance. If they are set properly, the information provided in response to standards will alert your people to problems and deviations, often before you know about them yourself.

Sound standards warn you when events occur that endanger accomplishment of your objectives. This helps you to concentrate time and effort at those points where the payoff in improved performance is most certain.

Confusing Standards with Plans

Although specific standards most often accompany specific objectives, it is important to recognize the differences between standards and the planning activities. There is a tendency to confuse program steps with specific standards because the program steps can also be used to measure progress toward the result. The two can be differentiated, however, by keeping in mind that standards provide evidence of accomplishment of the work involved, while a program step is the work step leading to the specific objective. For example, "Install word processing equipment" is a program step, while "Total direct costs are no more than $620,000" is a specific standard.

Standards are not plans; they are part of the control process. Specific standards, not specific objectives, are the best basis for measuring performance. For example, "To reduce overtime so that direct costs are kept within budget" is a specific objective. Performance can be appraised much more effectively if this is supported by a standard such as "Overtime payments are no more than $12,000—1st quarter, $16,700—2nd quarter, $18,750—3rd quarter, and $11,670—4th quarter."

How to Make Specific Standards Measurable

Good specific standards should be measurable. Only in this way can we be sure they will be within the capacity of the person being measured. Incorporating measures of quantity and quality helps make standards realistic but also ensures that they will require some "reach." We can maintain this measurability by revising and updating standards so they reflect current conditions.

Measuring anything requires some kind of quantification. You can measure 1 mile or 2 tons but not "a long distance" or "a heavy weight." Specific standards take on the major burden of measurability, for they always relate directly to the objectives that are to be measured. If a fully measurable standard cannot be developed, you can use a process standard. This is based on whether a given process or chain of actions is completed. For example, if you complete your position charter, this is a tangible, observable fact.

THE VITAL FACTORS

In developing measurable specific standards, you will want to determine the most important measurement factors that will lead to success or failure. For example, if your objective is to reduce costs by 10% so that prices can be maintained at present levels, the most important factors might be direct labor, materials charges, and productivity per hour. You know that if you can get direct labor, materials charges, and productivity per hour to the proper levels, you are almost sure to reduce costs by 10%; if not, nothing you do will enable you to achieve your objective.

For each specific objective, you will want to select the few factors that will account for the larger part of the results. Use these as the basis for your standards. For example, if you want to determine how well salespeople are doing, select vital factors such as number of sales presentations or number of orders booked. If you want to determine how well people are being trained, consider factors such as increased productivity or improved quality. The criterion for selection of vital factors is that if they are met, the desired level of performance will be achieved while if they are not met, failure will inevitably follow.

Typical Vital Factors

1. *Quantity:* number of units produced or sold; volume by straight or trend line (20 per hour or an additional 20 with each 100 units)

2. *Quality:* number of rejects or claims; accuracy; completeness; comparative quality ratings with other products or services; number of breakdowns; on-time deliveries; long, short cycle
3. *Costs:* direct, allocated, standard, estimated, per unit, and total
4. *Profitability:* return on sales or investment; gross, net profit; related to fixed assets, net worth, and total capital employed
5. *Materials Utilization:* efficiency of use; percent of damage; amount of waste or recovery; dependability of sources; cost of materials handling; storage
6. *Utilization of Human Resources:* number of quits, firings; amount of absence, lateness; number of grievances or formal complaints; percent of promotions from within; number in training; productivity per person
7. *Facilities Utilization:* cost of idle facilities; trend of machine hour rates; cost per facility hour; cost of maintenance; productivity of machines; security cost
8. *Social Responsibility:* hiring of minorities and women; minorities and women in management positions; corporate giving; employee morale; costs of social programs; number of people involved in programs; compliance with government standards
9. *Management Performance:* effectiveness of planning; organizational productivity; leadership competence; efficiency of controls

What Do the Vital Factors Measure?

The surest way to concentrate attention on something is to use it as a basis for measurement. Jogging a mile might be leisurely and pleasant until we set a standard of 6 minutes and try to beat it. If you measure your word processing system on the speed and accuracy with which it processes data, it will be set up to operate differently than if your vital factors are flexibility and convenience. Similarly, if you want concern for profitability to be dominant, you avoid setting standards that measure only gross sales volume.

For these reasons, you will want to anticipate how your choice of vital factors will influence the plans you develop and vice versa. This can be extremely difficult, for it seems to require a degree of clairvoyance. However, I have found that the easiest way to do this is to carry the control process to the next step and to identify the kinds of information that will be reported to you in response to the standards set. For example, if the reports you receive single out sales volume for attention and not profit contribution, you will want to question whether you selected the proper vital factor and not look with suspicion on your reporting system.

Using Specific Standards for Staff Performance

Managers of staff functions such as finance, accounting, human resources, or administration use two types of standards. In some cases their concern is to improve the performance of their own departments; specific standards then relate to their own accountability. Much of the time, however, staff managers provide advice and service in their specialties to other managers and components.

Frequently, there is an attempt to differentiate between standards for improving staff department performance and those for measuring the value or effectiveness of the advice and service provided. In most cases, however, work done for the organization as a whole will also apply to the staff department, and similar standards will apply to both.

For example, the manager of human resources in a Houston oil supply company developed two specific objectives. One was "to develop a program for nondiscrimination in hiring and for placing personnel so that government requirements will be met." The second read "to implement the company's nondiscrimination program in the human resources department." The standards for both were the governmental requirements for compliance.

Securing Understanding and Acceptance of Specific Standards

As with other aspects of management, the purpose of standards is to help other people to perform better. We know that motivation is the engine that drives improvement. Securing understanding and acceptance is at the heart of motivation and is vital in motivating people to *want* to use standards and to work hard to meet them.

This can be accomplished in several ways. One is to ask the people accountable to develop their own standards. Encourage them to talk with others, consult staff specialists, and go on the outside to secure expert help if necessary. Then, independently, develop what you believe to be a good set of standards. Discuss these with the accountable person and negotiate the final statement. Contracting is the key. This should be a mutual discussion, not a meeting in which you communicate your decision. You will probably find it easy to agree on most of the vital factors and standards, but on those few which need to be reconciled, the final agreement most often will represent a compromise.

We know where we want to go and we have a means of determining how well we are progressing. In the next chapter, we look to the more mechanical steps of developing the programs, schedules, and budgets that will set us on our course and keep us there.

KEY POINTS

1. *Deficiencies in Short-Term Plans.* Common problems in short-term planning are that operating plans often cover repetitive problems or needs, are too detailed or too general, or are isolated from the overall plan.

2. *The Action Plan.* This is a plan that is intended to be completed within a definite time period. An action plan prompts specific action by individuals in a critical few matters. It can either be short- or long-term (several days or several years). Action plans provide a basis for effective controls; they help you to delegate and to develop good working relationships.

3. *Logical Decision Making and Action Planning.* The same logic design holds for decision making and planning. Essential steps in the action planning process are (1) conduct a needs analysis, (2) identify the possible objectives that will satisfy the need, (3) select the best objective, and (4) determine the program, schedule, and specific budget necessary to achieve the specific objective.

4. *Using Action Plans Effectively.* Objectives are developed with reference to the overall system so that coordination and control are facilitated. Formalization of the action-planning process ensures clear and complete communication. Agreement on need, feasibility, and standards is central to effective action planning; contracting is a means of securing this agreement. Action plans are reviewed and revised with changing conditions. Measurability is vital to effective implementation of action plans; however, while plans should be the basis for controls, the objective should remain separate from and unencumbered by measurements.

5. *Provide Both Long- and Short-Term Action Plans.* To avoid artificial distinctions between long- and short-range planning, you may prepare action plans that extend for whatever time period is required for their accomplishment. In general, a manager's action plans tend to extend over a longer range than those of his or her team members because the manager's responsibilities are broader.

6. *Conducting a Needs Analysis.* To analyze needs, you identify deficiencies, current problems, potential problems, and new opportunities. To screen out the critical few, assess whether satisfying the need in question will contribute significantly to the key objective, whether action can be taken within a reasonable time, whether necessary resources are available, and

whether the desired result is within your area of accountability. Finally, the needs statements you derive should be clear and concise and should be readily convertible into specific objectives.

7. *Stating Specific Objectives.* Specific objectives should state both the work and the results. Use of action verbs ensures a meaning-packed objective. The objective should be measurable so that specific standards can be readily developed—the program, schedule, and budget provide further measurability.

Specific objectives should be clear and understandable. Avoid technical terms and unnecessary verbiage. Specific objectives should be reasonable but challenging; when they are either too high or too low, the people who must accomplish them become frustrated and lose motivation. Regular performance reviews help maintain reasonable expectations.

8. *Specific Standards.* These are the criteria used to measure progress and results in achieving specific objectives. Specific standards allow us to compare what is actually being done with what we set out to accomplish.

9. *Uses of Specific Standards.* Standards are most effective as a measure of progress. Specific standards generate information, facilitate control with the least amount of effort, and help improve performance. Sound standards alert you to problems before they become crises. Standards are not plans; they are part of the control process. Measures of quality and quantity are incorporated into specific standards.

10. *The Vital Factors.* These are the most important measurement factors that will lead to success or failure. For each specific objective, you select the few factors that account for the larger part of results.

11. *Specific Standards and Staff Performance.* Usually similar standards apply to both the staff department and the work done for the organization as a whole.

QUOTES FROM CHAPTER 15

Significant quotations from this chapter that you will want to consider and discuss in greater detail:

- The heart of the planning process is the work done by individual managers to plan the day-to-day actions of their own groups.

- Action plans ensure that each individual can have challenging tasks, the authority necessary to make most decisions, and a means of self-control.

- Action plans can help you make well-rounded performance appraisals and to counsel and coach your people.

- Every plan has imbedded in it a multitude of decisions.

- Contracting action plans gives you an opportunity to get suggestions from the people who will carry out the plan.

- Measurability does not always require quantification.

- A result is the outcome of work.

- People may be more capable than the goals that are set for them.

- Specific standards signal problems before they become crises.

- You can get the best from standards if you look upon them as a means of helping people to improve their own performance.

- Plans are useful to the extent that their articulation binds them to other plans.

- You can standardize repetitive programs and convert them into procedures.

- Measuring things is usually precise, quantifiable, and satisfying. Measuring people tends to be imprecise, elusive, and frustrating.

ACTION PLANNING: PROGRAMS, SCHEDULES, BUDGETS

It is not enough to be busy; so are the ants. The question is: what are we busy about?
HENRY DAVID THOREAU

THE CHAPTER IN BRIEF   Developing management programs, schedules, and specific budgets is a detailed and methodical aspect of management planning; however, since these plans generate action and guide the use of resources, they are very important. Management programs are a means of delegation as well as a detailing of work steps. They are developed by first establishing the priority and sequence of the primary steps, then filling in the details. Schedules involve estimating the time required. Specific budgets are a means of costing out the program and schedule and also of valuing the benefits to be received.

MANAGEMENT PROGRAMMING

The setting of objectives points us in the direction we want to go, but equally important is knowing what steps to take, how much time will be required, what it will cost, and whether the value of the results is worth the cost of achieving them. This calls for developing programs, schedules, and specific budgets. Although these are closely related, we'll look at each separately.

Value of Programming

Programming is a useful tool which many managers overlook. Since it applies to the daily work we do to accomplish objectives, the subject matter of programs is very familiar. As is true of other aspects of management, instead of proceeding spontaneously and by habit, we can usually get better results by thinking through in advance what work must be done and establishing a logical pattern for programming.

Definition and Characteristics of Programming

"Programming" is the work a manager does to establish the sequence and priority of steps to be followed in reaching an objective. Every

251

result is accomplished by the performance of work; an objective can be no better than the program steps carried out to accomplish it.

Programming has special value in the planning process because it helps us to make the best use of resources and it gives us an opportunity to consider alternatives before taking action. Programming enables us to lay out various work step sequences and to assess each deliberately before making a choice. We can determine the time required and the cost for each option and compare these to the value of the objective. Both PERT and zero-based budgeting formalize this characteristic of programming; however, we can use it most simply and directly in the process of action planning.

We usually fail to recognize that there is a difference between management and technical programs. Confusion also arises between programs and the other parts of the planning process. We will first try to sort these out.

Differentiating Between Management and Technical Programs. A management program is intended to guide the efforts of all the different people involved in working toward an objective. It helps you to get results through other people. Therefore, it is constructed so that accountability can be identified easily, so that timing and cost are related to the work done, and so that the separate steps can be delegated.

Technical programs apply to work that yields results directly and not through other people. Computer programs, for example, are technical programs. PERT is also built on technical programming. Although PERT is one of the few rigorously logical processes in conventional planning, it does not satisfy our criteria for management programs. For one thing, program steps, which are called "activities," usually do not identify accountability. PERT objectives, which are called "events," can be valued only indirectly through PERT/cost.

Differentiating Between Programs and Procedures. Procedure steps may be confused with programs. However, while procedures are siblings of programs, there are distinct differences. Procedures are arrived at by study of the best way to perform a task. Procedure steps are a means of standardizing work so it is done in the same way wherever it is performed. For example, if there is a procedure for terminating employees, everybody who has this task will do it in the same way. This not only capitalizes on experience, it ensures that all legal and policy requirements are satisfied. On the other hand, if employees are terminated without the guidance of procedures, there will be as many ways of accomplishing the task as there are people performing it.

When a program is carried out repeatedly in exactly the same way, it may become a procedure. You can standardize the way the work is done by studying the program steps, putting them in logical sequence, and issuing them as a procedure to all who must perform the work.

Differentiating Between Programs and Standards. We sometimes find it difficult to tell the difference between program steps and standards. The program step specifies the work to be done, that is, what mental and physical effort will be expended. A standard provides evidence that the work has been carried out as intended. For example, "Prepare specifications to include capacity and quality requirements," is a program step. The application standard is "Capacity is 50 tons and stress and quality are both ± 1.5%."

Differentiating Between Programs and Other Planning Activities. We may confuse programs with forecast and objectives. Consider that forecasting is an estimate; it does not obligate us to do anything. An objective is an expected end result. While it anticipates resources, it does not carry a commitment to use specific amounts of money, time, or materials.

A program requires direct commitment of resources; it is the channel for directing the flow of materials, tools and facilities, money and human effort. For example, if your objective is to hire a new employee, you must perform the work steps of determining the qualifications of the person you need, recruiting candidates for the position, selecting the best candidate, and placing and orienting the person to the job. Only when you know what work must be done can you determine what resources will be needed.

How to Develop Management Programs

Management programming helps us to minimize trial and error by narrowing down all the things we *might* do to the critical few we *must* do if we want to be certain of reaching our objective. We follow five steps to develop programs. First, we make sure we know what the objective and standards are, then we think through the work steps necessary to reach it. We check the sequence and determine the priorities. We decide who will be accountable for each step. And, throughout, we seek the involvement and participation of those who will do the work so it truly becomes a team effort.

Agree on Objectives and Standards. There is usually a time lag between determining your specific objectives and developing the programs for them. In this interval, new conditions may be identified. Your best safeguard is to review the specific standards and be sure you have understanding and agreement before you move on.

This initial agreement gives you a strong basis for delegation. If everybody has clearly in mind the results you want to secure, you can more easily assign part or all of the programming and scheduling tasks to others. You may have individuals in mind, or you may organize one or more task forces. If each is fully centered on the same objectives and standards, coordination is automatic instead of a laborious task you must perform personally.

Identify the Primary Steps. Program steps may vary from very large to very small. A program step in the reorganization of an international research institution was worldwide in scope: "Organize four international geographic divisions." A popular cookbook shows a program step in baking a chocolate cake as: "Add a pinch of salt." The magnitude of program steps depends upon the scope of the objective.

When you are ready to think through how the objective is to be achieved, you can anticipate that the more you know about the problem or situation, the more likely you are to develop highly detailed work steps. This will quickly get you into trouble; for in your attempt to sort out each separate small step, you will tend to lose sight of the really important things that must be done.

Which Steps Are Most Important? Your first concern is to identify the primary steps that must be completed to achieve the objective. One way is to ask those who will be doing the work; usually they are most knowledgeable. If the work is routine or repetitive, probably you can determine the primary steps readily. Keep in mind the ever-useful principle of the critical few: a relatively few steps will account for the greater part of your success in achieving the objective. If you want to test the importance of a step, ask yourself: "If I fail to complete this step, will I also fail to achieve the objective?"

Use Work Analysis. A good way to home in on these critical steps is to do a work analysis. Review the specific objective and specific standards. Then ask yourself: "What are the largest categories of work that must be performed to achieve the objective and satisfy the standards?" Write these down. Check them with as many people as you can find who will be working with you on the program. When you have agreement, you will have your road map to success in securing the results you want.

As an example, suppose you are a plant manager with a quality problem. Your specific objective is "to reduce rejects so that goods shipped to customers meet all quality standards." You think of the most important categories of work that must be performed to achieve the objective. They are:

Analysis

Identification

Correction

Training

These become the titles for four primary program steps. You might state the work as follows:

Analysis. Collect samplings of rejects from one complete cycle, and determine nature and causes of failure.

Identification. Specify the critical few causes, and confirm with supervisors.

Correction. Determine corrective measures, and secure agreement of engineering and supervision.

Training. Develop training procedures, and train all operators.

Determine Sequence and Priority. Sequence and priority of work steps are closely related: usually the most important things get done first. However, the flow of work may place high priority items far down the sequence. For example, agreeing on the salary to be paid is a vital step, but this could be one of the last program steps if our objective is to hire a systems engineer so that we can fill a vacant position.

Try Brainstorming. If you are dealing with a new situation, you may find it helpful to brainstorm the work steps first. As we discussed earlier, you review the objective and standards, then call upon members of the group to suggest any steps that come to mind. You list these, usually on a blackboard or chart, without comment or analysis. When the list is complete, the group joins in sorting out the primary steps and setting the priority and sequence for them.

Identify Detail Steps. Frequently you will delegate the primary steps to others, who will then convert them into their own specific objectives and repeat the steps we have just described. For example, suppose you are the plant manager with the specific objective that we identified earlier, "to reduce rejects so that goods shipped to customers meet all quality standards."

The first primary step is "Analysis. Collect sampling of rejects from one complete cycle, and determine nature and causes of failure." You know you will delegate this primary step to the chief inspector, who will make it his or her specific objective and who will work out the detail steps with day and shift inspectors.

At times, however, you will want to provide more guidance in your own action plan by specifying detail steps as well as primary steps. Here again you will probably get most help from those who will do the work.

As a rule of thumb, if you delegate a program step to one person who will be accountable for carrying it out, you can leave it to that individual to work out the detail steps. However, if the same detail steps must be carried out in the same manner by more than one individual, work out the detail steps and include them in your own action plan.

To return to the example we cited earlier, one program step was: "Analysis. Collect sampling of rejects from one complete cycle, and determine nature and causes of failures." There are nine inspectors, and you want all of them to carry out this primary step in the same way. You might break down the primary step into these detail steps:

1. *Analysis.* Collect sampling of rejects from one complete cycle.
2. *Document Failures.* Submit to Arlens Mass Laboratories to specify precise nature of failures.
3. *Determine Causes.* Inspect vehicle lines, interview operators, check with primary source.

Establish Accountability. If your people are trained in planning, you can probably delegate much or all of the task of developing the primary program steps. You can identify the person who will be accountable for each program step you delegate by placing the person's initials in the "Accountability" column on the form. If there are no initials, you, of course, remain accountable for those steps. Figure 16-1 gives an example.

Keep in mind that you are accountable for the entire action plan. You cannot rid yourself of this obligation by delegation. You may want to check some or all of the steps that are completed. If so, make the appropriate notation at the end of the program step. You can use something like: "Check with ABC" or "ABC/OK."

ACTION PLAN			
S.O. TITLE: Hire Electrical Engineer		**Acct:** P.B.	

S.O.:   To hire an electrical engineer so that Division energy usage can be maintained at standard.

Standards (the objective will be accomplished when):

    a. Need Analysis shows the work cannot be done by existing personnel.

    b. Qualifications   The person selected has demonstrated ability to work in a staff relationship and meets corporate technical specifications.

    c. Timing The position is filled by May 1.

    d. Cost The budget is no more than $6200.

	PROGRAM STEPS	ACCT.	SCHEDULE	BUDGET
1.	Conduct a work analysis	L.M.	2/1-2/12	$ 900
2.	Prepare job qualifications	L.M.	3/1-3/4	270
3.	Advertise internally and externally	F.O.B.	3/6-3/14	2100
4.	Solicit prospects at the Engineers' Convention	J.L.M.	3/10	1800
5.	Interview candidates	F.O.B.	3/12-3/27	825
6.	Select best candidate. Check with L.M.	P.B.	3/30	200
7.	Orient engineer to new job	R.J.K.	4/12	90
				$6185

FIGURE 16-1   Program Steps for Action Plan

How to Delegate Program Steps

Your program provides an excellent vehicle for delegation. It serves as a framework for assigning responsibility and authority to others and for controlling the results you want.

To understand the logic of delegation through programs, keep in mind that you can delegate to others the obligation both to do specified work and to secure specified results. The program steps identify the work to be done. But just knowing what work is to be done may not be enough for effective delegation. If you want to hold people accountable, it is well to agree upon both the work to be done and the results to be achieved.

As a simple illustration, suppose you are Paul Burnside, the engineering manager of the metal products division, Xxex Corporation, as shown in Figure 15-3. You develop an action plan to hire a new electrical engineer. The action plan you develop is shown in Figure 16-1.

You will delegate six of the seven steps. The work required in most steps is standardized and is covered by procedures, so further detail will not be required in the action plan.

The program contains one novel step: "Solicit prospects at the engineers' convention." This has never been done before, and you want to delegate it to Jack Marshall. To save time and ensure consistency, you ask J.L.M. to prepare an action plan, secure the understanding and agreement of Kay Stewart, the advertising supervisor, and get your approval. Jack Marshall brings you the action plan shown in Figure 16-2.

Everything needed is contained on one sheet of paper. Not only is the work clearly defined, but accountability is pinpointed and the work

ACTION PLAN				
S.O. TITLE: Recruit Engineer			**Acct:** J.L.M.	

To recruit for one Electrical Engineer at the Engineers' Convention so that at least three highly qualified, screened candidates are available for final interview.
 	
Standards:
    a. Evaluation Candidates are evaluated "Very Good" by F.O.B.
    b. Timing The candidates are available for final interview by 3/20 or before.
    c. Cost Total is no more than $1800.				

PROGRAM STEPS		**ACCT.**	**SCHEDULE**	**BUDGET**
1.	Prepare advertisement	K.S.	2/12-2/14	$ 120
2.	Insert advertisement in Engineering Newsletter	K.S.	2/20	450
3.	Write and print invitation	K.S.	2/13-2/26	220
4.	Post invitation on Convention bulletin board	J.L.M.	3/9	—
5.	Deliver invitation to room of each registered participant	J.L.M.	3/9	140
6.	Staff hospitality room at hotel	J.L.M.	3/9-3/11	630
7.	Confirm interview dates with candidates	J.L.M.	3/10-3/11	90
8.	Send confirmed list to F.O.B.	J.L.M.	3/12	—
				$1650

FIGURE 16-2   Delegated Program Steps

can be monitored with minimum intervention by the accountable manager. Brief weekly reports, in person or in writing, would keep everybody adequately informed.

MANAGEMENT SCHEDULING

People who use time poorly are most prone to complain there is too little of it. While time is easily measured, it is difficult to control. Scheduling is one means of putting a harness on time.

Definition and Characteristics

We define a "management schedule" as *the time sequence necessary to carry out the action steps in a management program*. We often look upon planning as a mechanical process in which we cut out a chunk of time and assign it to the work to be done; however, the management of time is the key to our personal effectiveness and, through us, to the effectiveness of those we manage.

Scheduling is the most easily quantifiable of the planning activities. It is measured everywhere in standard units. Because it is quantifiable, time is easily converted into money, for many costs are based on the value of the time required to perform work.

The people who will do the work are best qualified to determine the time required; if they will also be accountable for carrying out the program steps involved, their participation will ensure both realism and commitment.

How to Estimate the Time Required

Estimating how much time it will require to complete each program step appears clear and straightforward. However, several considerations will influence the accuracy and usefulness of your schedule.

Estimate Time, Not Dates. Management schedules are usually expressed as specific calendar dates, but in estimating the time required to complete each program step, it is best to consider only the number of hours or days. This treatment facilitates the development of budgets and makes it much easier to determine the people required to do the work. At the appropriate point, these time estimates can be converted into calendar dates.

Single and multiple time estimates are used in management scheduling. Each has advantages and disadvantages.

Single Estimates. In calculating the time required to carry out program steps, it is much easier and more practical to work with single schedule times, rather than with ranges. For example, if we're starting a new project, we want to know that it will require 45 days to organize and staff the project, rather than somewhere between 40 and 90 days. We are willing to accept some average in the estimate if it means we can depend on the number.

Making single estimates is faster and simpler than making multiple estimates. Single estimates are most appropriate when the work is clearly defined, when similar work has been done before, and when you have facts on the time required. Suppose, for example, a program step calls for ordering and installing a new composer. We have ordered and successfully installed three in the past year, all in 45 days. The supplier checks availability and delivery and again quotes 45 days. A schedule time of 45 days is evident.

Single estimates best originate with the people who will do the work. These individuals know most about the tasks. They should be asked for the time required under normal circumstances—with the usual number of problems and delays. One caution: Contrary to what you would expect, single estimates tend to be underestimated rather than overestimated.

Separate estimates should be secured of start and complete times. Calculate these in days or hours, not as calendar dates. You will find that if you follow the calendar, the person doing the estimating will tend to assume there is enough latitude in the next set of dates to compensate for any errors. Determining the number of days required for each individual step helps to avoid this. Another useful method is to determine the schedule times out of sequence; that is, estimate the first, fourth, and seventh steps, then come back and fill in the others, also out of sequence. This will ensure that each work cycle is discrete, with clear start and complete points.

The estimate becomes a commitment only after it is understood and agreed to by the person who will do the work. If staff groups have an important bearing on meeting the schedule, their agreement is also necessary.

Multiple Estimates. When the program step is new and people have little experience with it, you may arrive at a more realistic schedule by securing several estimates from knowledgeable individuals. You can then either calculate an average or agree upon some acceptable point between the extremes. Alternatively, you may use the minimax approach which is described later.

Multiple estimates are most effective when clearly validated single estimates are not available; they help you to arrive at a reasonable time commitment which will be better understood and agreed to than a single estimate. Multiple estimates are also indicated when you anticipate many problems and a high degree of uncertainty. They are particularly effective when there is emotional resistance by those who will have a part in meeting the schedule. The opportunity to consider different time alternatives and to consciously select the best one will help overcome feelings of coercion and unfairness.

The Minimax Technique. When there is a great deal of uncertainty about the time required, you may want to use the minimax method, which is used in making PERT time estimates. People most familiar with the work are asked to make three sets of estimates.

First an *optimistic* time is estimated. This is the shortest time in which the work step can be completed if everything goes right. We know this is unrealistic and that it will seldom be achieved; however, it gives up a top limit. The second estimate is the *pessimistic* time, which is what it would take if Murphy's law prevailed and everything that could go wrong did go wrong. While also unrealistic, it provides a bottom limit. People involved usually concur that the limits are improbable and will agree to a point in between, the *most likely* time. This is the time required under normal conditions.

In securing the estimates, be sure all three represent the same basic conditions; for example, don't assume more money or people will be available for the optimistic time and less for the pessimistic. The estimates will probably be more realistic if you set the optimistic time first, then the pessimistic. In all cases, those who will do the work and the managers accountable should be in agreement on the three estimates.

The three estimates may turn out to be balanced or unbalanced, for example:

	Optimistic	Most Likely	Pessimistic
Balanced:	4	6	8
Unbalanced:	1	7	7

We can see there is a higher degree of uncertainty in the second case than in the first. Our need now is to arrive at a single figure that will represent at least a 50% probability of accomplishment. We can do this by determining the statistical equivalent of an "average" or "mean," which is called the expected time (ET).

The expected time is calculated as the mean time of a beta distribution, using this formula:

$$ET = \frac{a + 4m + b}{6}$$

In the formula, "a" is the optimistic time; "m" the most likely time, and "b" is the pessimistic time. The expected time can be determined easily on a hand calculator.

SPECIFIC BUDGETING

As we have noted, profitability lies in providing products and services to satisfy the needs of people in such a manner that the value of what is produced is greater than the costs of producing it. The criterion of profitability applies to all aspects of planning, but in the activity of budgeting, we reduce it to numbers so we can use it as a convenient measuring stick.

Definition and Characteristics

We define "specific budgeting" as *the allocation of resources necessary to carry out an action plan.*

There are many different ways to allocate resources. Capital budgeting, expense budgeting, program budgeting, responsibility budgeting are commonplace. One of the primary shortcomings in conventional budgeting has been the tendency to sort out the money that would become available and to parcel it out to cover a list of categories. Often a primary determinant of how large a budget you get for next year is how much you spent last year. Approaches such as responsibility budgeting and zero-based budgeting have been attempts to relate money spent directly to the work done, so that the expenditures can be shown to have highest probability of generating profits. These budgeting approaches have succeeded to a degree and mark the desirable direction for development of budgeting in the future.

A specific budget is different from conventional budgets, although it becomes a valuable input to them. A specific budget is the calculation of the cost of implementing a given action plan. Carried to its logical conclusion, a specific budget enables us to determine the value of the result which we expect to get from the action plan and whether, in terms of its cost, it is worth doing.

Specific budgets are particularly valuable in pricing out alternative courses of action, that is, the costs of carrying out optional programs and schedules. Specific budgets also can help determine the priority assigned to programs: the greater the potential impact on profitability, the higher the priority will be.

Most budgets are developed within the framework of accounting conventions and thus become approximations of the actual costs, not the costs themselves. Specific budgets, on the other hand, are always related to the actual work that is to be done—the program steps—and hence are realistic and useful guides to action.

Determining the Cost of Program Steps

When we prepare a specific budget, we are largely concerned with determining the costs of the work done in the program steps and the time of people covered by the schedule. Direct costs, the cost of time, and indirect costs are involved.

Direct Costs. These are the costs of carrying out each program step within the schedule limits provided. They include the costs of materials, tools, equipment, and facilities. Direct costs may be incurred by any person or group that works to carry out program steps. This includes the costs of steps which you have delegated but for which you remain accountable.

Cost of Time. The cost of the hours of work required to carry out each program step is calculated separately. This includes both management and technical work. These figures may have to be estimated in part, especially for the time devoted by managers to individual program steps.

Indirect Costs. These are costs that do not enter directly into carrying out program steps but which must be incurred if the work steps are to be performed. These costs may vary from the costs of repair and maintenance for machines and equipment used to the expenses associated with training people.

Convert into Monetary Units. Although time and materials are the ingredients that go into the action plan, all of these are converted into monetary terms. On occasion there may be an attempt to show time only in terms of hours incurred, but this is inadequate.

Annualize Continuing Costs. Some costs continue beyond the life span of the action plan or are part of a continuing investment, such as a computer system or a new facility. To compare costs and value, you will want to calculate the value of what is accomplished and the cost of accomplishing it over the same time period. In the case of continuing costs, the simplest way is to convert them to an annualized basis.

Estimating the Value of the Expected Results

You can best judge the desirability of an action plan if you have a clear idea of its value. This will not only help you establish priorities, it will also enable you to determine the contribution to profitability of each action plan.

Difficulties. This task is not always straightforward or easy to perform. For example, if you conduct a management training program for supervisors, how do you calculate the value? If you are a hospital administrator and want to install a new oxygen system, how do you calculate the value of the potential lives saved or of the recovery time shortened?

Calculating the value of an objective always must be an estimate, for you can never know before the fact exactly what the outcome will be and what it is worth. However, as is true of forecasting, sales estimates, and weather predictions, it is better to estimate and establish guidelines for future action than to proceed blindly.

When Cost Is Not Decisive. In some cases, specific results must be achieved no matter what the cost. Legal requirements, company policy obligations, procedural demands must be carried out. Despite the difficulties, it is often worthwhile to know what the value is and how much of a cost burden you are carrying.

What Type of Benefits? You may derive direct, indirect, and intangible benefits from carrying out an action plan. You will want to consider each of these in estimating the value of the expected results from the plan.

Direct Benefits. You may derive direct benefits from achieving the specific objective, either in the form of an increase in revenue or in the form of a reduction in costs. An increase in sales is obvious, but also there is a direct value in reducing current costs, if the short-range reduction does not carry a long-range penalty. For example, you may eliminate a staff department at immediate savings, but with what long-term consequences? You can forego the recruiting of university graduates for the management succession program this year, but at what added costs 2 years from now?

Indirect Benefits. Accomplishment of a specific objective often leads to indirect benefits. The product or service may become more valuable to the user. A new package design that includes a pouring spout or a folding chair that can also become a step stool are cases in point.

Improvement of management work usually leads to indirect benefits. Better delegation leads to increased efficiency; improved motivation reduces turnover and helps both to increase productivity and to reduce selection and training expenses.

Intangible Benefits. Indirect benefits are sometimes so intangible it is difficult to assign a monetary value to them. How can we prove that improved motivation results in improved productivity? If we install an employee stock-option plan, what productivity improvement can we credit to it?

While indirect benefits are difficult to calculate, it is always helpful to make a reasonable estimate of their value; if nothing else, we can always ask, "How much do I stand to lose by *not* making this improvement?"

Using Standards to Value Objectives. Since standards provide evidence of accomplishment of objectives and since they are quantified, they can be of great help in determining the value of your specific objective. For example, suppose that the objective is as follows: "Provide training so that department supervisors control costs effectively" and that we set the following standards:

1. 80% of supervisors score 80% or higher on training criteria.
2. From the second quarter following training on, budget overruns are no more than 1½%.
3. Planned cost savings are 10% of direct costs.

These standards can be converted directly into dollar amounts that give a clear indication of the value of the objective.

Criteria for Estimating the Value of Benefits. When calculating the value of your specific objective, you will want to have several criteria in mind. First, calculate the value of direct benefits in terms of monetary savings or gains in the form of increased revenue or reduced costs. Second, calculate the value of indirect benefits in terms of improvements which have an identifiable value in the form of increased revenue or reduced costs. If the indirect benefit is intangible, get agreement from at least two knowledgeable people of its probable value. Third, always state your assumptions, do not merely state a monetary value. For example, if the intangible benefit is salary savings, state what salaries; if it is improved morale, make clear whose morale is affected. If each person who makes valuations follows the same procedure, meaningful and comparable numbers can be developed.

Specific Budgeting Considerations

Specific budgeting provides data that is valuable when you prepare your regular business or operating budget. Two points are important if you wish to get the best returns from this technique.

Maintain Integrity of the Specific Budget. There is often a tendency to use the specific budget as a means of reducing costs by changing the budget figures, but not the actions that lead to them. Unless there has been a miscalculation, each time a budgeted amount is reduced, a corresponding change should be made in the work it represents. For example, if the cost of the management time required is $12,000 and you want it to be no more than $9600, this cannot be achieved simply by changing numbers. You will need to delegate more effectively, develop a better work flow, figure out how to institute self-controls, or determine a more efficient way that requires less management.

Once set and agreed to, budget overruns and underruns should be equally suspect. If these are outside the zone of normal variance, prompt investigation and corrective action are indicated.

Establish Management Accountability

At times the task of preparing specific budgets is turned over to the accounting or budgeting department or controller. This is a mistake. These specialists do not have firsthand knowledge of your operations. They cannot determine the specifics of the various assumptions you must make and the costs you derive from them. Use accounting and other specialists to provide technical detail, to inform you of approved budgetary procedures, to secure data, and to check your work. But, to be accountable, you must make the final decisions concerning the budgets you submit to your superior for approval.

There is one exception. In some cases, managers are held accountable for allocated costs over which they have little or no control. For example, office space may be costed at $1.15 per square foot. If these costs change, the manager can hardly be held to account. With this clear understanding, however, these costs should be included in the specific budget so that total costs can be estimated accurately.

From the material we have covered, we can establish a number of guidelines that will be helpful in improving the planning effort. We will discuss these in the final chapter.

KEY POINTS

1. *Achieving Objectives.* Specific objectives may result in wasted time and money if we do not give careful consideration to the *means* of achieving them. The most effective approach is to support the statement of objectives with programs, schedules, and specific budgets.

2. *Programming.* This is the work a manager does in establishing the sequence and priority of steps to be followed in reaching an objective. Programs direct the flow of materials, tools and facilities, and money and human effort. Programming provides an opportunity to assess options before committing resources.

3. *Developing Programs.* We can logically arrive at program steps by assessing our objective, identifying the work steps necessary to achieve it, ordering and prioritizing these steps, and assigning accountabilities. It is important throughout this process to obtain the participation of those who will do the work.

4. *Identify the Primary Steps.* You can identify the critical few program steps by performing a work analysis and by consulting those individuals who will be doing the work. Brainstorming with the people involved is a good way to consider all aspects of a program.

5. *Basis for Delegation.* Programming provides an excellent opportunity to delegate responsibility. You can delegate not only specified work, but also specified results. Initial agreement and regular follow-up sessions are key to successful delegation.

6. *Developing Management Schedules.* Scheduling is one means of putting a harness on time. A management schedule is the time sequence necessary to carry out the action steps in a management program. Time is easily quantifiable, and thus readily converted into money. Involving the accountable people in determination of the schedule ensures realism and commitment.

7. *Determining the Schedule.* In estimating the time required to complete each step, we can use either single or multiple estimates. Single estimates are best if the work is defined and we are familiar with it; but otherwise multiple estimates or the minimax technique can provide a more realistic schedule.

8. *Developing Budget Inputs.* Specific budgets, because they are related directly to the work to be done, enable us to evaluate both specific costs and

potential benefits. In determining the cost of a program step, we consider direct costs, the cost of time, and indirect costs. In finalizing a specific budget, all costs are converted to monetary units and continuing costs are annualized.

9. *Estimating the Value of Expected Results.* We can assess the desirability of an action plan by evaluating the benefits as well as the costs. Benefits are calculated as direct, indirect, or intangible.

10. *Specific Budgeting Considerations.* It is important to maintain the integrity of the budget. Changes in budget figures must be balanced by changes in the work they represent. Once a budget is accepted, overruns and underruns beyond the normal variance are equally undesirable. Accounting and other specialists can provide expert advice and help in developing and refining your budget, but you are accountable for how wisely you use the money available to your position.

QUOTES FROM CHAPTER 16

Significant quotations from this chapter that you will want to consider and discuss in greater detail:

- There is a difference between management and technical programs.

- When a program is carried out repeatedly in exactly the same way, it may become a procedure.

- Programs provide excellent vehicles for delegation.

- The people who will do the work are best qualified to determine the time required.

- Multiple estimates are particularly effective when there is emotional resistance by those who will have a part in meeting the schedule.

- Responsibility budgeting and zero-based budgeting have been attempts to relate money spent directly to the work done.

- A specific budget is the calculation of the cost of implementing a given action plan.

- Specific budgets are particularly valuable in pricing out alternative courses of action.

- You can best judge the desirability of an action plan if you have a clear idea of its value.

GUIDELINES FOR MORE EFFECTIVE PLANNING

Wherever we are, it is but a stage on the way to somewhere else, and whatever we do, it is only a preparation to do something else that shall be different.
ROBERT LOUIS STEVENSON

THE CHAPTER IN BRIEF   To improve our planning we can make sure that managers clearly understand the planning work they must do. We can be flexible so we can change both our plans and planning methods. It is important to learn to concentrate both our resources and our efforts on the critical few rather than the minor many. Plans have a tendency to become as complex as the situations they reflect, but we need to keep them clear and simple if we want them to prompt confident, direct action. Our planning will evolve, whether we want it to or not, and it is best to anticipate and to prepare for the changes rather than to be overwhelmed by them. Managers do not learn to plan intuitively. This calls for intensive, continued training. Finally, we must know how to plan for people, for the freedom people want, and for the kind of future in which the computer will be either a bane or a boon.

HOW TO BENEFIT FROM THE EXPERIENCE OF OTHERS

While every planning system is different, there are universals of practice we can draw from the experience of effective planners. The guidelines that follow are based on interviews with managers and planning staffs in selected companies.

GIVE MANAGERS ACCOUNTABILITY FOR PLANNING

A great many managers do not plan effectively because they do not know what plans are expected of them, they have not had training in planning, and, in too many cases, they feel that it doesn't seem to make much difference whether they plan or not. Typical of the response to the question "What planning are you required to do on your job?" was the reaction of a production manager in a large manufacturing plant. "I get my budget from the budget director," he said. "Production control does my production planning, and the personnel department sends me my MBO targets."

269

The only realistic solution is to spell out clearly for managers the planning and controlling work for which they are accountable. Here is a checklist. All managers should:

- Forecast for their area of accountability. These forecasts should include estimates of future requirements and changes in the nature of whatever products or services are provided and similar data on internal or external clients or customers.

- Establish strategic, long-term, or continuing objectives.

- Develop and keep up to date short-term action plans.

- Establish budgets to guide the use of resources.

- Interpret, apply, and recommend changes in policies.

- Develop and maintain procedures necessary to ensure uniformity and effectiveness of the work performed.

- Develop performance standards to serve as criteria in determining how well work is done and objectives are achieved.

- Provide timely, accurate records and reports of work in progress and results accomplished.

- Evaluate performance by comparing actual results to standards and identifying variances and exceptions.

- Take prompt corrective action to correct deficiencies, and take advantage of opportunities.

To maintain accountability, managers must be given the authority they need to get the results expected of them. This calls for decentralization of authority to the operating levels, but it also demands reservation of the necessary centralized authority to maintain control.

This pattern of decentralized authority with the necessary balance of control was pioneered by General Motors under Alfred P. Sloan; however, many companies use it effectively today. General Mills, for example, has developed its planning system based on a decentralized concept of management. In General Mills, corporate management sets the basic corporate policies and objectives and establishes charters and general criteria to guide the divisions and other operating components. Within this framework, the operating divisions are delegated broad authority to develop their own plans for accomplishing the overall objectives and strategies. General Mills finds that this encourages innovation and cost effectiveness and stimulates the creative thinking that both satisfies and holds customers.

BE FLEXIBLE WHEN YOU PLAN

Most planning systems have their genesis in the budgeting process. For accounting purposes, budgets must be relatively unchanging and inflexible. One consequence is that the same characteristics have held for other aspects of planning. This is understandable. So much time and effort are invested in the initial effort of developing plans that there is a natural reluctance to undo the work by changing.

If circumstances change and plans do not, however, planning quickly falls into disrepute and either is abandoned or becomes stereotyped and sterile. The most useful answer is to make long-range objectives and strategies broad and comprehensive. They are intended to bracket sets of anticipated conditions, not to aim directly at precise points in time or specific events. Because they set direction and are not guides for daily action, long-range programs and budgets also can be generalized. For this reason, the review and revision periods for long-range plans can be reasonably long; most organizations find that an annual revision is adequate.

The more concrete and specific the plan and the more it is intended to provide guidance for daily and weekly actions, the more frequently it will need to be reviewed and, if necessary, revised. Thus, operating plans are analyzed and discussed weekly and monthly, or even more frequently. The objective is to revise plans often enough so that they continue to be useful guides to action but not so often that they become burdens instead of benefits.

Western Electric Co., Inc., for example, finds that its operational plans require continuous monitoring, while long-range and strategic plans need be revised only as conditions change. Since Western Electric provides the products and services of the Associated Bell Telephone Companies, it must probe constantly to assess a rapidly changing future. Historical precedents often are few or nonexistent so the task centers largely on interpreting the environment to provide data that will help the decision makers to develop sound assumptions about the future. In many situations, the real problem becomes one of identifying the problem.

PLAN FOR THE CRITICAL FEW

Planning often gets out of hand because we try to plan for everything. One consequence is that paperwork proliferates; another is that planning consumes so much time it keeps people from their other work.

The best way to conserve time is to concentrate planning on those critical few issues that account for the largest proportion of results. The "critical few" means only the events that will significantly influence objectives or will require substantial resources. There is little point in developing detailed plans to do an outstanding job if it doesn't matter at this time whether we do the work at all. For example, it may be desirable to plan entry into a completely new market 5 years from now, but it probably is not worthwhile to determine now the number of people who will be needed in each sales district to make sure we meet our quota, what media schedule will be followed, or how sales representatives will be trained.

The best reference point in determining how far to go with plans is to ask, "If we *don't* plan for this now, will it significantly alter our ability to achieve the objective we want?" In many cases, it will have little or no effect; the planning can then be postponed.

Identifying the critical few also can help in determining *what* plans we need to develop. For example, everything we expect to do, no matter how important, does not require a full array of plans. In some cases, we will need objectives only, to give clear direction. When pace and timing become important, schedules are in order. And when we need to make a definite commitment of resources, programs and budgets become necessary.

REMEMBER THAT PLANS ARE NOT AS IMPORTANT AS PLANNING

An effective planning system will force managers to think in an orderly and logical fashion about the courses of action they will carry out in the future. The prime value of planning lies in the thought and analysis that takes place. A written plan is valuable only to the degree it records sound and useful ideas that have emerged from the planning process.

What should be the nature and extent of the thought processes involved? Any plan is actually a set of decisions that we make now about what we will do in the future. Therefore, each vital activity—whether it be forecast, objective, program step, schedule time, or budget—should be developed in accordance with the techniques of logical thinking.

We need to be sure we are dealing with the real problem or issue, not the apparent one. For example, if we are engaged in developing an objective to increase sales, is sales revenue really the problem or is our concern pricing, outmoded products, or inadequate service?

Consideration of options is also important. Usually there are several ways to do almost anything. Rather than taking the first option that comes to hand, we are better advised to weigh all the options in terms of the objective or standards we have set and to select the option that gives greatest promise of success.

KEEP PLANNING SIMPLE

Most plans are carried out under operating pressures. Managers have little time or opportunity to deal with a large variety of actions that must be coordinated frequently. The ability of accountable managers to use the plans provided is the key factor. If plans are too complex, if they incorporate intricate models, if they rely on detailed arrays of options, they will get a cold reception.

Complex plans should be broken down into simple ones so they can be understood readily. Eventually every plan must become a work package that one individual can carry out in a normal work situation. A few simple plans, clearly understood and addressed to the critical few needs are most likely to succeed.

Planning staffs, which are organized to help managers to plan more effectively, sometimes become obstacles on the road to success. It is natural for planning staffs to be proud of their technical ability to produce complex plans that are built on sophisticated models or intricate mathematical computations. When this becomes prevalent, the people who deal with the complex plans become incapable of dealing with simple ones and, in fact, will contend that simplification is impossible or undesirable. They are much like the skilled cabinet maker who, asked to build a simple, inexpensive stool, produces one with complex miters and intricate inlays.

ANTICIPATE THE NECESSARY EVOLUTION

No matter how much money and personpower you invest, you will find that planning implementation can be hastened very little. While you may drive and push, it will find its own pace, geared to the needs and receptivity of your people and the special environment of your organization. Whatever your eagerness to set up a well-ordered planning system, you will proceed with greatest effectiveness if you trace the evolutionary development of the planning process and follow its natural path.

Arcata Corporation, a diversified wood products company, is a case in point. Arcata owned extensive redwood lands. It harvested and sold redwood lumber. That was its business. Success generated a large cash flow. At first, financial planning was adequate to keep track of the money and to invest it. The important decisions were made easily enough by the top operating and financial heads. Planning was largely a matter of the chief operating officer telling the functional heads what they were expected to do in the following year.

With money in the bank, Arcata looked to diversification. It decided to go into the "information transfer" business. First it bought up several printing companies, which formed the nucleus of its printing services group. It then formed information services and a communications group. The latter soon became a volume leader in the interconnect telephone industry. But Arcata did not have the technology or manufacturing capability of competitors such as ITT and the Bell System. Accordingly, Arcata took a bath in communications services.

Planning was still largely in the minds of the key officers. But the downturn called also for a changing of the guard. New management sold off the deviant organizations and cherished with renewed solicitude the profit-producing wood products. From this core, they extended the business into such end-use consumers and retail markets as gift wrap, greeting cards, and disposable tableware.

As is true of every company, once Arcata had passed beyond the grasp of its strong natural leaders, planning became a necessary adjunct to successful growth. At first, the line officers resisted advice or help. They felt that if they were considered capable enough to run their own businesses, they were capable enough to be left alone. But the need was clear for integration and for judicious use of the generous flow of cash. A strong, formalized planning effort was instituted and once more set the company on the path to success.

If planning is to be successful, planners must, at their own pace, evolve a consistent, logical structure. People must know what to do in order to take part in the enterprise planning process. If some set objectives, while others do not, if forecasting is done in operations but not in sales, the planning effort will fall apart once it gets beyond the scope of the central authority at the top. If planning is to evolve from centralization to decentralization of the function, people must learn how to do their planning work. There must be a certain amount of standardization simply to add and subtract similar quantities and to make results comparable. If some do zero-based budgeting while others prefer simple line-item budgeting, the outcomes may be perfectly acceptable in themselves but they can't be analyzed, compared, or evaluated in similar terms. People who plan must also speak the same language. If to one a strategy is a long-range plan while to another it is a program to accomplish a long-range objective, meaning and minds will never meet.

TRAIN MANAGERS TO PLAN

As we have seen, formalization and standardization of planning requires time and constant attention. Many companies find that education and training are essential parts of the process.

Running managers through a planning seminar will not do the job. For real results, an organizationwide effort is required. A large New Jersey company with worldwide operations has instituted and successfully maintains an effective program that has eight steps.

1. *Determine Planning Needs.* The company thought through its overall, long-term planning requirements and developed a critical objective with accompanying standards that expressed its commitment to planning. It expanded the standards by developing a checklist for the desirable features of each of the planning activities. A task force was appointed. Using the objective and standards as the model, it evaluated the state of planning in the company as a whole and for each component. For this it developed a detailed list of needs. Specific objectives, programs, schedules, and specific budgets were prepared, itemizing the effort required.

2. *Prepare Training Program.* An educational program was developed, criterion referenced to the specific standards and needs that had been itemized. The program was designed so that it could be taught by selected internal line and staff managers trained as instructors.

3. *Orient Top Executives.* Since the planning system needed the support and inputs of the top management group, the training process began with the chief executive and his immediate line and staff officers. They scheduled a long weekend to make a 5-day session at a secluded country location. The corporate planning staff had been trained as instructors. Armed with forecasts and a *pro forma* set of the proposed planning documents, the staff worked with the top group to develop the initial set of position charters and to orient the executives to the essentials of the new planning system. A commitment was made by this group to install and implement the system that they had decided would best serve their needs.

4. *Secure Understanding of Key Managers.* The planning methods and plans established at the top depended for implementation on the participation and support of key line and staff middle managers. Accordingly, the format for the top-executive sessions was modified slightly to fit the needs of other management levels. These sessions then served as the vehicle for cascading both the position charter and the new planning system. Since the position charters and action plans provided the basis for performance appraisal and incentive

awards, the participating managers worked hard to master the new procedures.

5. *Formalize Planning Procedures.* By now the planning system had received its baptism of fire from the managers who would be accountable for using it. Adjustments were made, and the planning procedures were finalized. They served as the basis for extending the training throughout the company. The educational program was converted to an audiovisual, facilitator-led format, using the planning procedures as instructional criteria.

6. *Train Internal Facilitators.* Instructors were selected from each major component of the company, together with counselors, who would work closely with managers on the job to provide continuing and consistent guidance. These facilitators participated in a 10-day training session, during which they mastered the more complex aspects of the planning system and had the opportunity to practice their roles as instructors and counselors. The facilitators were selected from among the most capable younger managers, so that this training became an important element in their preparation for career advancement.

7. *Cascade Throughout the Organization.* Training sessions were scheduled to coincide with the first phase of the new planning cycle. This gave participating managers the opportunity to develop their own plans as part of the training process and made the training assignments both timely and practical. At the conclusion of the sessions, each manager made a personal contract to follow through by implementing the new system on his or her job.

8. *Provide Coaching and Counseling on the Job.* Since managers completed the training program before their subordinates, they were well prepared to advise and counsel. In fact, managers took considerable pride in their ability to help their people to prepare position charters and action plans on the job. The counselors who had been trained previously were also available in each organizational component to help with special problems and to fill in when accountable managers were not available.

A well-integrated training program is mandatory if managers are to speak the same planning language, use the same methods, and implement a common set of procedures. In too many cases, managers are expected to become planners by edict. This rarely works.

PLAN FOR PEOPLE

When we plan, we tend to become absorbed in the physical things involved, and in the process we forget the punch line: no plan is any better than the willingness of people to carry it out. To prove this, glance over the list of program steps you have developed for a recent action plan. Rarely will you find specific mention of the action necessary to get people to support your plan; for example, steps such as "Conduct meeting to secure understanding and acceptance," or "Prepare and distribute memo explaining the new project."

There are three key words in building consideration for people into your plans. These are "participation," "communication," and "delegation." We often assume that the actions implied by these terms will take place automatically; we can be much more certain if we specify exactly what we want to occur in the programs we develop.

Encourage Participation

Participation involves giving people an opportunity to offer their suggestions and recommendations in creating the plan. People who see their ideas in your plans become part owners of what you are trying to accomplish. Mental parenthood is almost as strong as physical.

Many Japanese companies use what is to westerners a unique but unusually effective way to get participation. When a new approach is planned, it is summarized on a "consensus form" and circulated to the people who should participate. This may be as many as 40 or 50. The names are all listed, from lowest to highest levels, with space for comments. Before the form is sent on, the recipient stamps it with his or her seal—a stylized symbol that represents the person's name. By the time the consensus form reaches the top executive, it represents an accurate cross section of opinion and ensures that each person has had a chance to examine the plan.

Communicate

Communication is also vital to effective planning. Too often people let their creative ideas pour into somebody's plan, then hear nothing more.

There is no better way to slam shut the gate. No matter how small the contribution, the rule of thumb is to keep everybody who participates in helping you develop and carry out your plan informed. Nothing elaborate is required: a brief memorandum will usually help people feel they were important enough to be kept informed.

Delegate Responsibility and Authority

Delegation is a potent factor in making people part of your plan. Assign as much of the work as possible to members of your team. Be sure to delegate authority along with responsibility. Specify that you want the person to whom you delegate to make the important decisions so he or she can do the work with minimal intervention on your part.

One aspect of delegating planning work that we often overlook is that it must be controlled. Giving people their heads with no way of checking what they do is courting disaster. If you quantify your standards, they provide excellent control points. You can also identify the program steps that are vital to success and require spot reports at these points.

When all is said and done, getting people to support your planning is a frame of mind. If you trust people, if you recognize that mistakes are opportunities for improvement and not mortal flaws, and if you are prepared to share your experience and judgment, you will find that you will get solid support from the people who must make your plans work.

PLAN FOR FREEDOM

Usually we think of plans and controls as restraints on our freedom. When we generate a bold idea or a brilliant new project, we want to run free with it. We chafe when we have to process it through critical reviewers and finally embalm it on some aseptic form.

But when many people must work together, freedom of action can exist only in the presence of control. If we want maximum freedom, we must learn to understand and use the controls necessary to provide maximum freedom. The necessary constraints and limits are onerous only if we make them so. Violinists do not consider the demands of their instruments an unfair abridgement of their personal freedom.

Our organization structures and our planning structures can offer us more rather than less freedom if we understand and use them properly. They are tools, not constraints. A planning structure can facilitate freedom of personal action by providing boundaries and guidelines which will enable us to concentrate our creative energies upon our own plot of ground and not to encroach upon that of our neighbors. To be free ourselves, we need to refrain from limiting the freedom of others.

Freedom and Growth

If they are to exist, these limits cannot be free-form and adventitious. They must be rational, consistent, and continuing. This reiterates the idea that organizations are made up of positions, which are groups of work that are maintained on a continuing basis. Here our concern is to help people to grow and to fit the requirements and challenges of the positions they occupy, rather than to tailor and shrink the positions to fit the people. You can only grow into something bigger than you are; you cannot grow to fill something you already occupy.

PLAN FOR THE FUTURE

A plan *is* the future, but often we forget that the process of planning itself must change and adapt as effectively as the subject matter or both will inevitably fail. In looking ahead, we can write a number of scenarios for what planning will be like in both the short- and long-range future, but the computer is a central feature in each.

We have been talking about the computer revolution since the General Electric Company some 30 years ago installed the first digital computer for business use, the UNIVAC, at its Appliance Park near Louisville, Kentucky.

The computer industry has followed the same type of evolutionary growth as other industries. In the early days, which date no further back than 1930, a primary aim of the leaders was to develop proprietary systems to keep others out. Manufacturers developed their own machine configurations. Both hardware and software grew spontaneously, generating independent technologies, different languages, and specialized procedures.

This brought the inevitable crisis of incompatibility, limited sales, and indifferent service. The independent, innovative entrepreneurs who created the industry discovered that standardization and control were the price of the freedom to grow.

It seems clear now that the objective of computerization is not primarily speed, efficiency, or storage capacity. The end result we want is communication. What ties together the enterprise in Tokyo and its branches in New York and Munich is communication. Top executives and line operators can combine their efforts effectively only to the degree they understand one another. Communication demands the same language, a similar logic that applies everywhere, and methods that work in Oslo as well as in Melbourne. The key to communication is computer software, and the key to software is compatibility.

Compatibility does not occur spontaneously. It must be planned. Increasingly, we will see that our planning systems must provide the logic for the installation of communication networks which are based on standardized software application packages. These will be the source for the operating directions that are already beginning to power a vast array of production and office tools and technologies.

One consequence will be that dependence upon mainframe processors will be replaced by extensive use of distributed data processing in which the load will be shifted to minicomputers scattered throughout the data processing network. The entire system will then be available to every person in the enterprise through intelligent/video terminals.

But this will still not give us what we want. Some 30 years ago, one of General Electric's early problems with the UNIVAC was that of using magnetic tape to store information. At that time, the company identified what turns out to be an even more basic concern—one which we still have in this day of silicon software and thin-film technology. This was the difficulty of computerizing planning systems which were essentially ad hoc and not logically consistent.

We know that compatible software will be the key to improving planning with the help of the computer. But as we discovered long ago with hardware, compatibility depends upon similar logics and identical vocabularies. The developers of software are now discovering that good programs must be criterion-referenced and as rigorously logical as the hardware.

For managers concerned with planning and planning systems, this means a return to the basics. In most cases, the planning systems we have are improvised and empirical. What is required is a clear, consistent logic for the planning process, a precisely defined vocabulary, and methods that permit ready duplication and interchangeability.

Planning will undergo many changes because of these pressures. Some people will find frustration and confusion in these changes. Others will discover new opportunities to probe the unknown that lies ahead and to develop limits for confident action and will discover the freedom to create a more challenging and rewarding future.

KEY POINTS

1. *What Planning Work Should Managers Do?* A first requirement in effective planning is to identify exactly what planning work we expect from man-

agers. These responsibilities should cover all activities of planning and controlling.

2. *Maintain Flexibility.* The only certainty about the future is that it will change. Fixed plans are useless if not dangerous, so we must purposely review and update our plans periodically. The lower in the organization, the more frequent the reviews should be.

3. *Plan for the Critical Few.* We tend to generate voluminous plans that frustrate and discourage people instead of guiding them. It is far better to develop only a few plans that cover the critical few situations that directly influence our end results than to develop a plethora of plans that cover everything.

4. *Planning Is More Important Than Plans.* The chief value of any plan is the thinking that goes into it. Instead of encouraging managers to prepare plans to satisfy procedures, it is better to use the time to discuss the problems and situations with others, to weigh and assess alternatives, and to develop a few action plans that provide a record of our thoughts and conclusions.

5. *Keep Planning Simple.* Staff planners often show their virtuosity by developing complex scenarios, intricate strategies, and involved models. These are of little value to practicing managers because they do not have the technical background to use them. It is best to use simple, logical plans that are easily understood and put to use.

6. *Prepare to Evolve.* Planning changes predictably, and it is better to prepare for increasing formalization and decentralization than to be hanging on to a past that is already obsolete. A logical structure of planning is the best preparation, for it can accommodate changes as they become necessary.

7. *Train Managers to Plan.* Managers learn to plan in the same way they become proficient in other skills. The educational process should begin at the top so the planning methods and terminology will be consistent and will be supported. The program can then be cascaded to lower levels by internal instructors. Provision should be made for follow-up coaching and counseling in planning on the job.

8. *Plan for People.* Since people are the engine that makes plans work, it is wise to build into our plans provision for participation, communication, and delegation. Participation helps people "own" the plans, communication makes sure they understand them, and delegation encourages them to use their creative ideas in developing and carrying them out.

9. *Plan for Freedom.* We can give people the greatest freedom by setting up limits within which they can have free play without encroaching on others. Instead of building organizations around people, we will do better to plan positions which give people a chance to expand and grow to fit increasing responsibilities.

10. *The Computer and Planning.* Distributed data processing will greatly increase the range and versatility of our plans. However, just as logical standardization is basic to hardware compatibility, it is also vital if we expect to provide the software that will enable us to realize the potential of the computer in planning for the future.

QUOTES FROM CHAPTER 17

Significant quotations from this chapter that you will want to consider and discuss in greater detail:

- To maintain accountability, managers must be given the authority they need to get the results expected of them.

- General Mills has developed its planning system based on a decentralized concept of management.

- The more concrete and specific the plan, the more frequently it will need to be reviewed.

- Western Electric Co., Inc. finds that its operational plans require continuous monitoring.

- The best way to conserve time is to concentrate planning on those critical few issues that account for the largest proportion of results.

- A plan is a set of decisions that we make now about what we will do in the future.

- Eventually every plan must become a work package that one individual can carry out in a normal work situation.

- It is natural for planning staffs to be proud of their technical ability to produce complex plans.

- If planning is to evolve from centralization to decentralization of the function, people must learn how to do their planning work.

- In too many cases, managers are expected to become planners by edict. This rarely works.

- The three key words in building consideration for people into your plans are "participation," "communication," and "delegation."

- Giving people their heads with no way of checking what they do is courting disaster.

- Planning structures can offer us more rather than less freedom if we understand and use them properly.

- To be free ourselves, we need to refrain from limiting the freedom of others.

- Our planning systems must provide the logic for the installation of communication networks which are based on standardized software application packages.

BIBLIOGRAPHY

GENERAL PLANNING

Abell, Derek F. *Defining the Business: The Starting Point of Strategic Planning*, Prentice-Hall, Inc., Englewood Cliffs, NJ, 1980.

Ackoff, Russell Lincoln. *A Concept of Corporate Planning*, John Wiley & Sons, Inc., New York, 1970.

Allio, Robert J. *Corporate Planning: Techniques and Applications*, AMACOM, New York, 1979.

Argenti, John. *Systematic Corporate Planning*, John Wiley & Sons, Inc., New York, 1974.

Brandt, Stephen C. *Strategic Planning in Emerging Companies*, Addison-Wesley Publishing Company, Reading, MA, 1981.

Buckner, Hugh (ed.), *Business Planning for the Board*, Gower Press, Limited, London, 1971.

Cotton, Donald B. *Company-Wide Planning: Concept and Process*, The Macmillan Company, New York, 1970.

Denning, Basil (ed.), *Corporate Planning: Selected Concepts*, McGraw-Hill Book Company, Inc., New York, 1971.

Ewing, David W. (ed.), *Long-Range Planning for Management*, Harper & Row, New York, 1972.

Halford, David Reece Charles. *Business Planning: A Practical Guide for Management*, David and Charles, Newton Abbot, 1971.

Harvard Business Review. *Planning, Part V*, Cambridge, MA, 1978.

Hussey, David H. *Corporate Planning: Theory and Practice*, Pergamon Press, Oxford/New York, 1974.

Jones, Harry. *Preparing Company Plans: A Workbook for Effective Corporate Planning*, John Wiley & Sons, Inc., New York, 1974.

Kastens, Merritt L. *Long-Range Planning for Your Business: An Operating Manual*, AMACOM, New York, 1976.

King, William Richard. *Strategic Planning and Policy*, Van Nostrand Reinhold Co., New York, 1978.

283

Lorange, Peter. *Strategic Planning Systems*, Prentice-Hall, Inc., Englewood Cliffs, NJ, 1977.

Miller, Ernest Charles. *Advanced Techniques for Strategic Planning*, American Management Association, New York, 1971.

Mockler, Robert J. *Business Planning and Policy Formation*, Appleton-Century-Crofts, Inc., New York, 1971.

Rothschild, William E. *Putting It All Together: A Guide to Strategic Thinking*, AMACOM, New York, 1976.

Rothschild, William E. *Strategic Alternatives: Selection, Development, and Implementation*, AMACOM, New York, 1979.

Schendel, Daniel E., and **Charles W. Hofer** (eds.), *Strategic Management: A New View of Business Policy and Planning*, Little, Brown and Company, Boston/Toronto, 1979.

Smith, Shea. *Strategies in Business*, John Wiley & Sons, Inc., New York, 1978.

Steiner, George A. *Strategic Planning: What Every Manager Must Know*, Free Press, New York, 1979.

Ward, Edward Peter. *The Dynamics of Planning*, Pergamon Press, Oxford/New York, 1970.

FORECASTING

Armstrong, Jon Scott. *Long-Range Forecasting: From Crystal Ball to Computer*, John Wiley & Sons, Inc., New York, 1978.

Bacon, Jeremy. *Planning and Forecasting in the Smaller Company*, The Conference Board, New York, 1971.

Butler, William F., Robert Kavesh, and **Robert Platt** (eds.), *Methods and Techniques of Business Forecasting*, Prentice-Hall, Inc., Englewood Cliffs, NJ, 1974.

Cantor, Jeremiah. *Pragmatic Forecasting*, American Management Association, New York, 1971.

Chambers, John Carlton, Satinder K. Mullick, and **Donald D. Smith.** *An Executive's Guide to Forecasting*, John Wiley & Sons, Inc., New York, 1974.

Chisholm, Roger K., and **Gilbert R. Whitaker, Jr.** *Forecasting Methods*, Richard D. Irwin, Inc., Homewood, IL, 1971.

Dauten, Carl Anton, and **Lloyd M. Valentine.** *Business Cycles and Forecasting*, South-Western Publishing Company, Cincinnati, 1974.

Firth, Michael Arthur. *Forecasting Methods in Business and Management,* International Ideas Inc., Philadelphia, 1977.

Granger, Clive William John. *Forecasting in Business and Economics,* Academic Press, New York, 1980.

Gross, Charles W., and **Robin T. Peterson.** *Business Forecasting,* Houghton Mifflin Company, Boston, 1976.

Harvard Business Review. *Forecasting,* Cambridge, MA, 1971.

Milne, Thomas E. *Business Forecasting: A Managerial Approach,* Longman, Inc., London/New York, 1975.

Morrell, James (ed.), *Management Decisions and the Role of Forecasting,* Penguin Books, Inc., Harmondsworth, Middlesex, England, 1972.

Nelson, Charles R. *Applied Time Series Analysis for Managerial Forecasting,* Holden-Dary, Inc., San Francisco, 1973.

Silk, Leonard Solomon, and **M. Louise Curley.** *A Primer on Business Forecasting, With a Guide to Sources of Business Data,* Random House, Inc., New York, 1970.

Sullivan, William G., and **W. Wayne Claycombe.** *Fundamentals of Forecasting,* Reston Publishing Company, Reston, Virginia, 1977.

Ward, A. John. *Forecasting Practices and Techniques, Industrial and Commercial Techniques,* London, 1970.

Wheelwright, Steven C., and **Spyros Makridakis.** *Forecasting,* North-Holland Publishing Company, New York, 1979.

Wheelwright, Steven C., and **Spyros Makridakis.** *Forecasting Methods for Management,* John Wiley & Sons, Inc., New York, 1980.

Wood, D., and **R. Fildes** (eds.), *Forecasting and Planning,* Saxon House, Farnborough, England, 1978.

OBJECTIVES AND MANAGEMENT BY OBJECTIVES

Albrecht, Karl G. *Successful Management by Objectives: An Action Manual,* Prentice-Hall, Inc., Englewood Cliffs, NJ, 1978.

Carroll, Stephen J., and **Henry L. Tosi, Jr.** *Management by Objectives: Applications and Research,* The Macmillan Company, New York, 1973.

Giegold, William C. *Management by Objectives: A Self-Instructional Approach,* McGraw-Hill Book Company, Inc., New York, 1978.

Giegold, William C. *Objective Setting and the MBO Process,* McGraw-Hill Book Company, Inc., New York, 1978.

Giegold, William C. *Performance Appraisal and the MBO Process*, McGraw-Hill Book Company, Inc., New York, 1978.

Humble, John William (ed.), *Management by Objectives in Action*, McGraw-Hill Book Company, Inc., New York, 1970.

McConkey, Dale D., and Ray Vander Weele. *Financial Management by Objectives*, Prentice-Hall, Inc., Englewood Cliffs, NJ, 1976.

McConkey, Dale D. *How to Manage by Results*, AMACOM, New York, 1976.

McConkey, Dale D. *MBO for Nonprofit Organizations*, AMACOM, New York, 1975.

Mager, Robert F. *Goal Analysis*, Fearon Publishing Company, Belmont, CA, 1972.

Mali, Paul. *Improving Total Productivity: MBO Strategies for Business, Government, and Not-For-Profit Organizations*, John Wiley & Sons, Inc., New York, 1978.

Migliore, R. Henry. *MBO: Blue Collar to Top Executive*, Bureau of National Affairs, Washington, DC, 1977.

Morrisey, George L. *Management by Objectives and Results for Business and Industry*, Addison-Wesley Publishing Company, Reading, MA, 1977.

Odiorne, George S. *MBO II: A System of Managerial Leadership for the 80s*, Pitman Learning, Inc., Belmont, CA, 1979.

Raia, Anthony P. *Managing by Objectives*, Scott, Foresman and Company, Glenview, IL, 1974.

Reddin, W. J. *Effective Management by Objectives: the 3-D Method of MBO*, McGraw-Hill Book Company, Inc., New York, 1971.

Varney, Glenn H. *Management by Objectives*, The Dartnell Corporation, Chicago, 1971.

PROGRAMS AND SCHEDULES

PERT

Brennan, Maribeth. *PERT AND CPM: A Selected Bibliography*, Council of Planning Librarians, Illinois, 1968.

Hardy, D. D. *PERT for Small Projects*, Royal Aircraft Est., Farnborough, England, 1965.

Stilian, Gabriel N. *PERT, A New Management Planning and Control Technique*, American Management Association, New York, 1962.

Critical Path Analysis

Barnetson, Paul. *Critical Path Planning: Present and Future Techniques,* Brandon/Systems Press, Princeton, NJ, 1970.

Moder, Joseph J., and **Cecil R. Phillips.** *Project Management with CPM and PERT,* Van Nostrand Reinhold Company, New York, 1970.

Wiest, Jerome D., and **Ferdinand K. Levy.** *A Management Guide to PERT/CPM: With GERT/PDM/DCPM and Other Networks,* Prentice-Hall, Inc., Englewood Cliffs, NJ, 1977.

Network Analysis

Battersby, Albert. *Network Analysis for Planning and Scheduling,* John Wiley & Sons, Inc., New York, 1970.

Bazaraa, M. S. *Linear Programming and Network Flows,* John Wiley & Sons, Inc., New York, 1977.

Hoare, Henry Ronald. *Project Management Using Network Analysis,* McGraw-Hill Book Company, Inc., New York, 1973.

Scheduling

Baker, Kenneth R. *Introduction to Sequencing and Scheduling,* John Wiley & Sons, Inc., New York, 1974.

Mather, Hal F., and **George W. Plossl.** *The Master Production Schedule: Management's Handle on the Business,* Mather and Plossl, Atlanta, 1978.

Tainiter, M. *Scheduling and Control for Industry and Government,* Time Table Press, Syosset, NY, 1971.

BUDGETS

Amey, Lloyd R. *Budget Planning and Control Systems,* Pitman Publishing Company, Marshfield, MA, 1979.

Austin, L. Allan. *Zero-Base Budgeting: Organizational Impact and Effects,* AMACOM, New York, 1977.

Bacon, Jeremy. *Managing the Budget Function,* National Industrial Conference Board, New York, 1970.

Bower, Joseph L. *Managing the Resource Allocation Process: A Study of Corporate Planning and Investment*, Harvard University, 1970.

Jones, Reginald L., and **H. George Trentin.** *Budgeting: Key to Planning and Control: Practical Guidelines for Managers*, American Management Association, New York, 1971.

Matthews, Lawrence M. *Practical Operating Budgeting*, McGraw-Hill Book Company, Inc., New York, 1977.

Olve, Nils-Göran. *Multiobjective Budgetary Planning: Models for Interactive Planning in Decentralized Organizations*, Stockholm School of Economics, Stockholm, 1977.

Pyhrr, Peter A. *Zero-Base Budgeting: A Practical Management Tool for Evaluating Expenses*, John Wiley & Sons, Inc., New York, 1973.

Sweeny, Allen. *Budgeting Fundamentals for Nonfinancial Executives*, AMACOM, New York, 1975.

Swieringa, Robert J., and **Robert H. Moncur.** *Some Effects of Participative Budgeting on Managerial Behavior*, National Association of Accountants, New York, 1975.

Thomas, William Edgar, Jr. (ed.), *Readings in Cost Accounting, Budgeting and Control*, South-Western Publishing Company, Cincinnati, 1978.

Welsch, Glenn A. *Budgeting: Profit Planning and Control*, Prentice-Hall, Inc., Englewood Cliffs, NJ, 1976.

BUSINESS POLICY

Christensen, Carl Roland, Kenneth R. Andrews, and **Joseph L. Bower.** *Business Policy: Text and Cases*, Richard D. Irwin, Inc., Homewood, IL, 1978.

Glueck, William F. *Business Policy: Strategy Formation and Management Action*, McGraw-Hill Book Company, Inc., New York, 1976.

Glueck, William F. (ed.), *Readings in Business Policy from Business Week*, McGraw-Hill Book Company, Inc., New York, 1978.

McCarthy, Daniel J., Robert J. Minichiello, and **Joseph R. Curran.** *Business Policy and Strategy: Concepts and Readings*, Richard D. Irwin, Inc., Homewood, IL, 1979.

Rogers, David C. D. *Business Policy and Planning: Text and Cases*, Prentice-Hall, Inc., Englewood Cliffs, NJ, 1977.

PROCEDURES/SYSTEMS

Argenti, John. *A Management System for the Seventies*, Allen and Unwin, Inc., London, 1972.

Coyle, R. G. *Management System Dynamics*, John Wiley & Sons, Inc., New York, 1977.

Neuschel, Richard F. *Management Systems for Profit and Growth*, McGraw-Hill Book Company, Inc., New York, 1976.

Schoderbeck, Peter P. (ed.), *Management Systems*, John Wiley & Sons, Inc., New York, 1971.

CONTROLLING

Anthony, Robert Newton. *Management Control Systems: Text and Cases*, Richard D. Irwin, Inc., Homewood, IL, 1976.

Cummings, Larry L. *Performance in Organizations: Determinants and Appraisal*, Scott, Foresman and Company, Glenview, IL, 1973.

Eilon, Samuel. *Management Control*, Pergamon Press, Oxford/New York, 1979.

Ferguson, Charles R. *Measuring Corporate Strategy*, Dow Jones, Irwin, Homewood, IL, 1974.

Harvard Business Review. *Control, Part III*, Cambridge, MA, 1974.

Herbert, Leo. *Auditing the Performance of Management*, Lifetime Learning Publications, Belmont, CA, 1979.

Koontz, Harold. *Appraising Managers as Managers*, McGraw-Hill Book Company, Inc., New York, 1976.

Lindberg, Roy A. *Operations Auditing*, AMACOM, New York, 1972.

Mockler, Robert J. *The Management Control Process*, Appleton-Century-Crofts, Inc., New York, 1972.

Patz, Alan L., and **Alan J. Rowe.** *Management Control and Decision Systems: Text, Cases, and Readings*, John Wiley & Sons, Inc., New York, 1977.

Sawyer, Lawrence B. *The Manager and the Modern Internal Auditor: A Problem-Solving Partnership*, AMACOM, New York, 1978.

Scantlebury, D. L., and **Ronnel B. Raaum.** *Operational Auditing*, Association of Government Accountants, Arlington, VA, 1978.

Sloma, Richard S.   *How to Measure Managerial Performance,* The Macmillan Company, New York, 1980.

Steffy, Wilbert.   *Management Control Systems for Small and Medium-Sized Firms,* University of Michigan Press, Ann Arbor, MI, 1975.

Thierauf, Robert J.   *Management Auditing: A Questionnaire Approach,* AMACOM, New York, 1980.

Washbrook, Harry.   *The Board and Management Audit,* Business Books, London, 1978.

Williamson, Oliver E.   *Corporate Control and Business Behavior,* Prentice-Hall, Inc., Englewood Cliffs, NJ, 1970.

Wilson, Richard M. S.   *Management Controls and Marketing Planning,* John Wiley & Sons, Inc., New York, 1979.

INDEX